The Campus History Series

CLINTON JUNIOR COLLEGE

The Campus History Series

CLINTON JUNIOR COLLEGE

PIPER PETERS AHERON, ELAINE JOHNSON COPELAND, PH.D.,
CHERYL J. MCCULLOUGH, AND CYNTHIA P. RODDEY, D.MIN.

ARCADIA
PUBLISHING

ISBN 978-0-7385-1729-2

Published by Arcadia Publishing
Charleston, South Carolina

Printed in the United States of America

Library of Congress Catalog Card Number: 2004110459

For all general information, please contact Arcadia Publishing:
Telephone 843-853-2070
Fax 843-853-0044
E-mail sales@arcadiapublishing.com
For customer service and orders:
Toll-Free 1-888-313-2665

Visit us on the Internet at www.arcadiapublishing.com

This book is dedicated to the late Juanita Simon Scott, Ph.D. (Class of 1956) and the late Mrs. Katherine Rogers Wood (Class of 1968), dedicated alumni and memebers of the board of trustees.

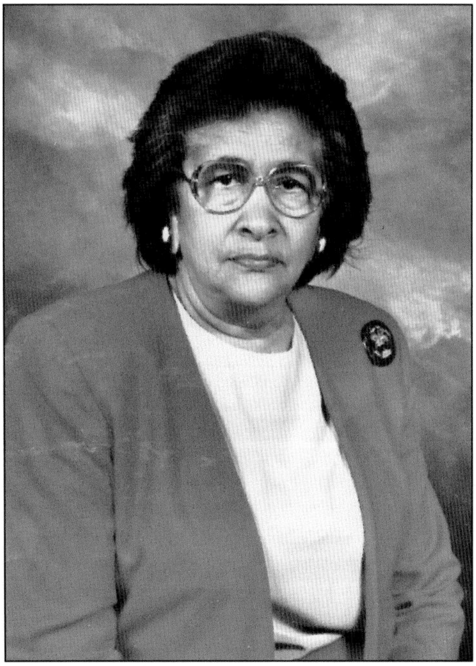

DR. JUANITA SIMON SCOTT, CLASS OF 1956.

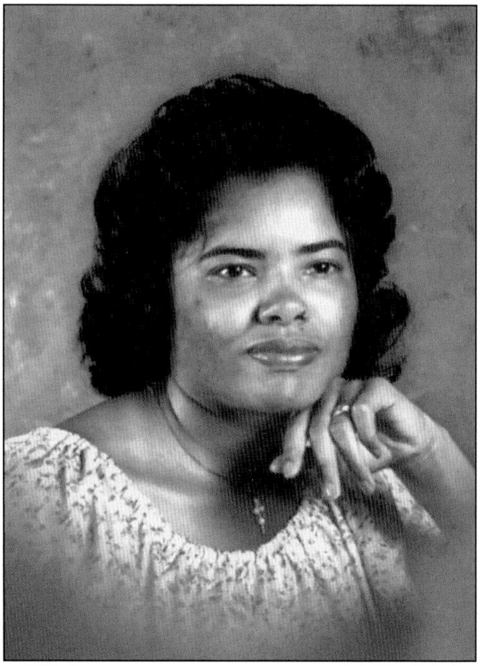

MRS. KATHERINE ROGERS WOOD, CLASS OF 1968.

CONTENTS

Acknowledgments 6

Introduction: A History of Distinction 7

1. The Freedom Church 9

2. Growth: Creating Opportunity 13

3. Education: Inspire and Instruct 29

4. Progress: Keep the Light Shining 65

5. Growth and Development 73

6. Challenges: A Legacy of Liberation 81

7. The Church's Legacy 109

8. 110 Years of Excellence in Education 113

9. The Mission of the College 119

10. The Presidents 123

ACKNOWLEDGMENTS

Through the compilation of photos and captions, this book was created to provide a brief glimpse into Clinton Junior College's 110-year history. It is the first of its kind for the college, and hopefully, it will inspire a more academic and scholarly accounting in the future. This book would not have been possible without the support of the dedicated staff and educators of Clinton Junior College; the Schomburg Center for Research in Black Culture, a division of the New York Public Library in New York City; Gina Price White, archivist at Winthrop University's Dacus Library; and Mark Herring, dean of library sciences at Winthrop. Special thanks go to *The Herald*. Also, special thanks go to Mr. Harold Tyson and Mr. Melvin Poole, photographers, and to the members of the 110th Anniversary Committee: Mr. Tommie Chambers, president of the 2003 Student Government Association; Ms. Carrie Massey, book store manager; Mr. Sylvester Owens, registrar and academic advisor; Ms. Janis Pendleton, dean of academic affairs; and Mrs. Daisy C. Wylie. An extra special thank you to Rev. Lloyd Snipes for his invaluable memory.

A number of periodicals were studied, and these include *The Evening Herald*, *The Star of Zion*, and *The Community Voice*. Past issues of *The Charlotte Observer* also provided a variety of informative articles. Documents from the Library of Congress and U.S. Census data accessed via the Internet were incorporated into the research process as well.

Unless otherwise specified in the courtesy notes, photographs are from the Clinton Junior College Library and Archives.

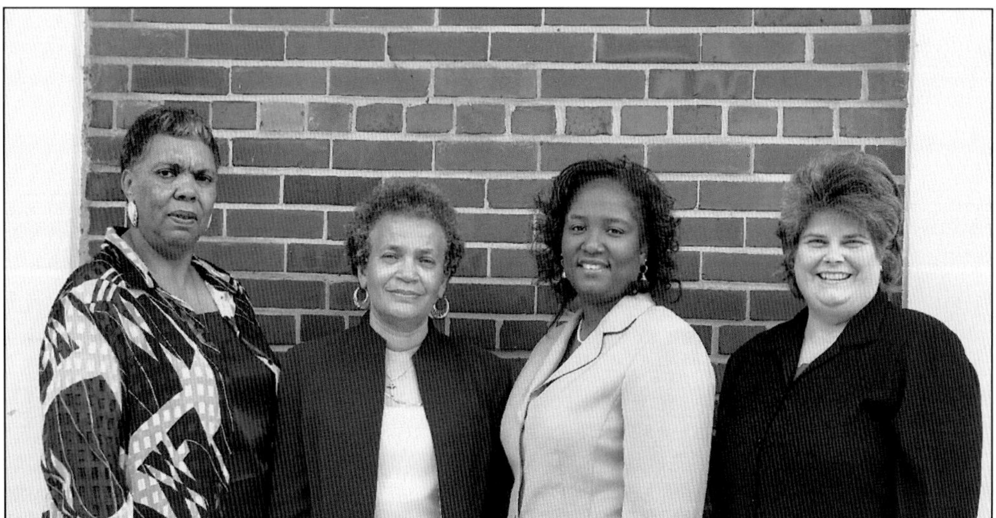

Pictured from left to right are authors Dr. Cynthia P. Roddey, Dr. Elaine J. Copeland, Cheryl J. McCullough, and Piper Peters Aheron.

INTRODUCTION

A HISTORY OF DISTINCTION

Upon arrival in the Colonial United States, enslaved Africans were restricted from practicing tribal faith and mystic customs. They were introduced to Christianity only to have whites refuse them the right to worship within Anglo-American churches. Pioneering evangelists protested. Those who seemed most vocal identified themselves as Methodists. They had entered North America in 1766, and their mission was to comfort and educate the laity wherever the Holy Spirit directed them.

Methodism, a reform movement within the Church of England, traditionally made no spiritual or righteous appraisals based on a person's skin color. As a result, Methodism appealed to many free and enslaved people of African descent. United worship services by the races within Methodist churches became celebrated, but by the end of the 18th century, African Americans were disenchanted. White Methodists had become timid about slavery. Congregations fragmented over the issue, with Richard Allen and Absalom Jones organizing the African Methodist Episcopal Church in Philadelphia in 1787. The second major reorganization occurred in 1796 when the John Street Methodist Episcopal Church congregation in New York City divided. James Varick and other members from John Street severed ties with the Methodist Episcopal Church in 1821. They established the African Methodist Episcopal Zion (A.M.E. Zion) Church, adding the word "Zion" (the name of the mother church, the first church of the denomination), to distinguish themselves from the Philadelphia group.

It was legal to oppress African Americans by 1740. Slaves could no longer be taught to read and write, a surprising turn of events considering that 45 years earlier, Samuel Thomas, a white cleric with a passion to improve life in the New World, founded the first-known school for African Americans in Charleston, South Carolina. The irony was lost on the greedy, but it was not lost on the dedicated ministers. Methodists continued organizing schools, with one of the first being Wilberforce University in Ohio. By 1862, A.M.E. minister Daniel A. Payne served at the helm of Wilberforce, becoming the first African-American college president in United States. Livingstone College, the former Wesley Institute, became the first college of the A.M.E. Zion denomination when it was founded in 1879.

Progress crawled in the South. In 1860, Abraham Lincoln became President, and South Carolina seceded from the Union. By that time, the U.S. African-American population stood at 4,441,830 (14.1 percent). Between 1862 and 1864, roughly four million enslaved African Americans were freed by acts of Congress. When the War Between the States finally ended in 1865, the Holy Spirit engulfed the South and church congregations affiliated with A.M.E. Zion enjoyed explosive growth. National membership increased from 25,000 in 1860 to 200,000 in 1870. In 1894, the A.M.E. Zion ordained women to preach. It also ordered the eradication of illiteracy among freedmen and encouraged more schools and colleges to be developed in each bishop's district.

The call to educate freedmen particularly moved stoic Rev. Nero A. Crockett, presiding elder of the Yorkville District, South Carolina. Reverend Crockett met with Rev. W.M. Robinson, pastor of Clinton Chapel, A.M.E. Zion. The two founded Clinton Normal and Industrial College on a rock-ribbed field roughly three miles from a railroad depot identified on maps as Rock Hill. The college was named after Bishop Isom Caleb Clinton, who was elected bishop at the general conference in 1892 and was the presiding bishop in the Palmetto State in 1894, when the college was founded.

Clinton Normal and Industrial College became a connectional institution under the auspices of the A.M.E. Zion Church, and the school began to train and certify the state's future teachers and preachers.

Many obstacles existed in the South: first the Civil War, then Reconstruction, and later the Depression. Many local Christian families sacrificially committed themselves to continuing the A.M.E. Zion Church mission, and by the dawn of the 20th century, Clinton Junior College had become a beacon for ambitious students. The progressive school and its educators guided a generation burdened by narrow-minded prejudices, and they gave hope to the community whenever segregation created despair.

Poverty prevailed in the South until after the World Wars. While other institutions folded, Clinton Junior College flourished. Presently, Clinton Junior College is the only African-American junior college in continuous operation in the two Carolinas. For more than 110 years, Clinton Junior College has provided an environment that nurtures intellectual growth. International people and students from across the nation gain positive moral, ethical, and spiritual values, while the college continues to grow and share its Christian heritage. The college serves to encourage each individual, no matter their race or gender, to become active citizens and good stewards at all times.

Although this book is an incomplete, pictorial history of this inspirational college, it is complete in its intention to provide the reader with a sense of evolution about one of the South's most unique two-year institutions. Some of the photographs have been published before, but many appear here for the first time. In all, the images here depict the optimism and the hardships, the architecture and the landscape of this group of ministers and educators who serve at Clinton Junior College.

It is our hope that from beginning to end, young and old, white and black, and newcomers and visitors alike will find this book to be not only a delightful addition to the family library but also a fun, leisurely read for many years to come.

One

THE FREEDOM CHURCH

"In October 1796, the African Methodist Episcopal Zion Church was founded in New York City. The organization grew out of the well-known dissatisfaction among the people of color over the kind of treatment they received in the services of the church."

—Bishop William Jacob Walls, *The African Methodist Episcopal Zion Church: Reality of the Black Church* (1974)

The A.M.E. Zion church divested from the Methodist Episcopal Society (Church) under the leadership of James Varick, who became the first bishop. Bishop Walls noted, "Thus we have the comprehensive and living definition of small, restless, dissatisfied group, who with wholehearted determination and zeal made the giant step in eliminating brutal slavery and proscription. From then on they moved with magnifying force, not only to produce some of the world's greatest freedom fighters and advocates, but to shine as a beacon light for individual rights and privileges, in becoming prominent and well known as 'The Freedom Church.' "

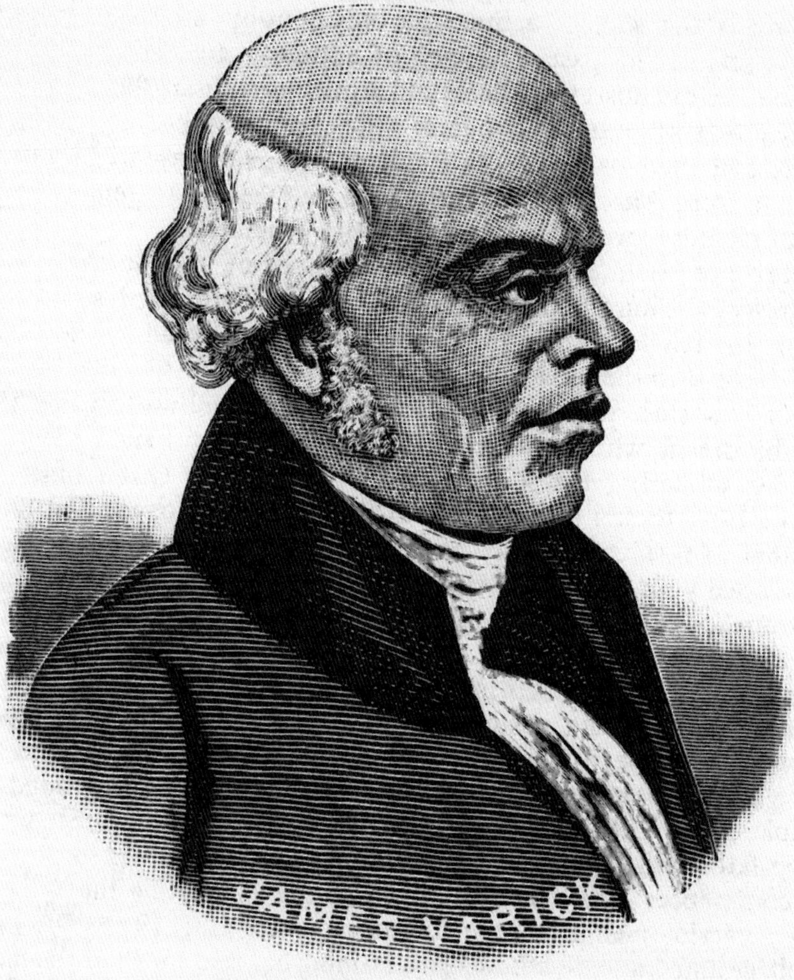

1750 – 1827
Founder and First Bishop of the African Methodist Episcopal Zion Church

James Varick became the first bishop of the A.M.E. Zion Church. He was elected in 1822 and died in 1827.

Harriet Tubman, *c.* 1820–1913, was called the "Conductor of the Underground Railroad." The A.M.E. Zion Church is restoring her home in Auburn, New York.

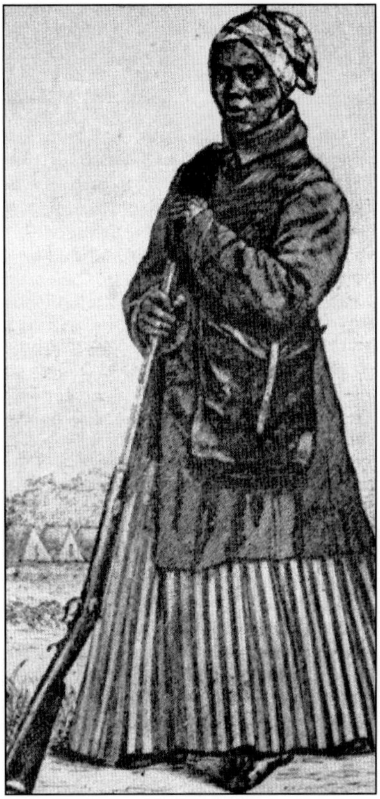

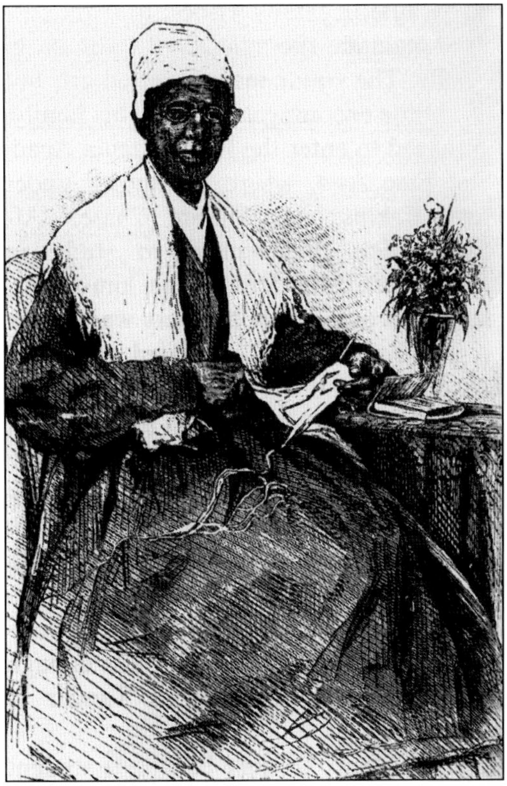

Sojouner Truth (1797–1883) was a Civil War heroine and abolitionist. A notable and unusual antislavery speaker, she was also an early fighter for women's rights.

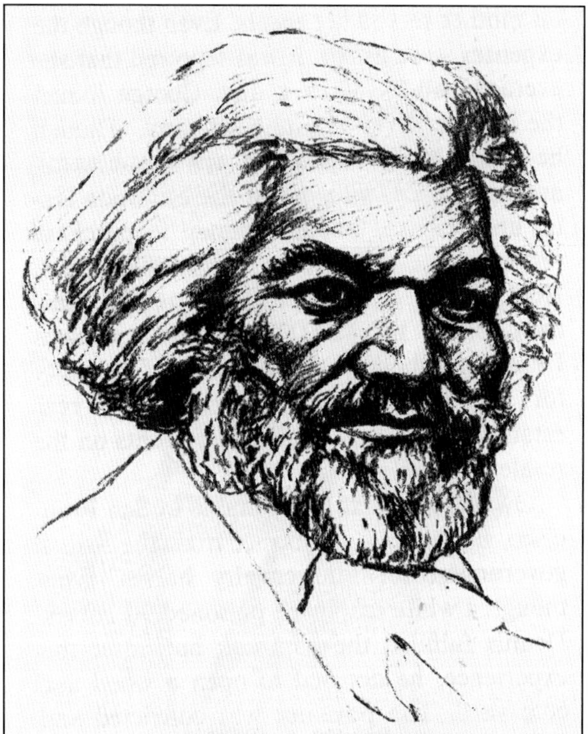

Frederick Douglass (1817–1895) was an abolitionist. He escaped bondage in 1838 and went on to become a great orator, writer, and publisher.

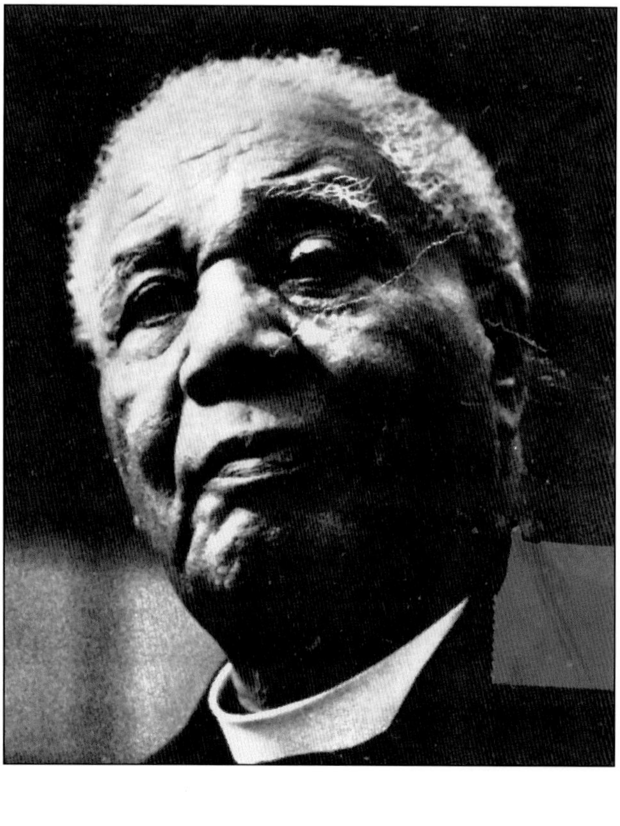

William Jacob Walls was the 42nd bishop elected to the A.M.E. Zion Church. He was elected bishop in 1924. He was a great scholar and authored the book *The African Methodist Episcopal Zion Church: Reality of the Black Church*, a history of the A.M.E. Zion Church. According to Bishop Walls, the A.M.E. Zion Church has sponsored institutional education practically since its beginning. After the establishment of what is now Livingstone College in 1885, "efforts were made to establish schools in every section of the country where the A.M.E. Zion Church had a large or average following.

Two

GROWTH

Creating Opportunity

Clinton Junior College is named in honor of Bishop Isom Caleb Clinton (1859–1921). Born to a slave woman in the Mount Carmel community of Lancaster County, South Carolina, Isom Clinton respected his teachers, particularly a West Indian instructor who encouraged young Clinton to obtain a college education. In 1874, I.C. Clinton enrolled at South Carolina College (founded in 1896 and now known as South Carolina State University), but in 1876, state and local governments refused African Americans access to many colleges. Determined to reach his goal, Isom Clinton returned to Mount Carmel and attended Brainerd Institute in Chester, South Carolina. In 1879, Isom Clinton became licensed to preach. His career flourished, and he presided over the state's conference of the African Methodist Episcopal (A.M.E.) Zion Church in 1894. At the same time, Rev. Nero Crockett and Rev. W.M. Robinson founded Clinton Institute in Rock Hill. When Clinton died at age 62, World War I had ended, and Alain Locke, a 1907 graduate of Harvard, had become the first African American to win a Rhodes Scholarship. Clinton had lived to see progress. He lived to see Clinton Junior College incorporated (June 22, 1909) as Clinton Normal and Industrial Institute. A 1965 charter amended the name to Clinton Junior College, and currently, some local residents refer to the two-year, private institute as simply Clinton College.

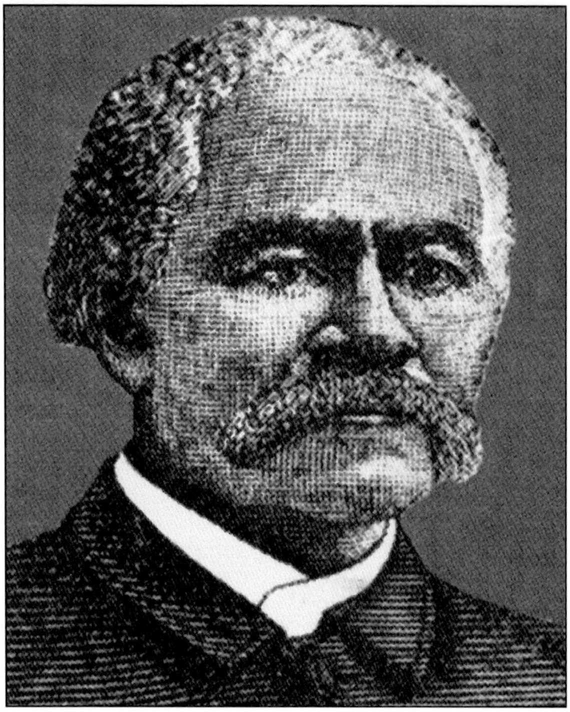

Clinton Junior College is named for Bishop Clinton (1859–1921), who lived to see the college incorporated in 1909.

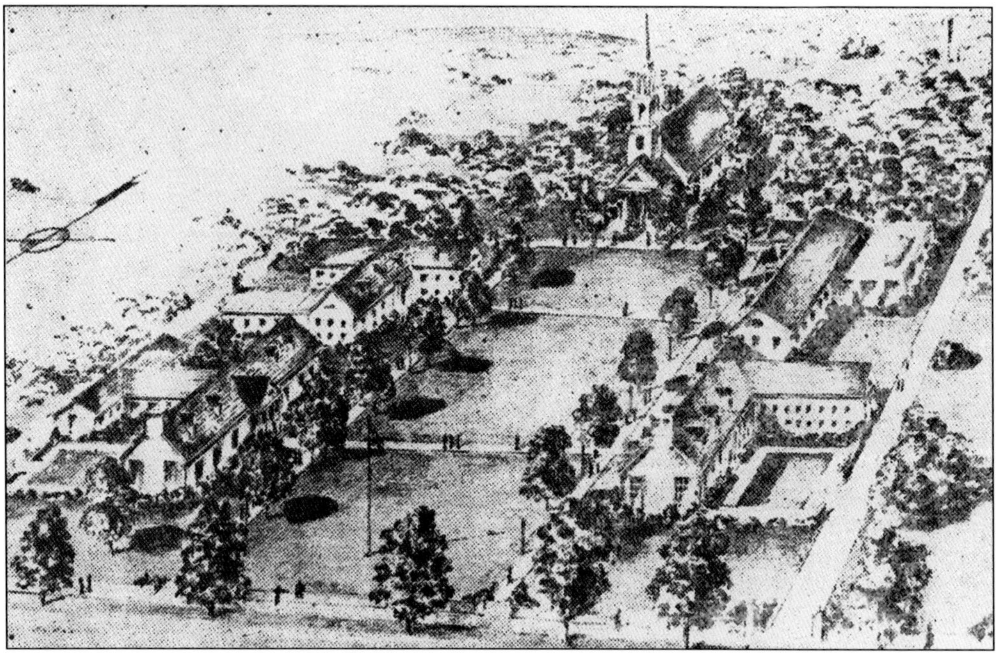

White landowners L.M. Davis and W.L. Roddey ceded about 19 acres of rock-ribbed, flat land at the intersection of Crawford Road and Heckle Boulevard to the trustees at Clinton Normal and Industrial Institute. Depicted is an early 20th-century architect's concept of the college's first campus. This campus never materialized, but Clinton Junior College continued to grow. It flourished among shady groves, an inviting, scholarly atmosphere that is still part of the college's main campus.

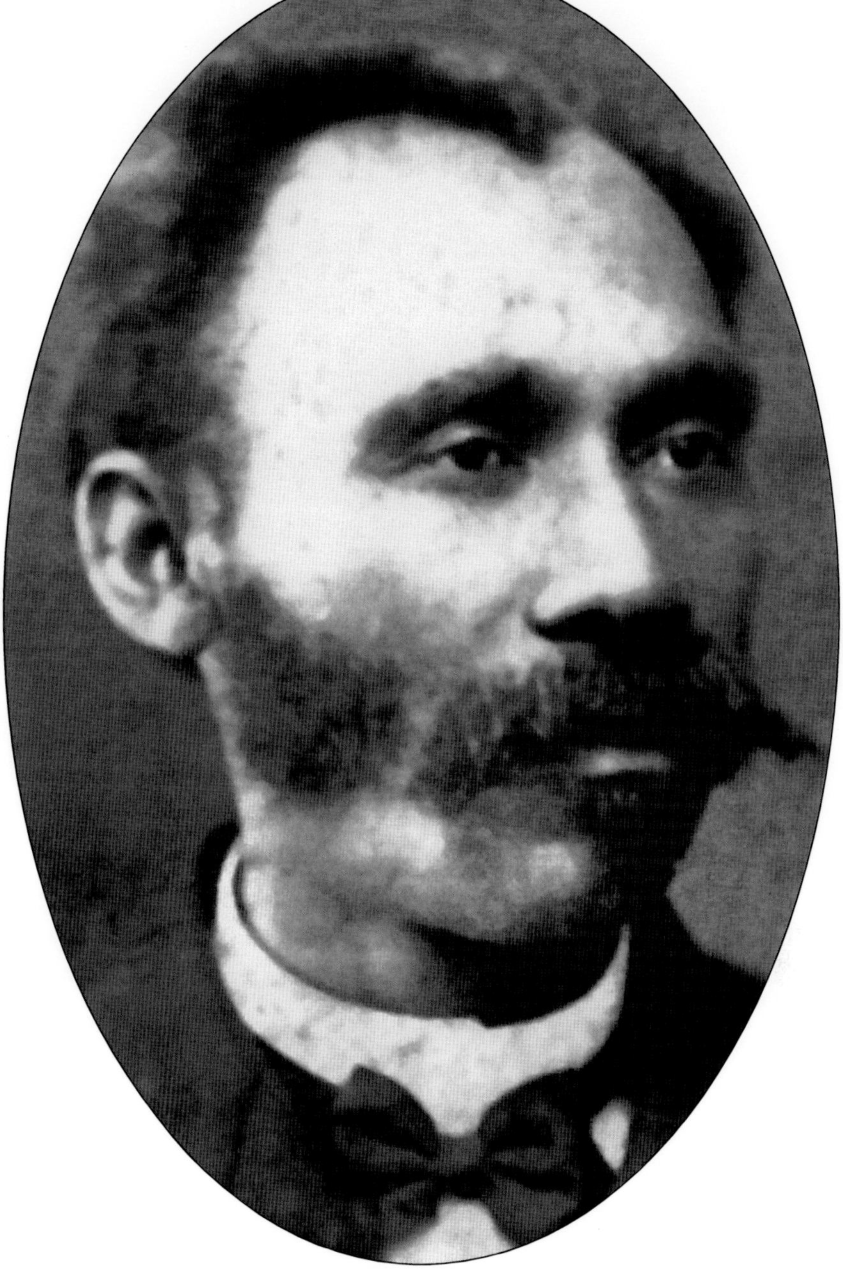

Most people in Rock Hill are surprised to learn that two African-American colleges existed prior to the arrival of the all-female school that became Winthrop University. In 1891, Friendship Junior College, or the Friendship Normal and Industrial Institute, was founded by Rev. M.P. Hall in the old Mount Prospect Baptist Church. Three years later, in 1894, Rev. W.M. Robinson founded Clinton Junior College with Rev. N.L. Crockett. Pictured is Rev. W.M. Robinson, then pastor of the Clinton Chapel A.M.E. Zion Church in York, South Carolina. No picture is available of Rev. Nero Crockett, the presiding elder of the A.M.E. Zion Church, Yorkville District in the South Carolina Conference.

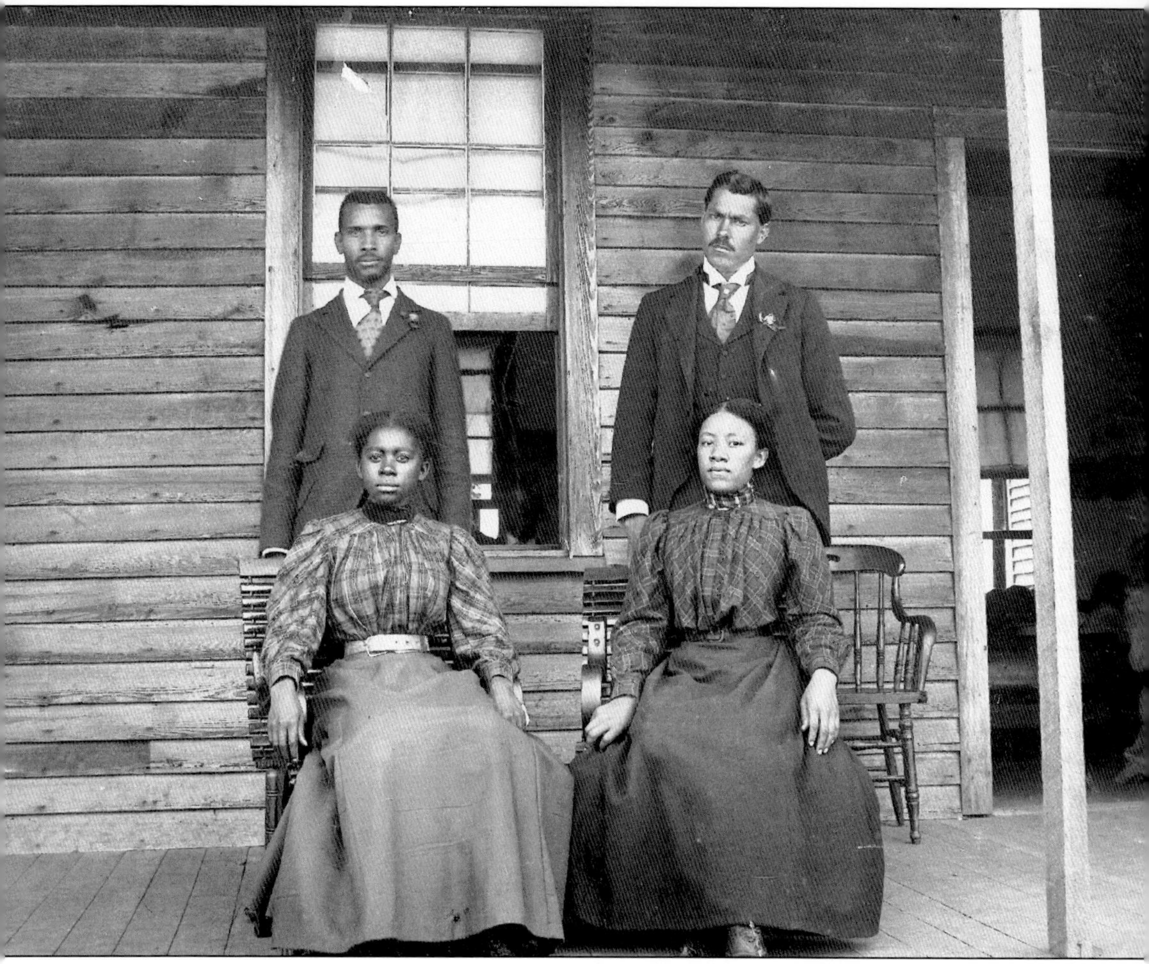

After the Civil War, shortages abounded. Sugar, salt, and dry goods were hard to find. Confederate money was worthless, but African Americans were finally free. This fact intimidated many adult white males, who therefore joined the Ku Klux Klan in an effort to suppress the freedmen and new citizens of the United States. Violence ensued. In 1871, President Ulysses S. Grant ordered martial law for York and other rebel counties. In 1876, Wade Hampton ran for South Carolina governor. When he won, federal troops withdrew from the state, and Klan activity diminished. Prejudices did not. The state embraced industrialization and began to improve education for whites. Free public education for African Americans would not come to Rock Hill until 1916, but these social, economic, and physical obstacles did not deter the Class of 1899, a group dedicated to the eradication of illiteracy among freed men and women and the first graduating class of the college.

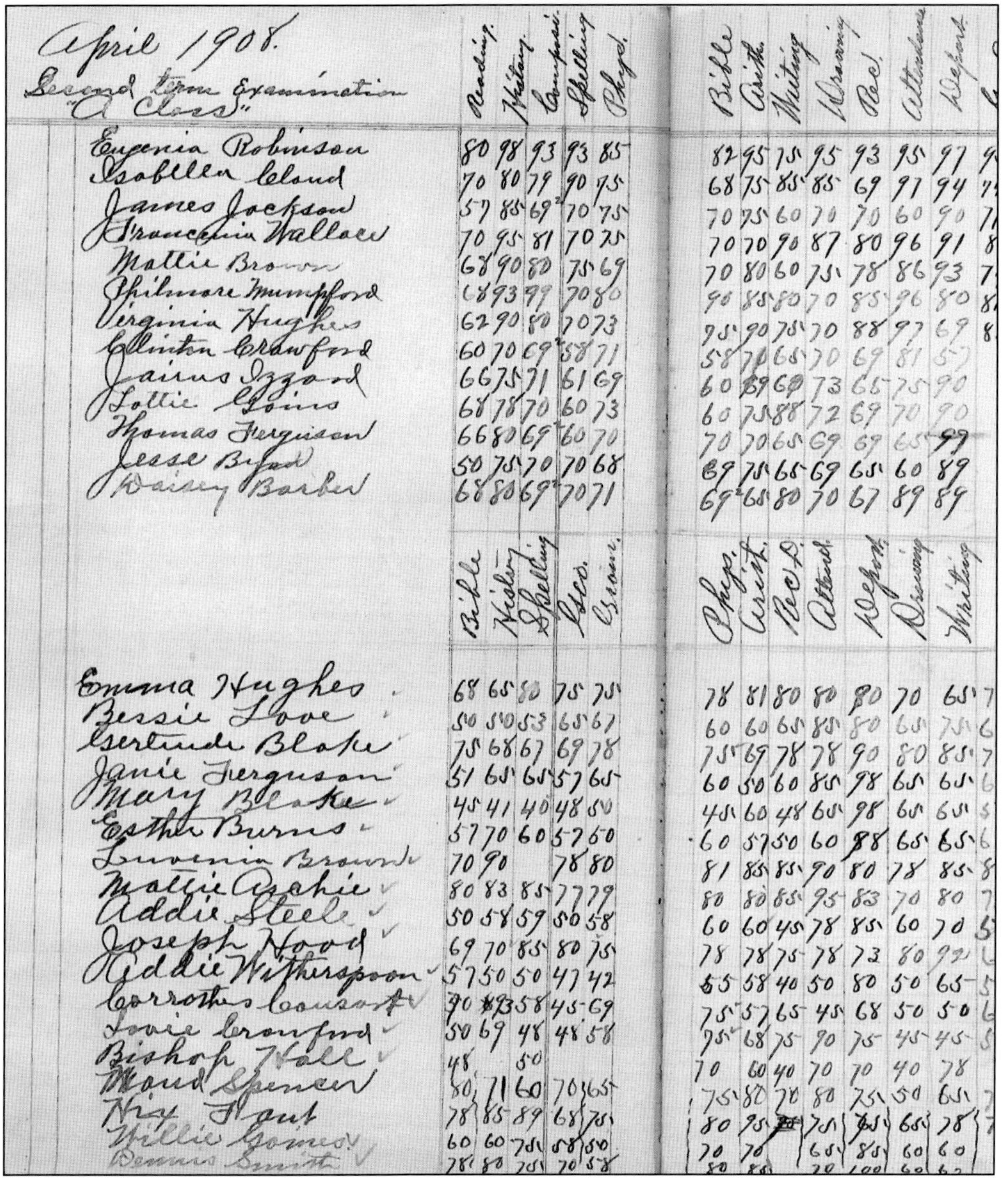

In the early days, Clinton Junior College served as a boarding school for students. Grade books at the college include third graders' names and courses such as spelling, geography, arithmetic, and drawing. Depicted is one of the entries from April 1908. The subjects on the ledger include history and the Bible. Classes were small then, and the school struggled. Generations of families sacrificially committed themselves to keeping the school alive, and today, Clinton Junior College is the only historically black junior college operating in the two Carolinas.

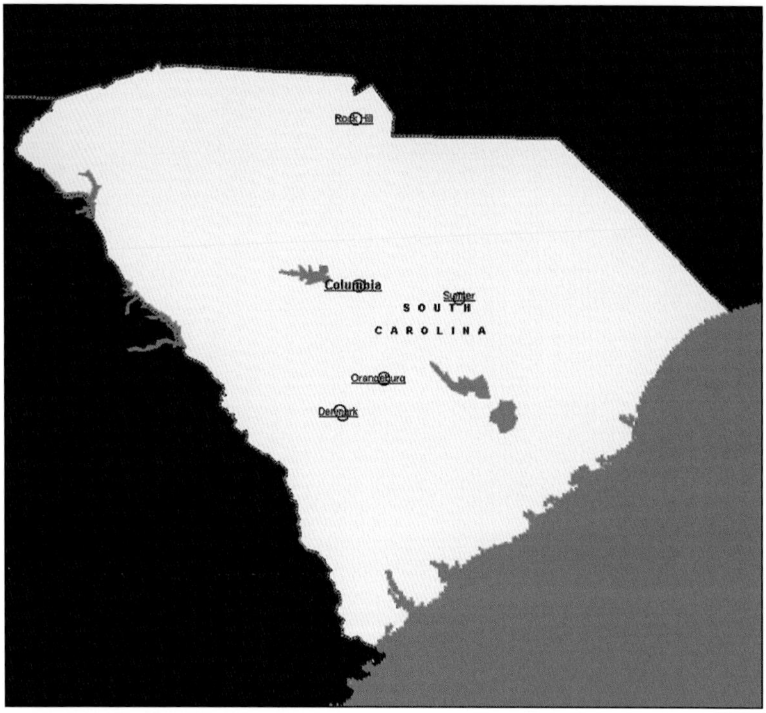

The world changed drastically between 1866 and 1904. During the 35 years that followed the Civil War, more than 24 colleges and universities for African Americans were founded in the South. Education meant the world to these scholars, and they studied diligently.

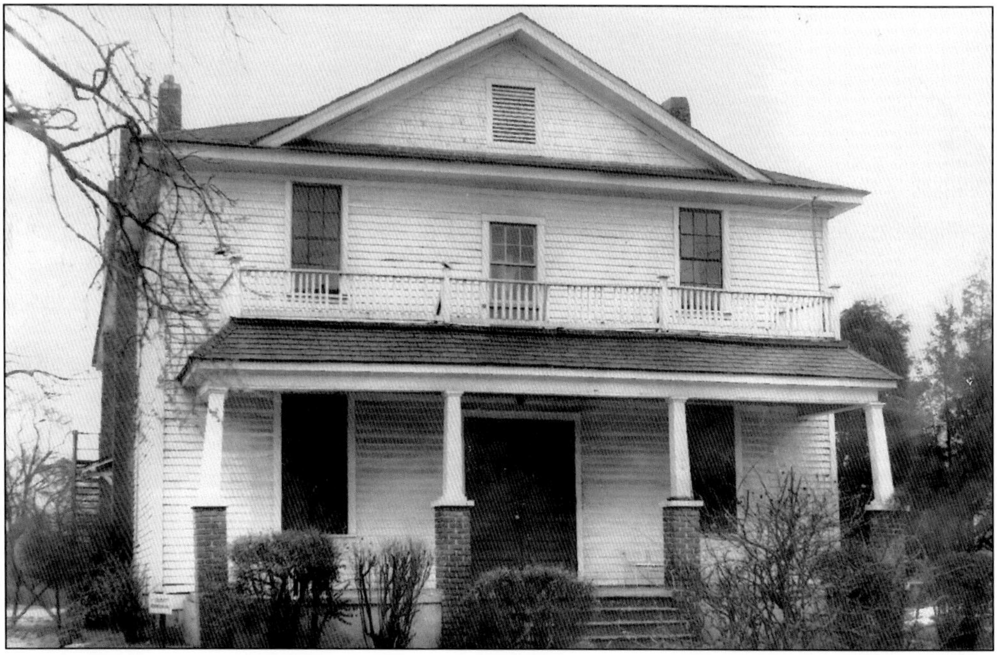

Clinton's campus is a mixture of historical architecture, but this building no longer stands. Named for the founders of the college, Crockett-Robinson Hall housed the president's office on the first floor. Donated by Mr. H.A. Kelsey of Washington, D.C, the Kelsey Library, Clinton's first library, shared the first floor with a dining room, kitchen, and small auditorium. The second floor of Crockett-Robinson Hall functioned as the women's residence hall, the first of its kind at Clinton Junior College.

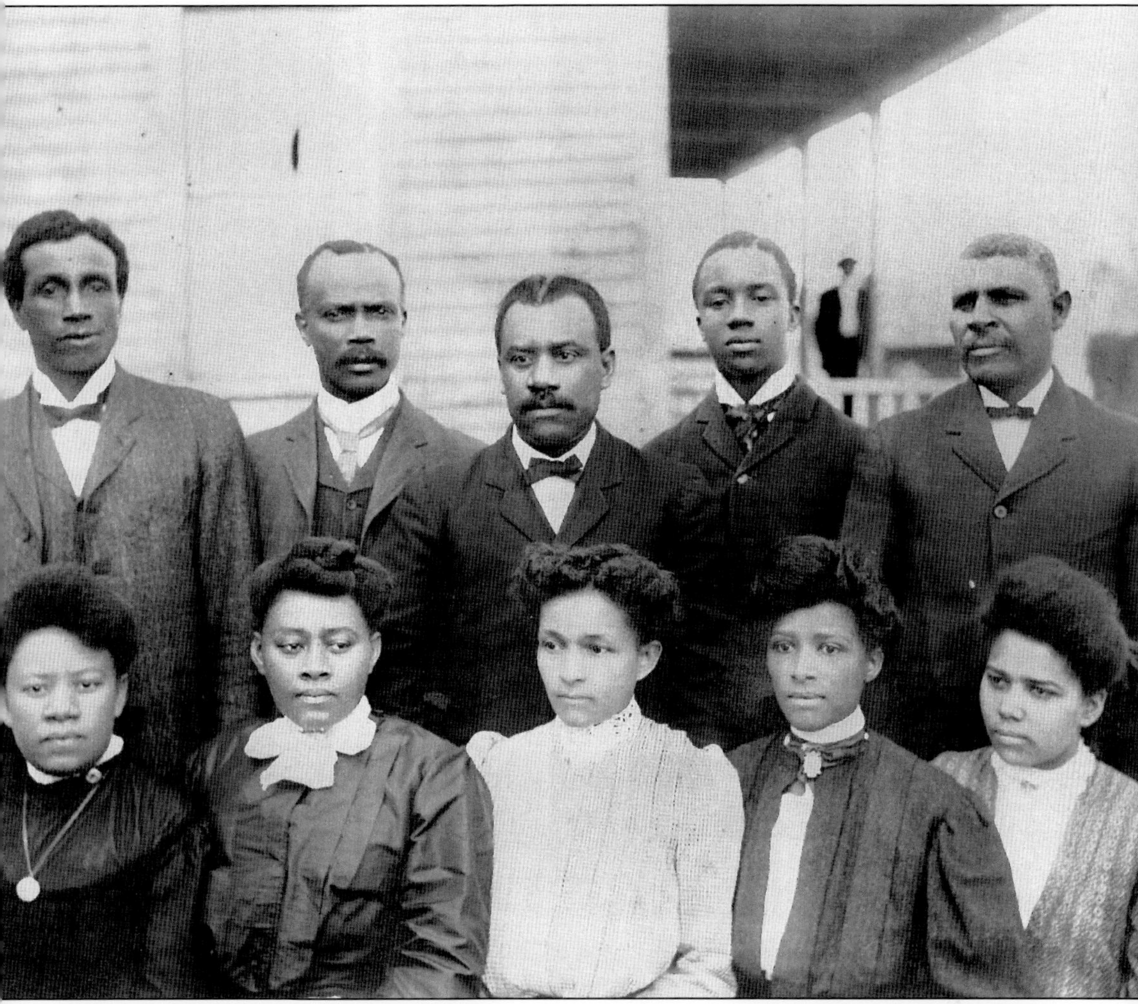

This early 1900s image shows the first faculty photographed at Clinton Junior College, then known as the Clinton Normal and Industrial Institute. The institute operated like a boarding high school, providing a high-quality education to hundreds of newly freed African Americans. From left to right are (front row) Miss Nettie C. Crockett (music), Mrs. Ella B. White (dietitian), Mrs. Alice V. Jones, Miss Fannie Beatty, and Miss Hattie E. Ramseur; (back row) Mr. Robert J. Boulware (math), Dr. I.A. Macon (science), Pres. Robert J. Crockett, Dr. James W. Eichelberger, and Charles H. Jones.

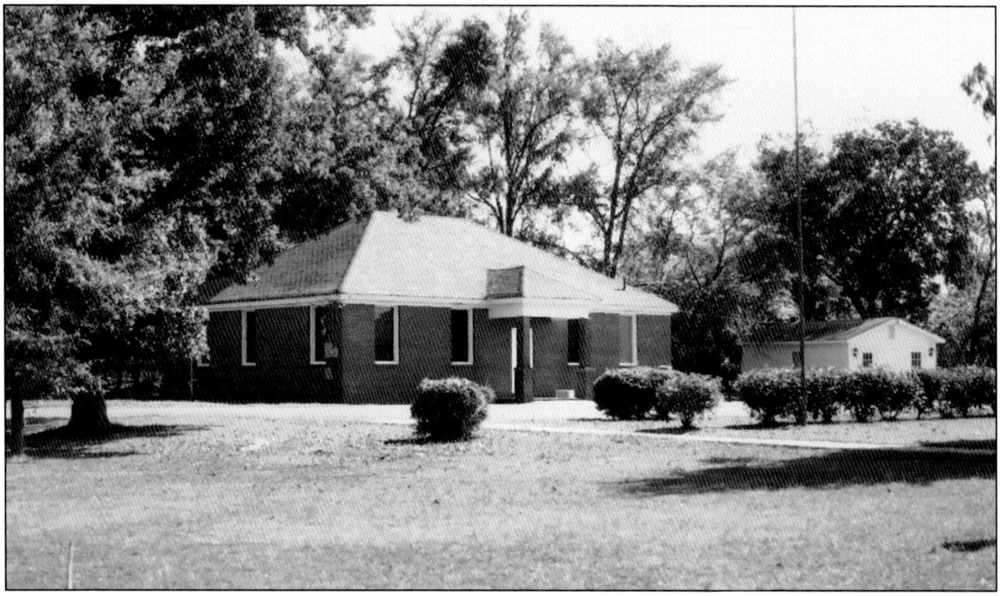

In 1872, the South Carolina Agricultural and Mechanics Institute, a state college for African Americans, was established in Orangeburg. In 1879, Zion Wesley Institute, now Livingstone College, was established in North Carolina. It closed during 1880–1881 and re-opened under Joseph Charles Price, noted scholar and orator. In 1894, Clinton Normal Institute was founded, and in 1936, a second building was constructed on the Clinton campus. Shown *c.* 1942, it is described in documents as the Academic Building.

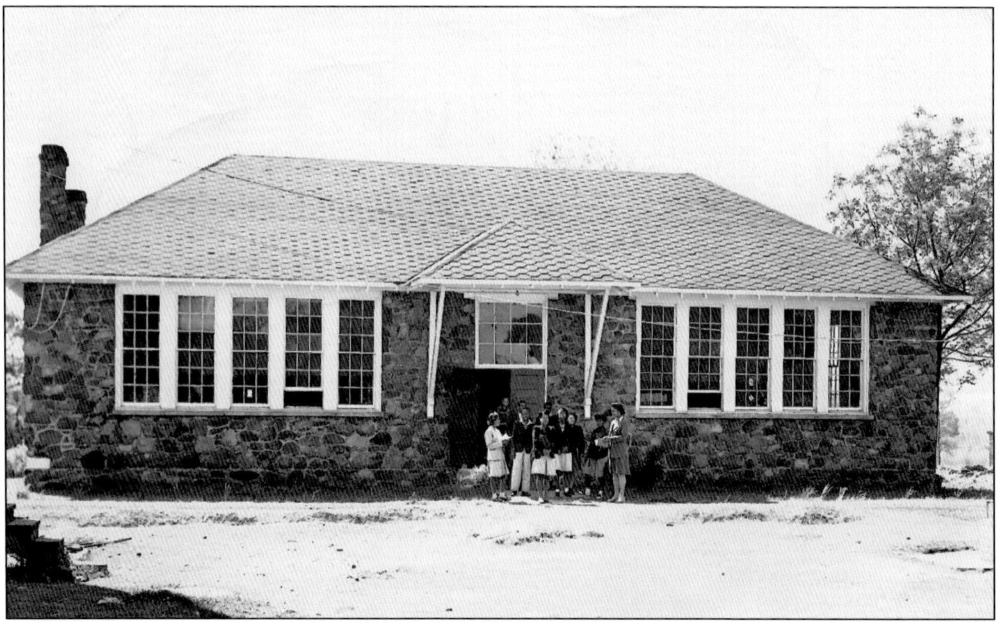

In the 1930s, the Work Progress Administration (WPA) constructed a number of buildings out of rubble rock and field stone, the kind utilized on the 1936 Administration Building at Clinton Normal and Industrial College. Many of these buildings in South Carolina have been razed, including the Administration Building, which was replaced by the brick W.W. Slade Memorial Hall in the 1940s. (Courtesy of Thaxton's Studio, Rock Hill, South Carolina.)

At the turn of the 20th century, African-American leadership came from the church, the only institution where they were encouraged to express their dreams. According to the book *Black Carolinians* by Idus Newby (USC Press, 1973), "African Americans yearned for a quality education and a public forum in order to solve their socio-economic problems." People like Booker T. Washington (right) stressed a doctrine of self-help and vocational education for African Americans. Booker T. Washington (below) visited South Carolina several times. In 1923, George Washington Carver, peanut butter inventor and agricultural specialist, also lectured at colleges in the Carolinas. There is no hard copy or surviving historical evidence that the two men ever visited Clinton Junior College, but their positive messages echoed a similar inspiration ringing throughout the sanctuaries of the A.M.E. Zion churches.

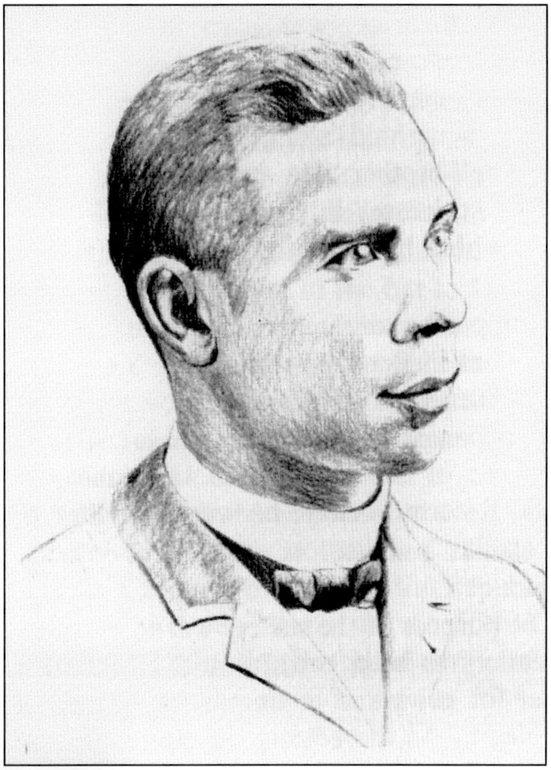

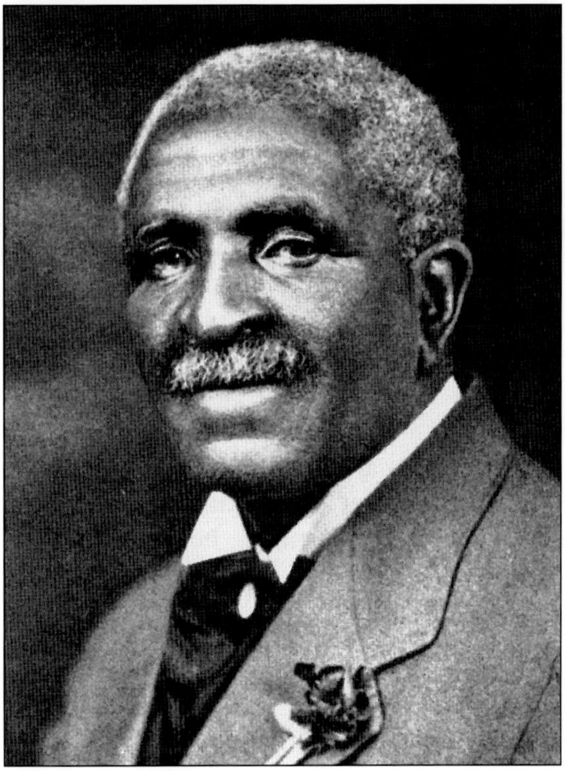

ficial Voice Of The African Methodist Episcopal Zion Church

The Star

celerating Communication About The Freedom Church

OLUME 127 NO. 19-20

In 1933, the NAACP began its campaign to eliminate segregation and discrimination in the educational systems. By the mid-20th century, the A.M.E. Zion Church regularly published *The Star of Zion*, *Quarterly Review*, and many other periodicals for distribution throughout the world. In the South, however, receiving mail or newspapers proved difficult. Many

Clinton College attains full accreditation

BY ERICA PIPPINS
reprinted from
THE HERALD

For three years, Clinton Junior College administrators, students and alumni have hoped and prayed for the day where a single decision would reshape the college's future.

In the end, it took less than five minutes for them to get their wish.

After a brief closed-door meeting April 9 in Raleigh, NC, the 23-member accreditation commission of the Transnational Association of Christian Colleges and Schools delivered the news Clinton President Elaine Johnson Copeland had been waiting to hear: "The college has been approved for full accreditation."

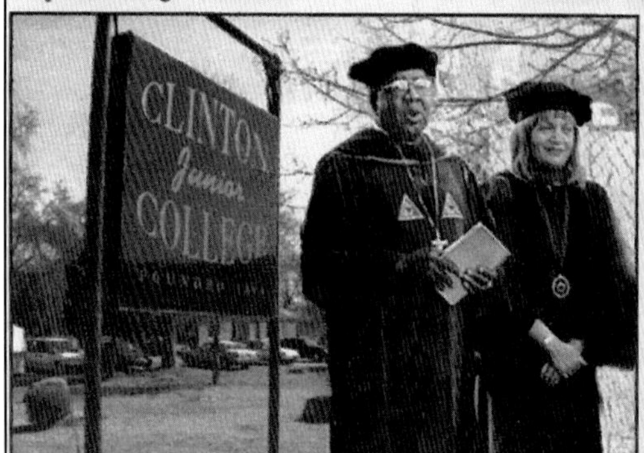

Star photo

Bishop Johnson and Dr. Elaine Copeland stand together in front of the new Clinton Jr. College sign.

Dr. Copeland, along with area Bishop Joseph Johnson, chairman of the college's board of trustees, were representatives from one of the eleven institutions considered for accreditation. However, the outcome for all schools will not be announced until November, Copeland said.

Approved by the U.S. Department of Education as a nationally-recognized institutional accrediting agency, TRACS was developed in 1979 to promote the development of post-secondary Christian institutions. Clinton Junior College, located at the intersection of Heckle Boulevard and Crawford Road, is supported by the A.M.E. Zion Church.

Copeland said she was "delighted" the two-year historically black college, which was evaluated by TRACS representatives in February, was granted full accreditation. An added honor, she said, was the commission's request that she become a member of the TRACS accreditation board.

"The accreditation process was an activity that brought everyone together;

See Clinton accreditation.../pg. 12

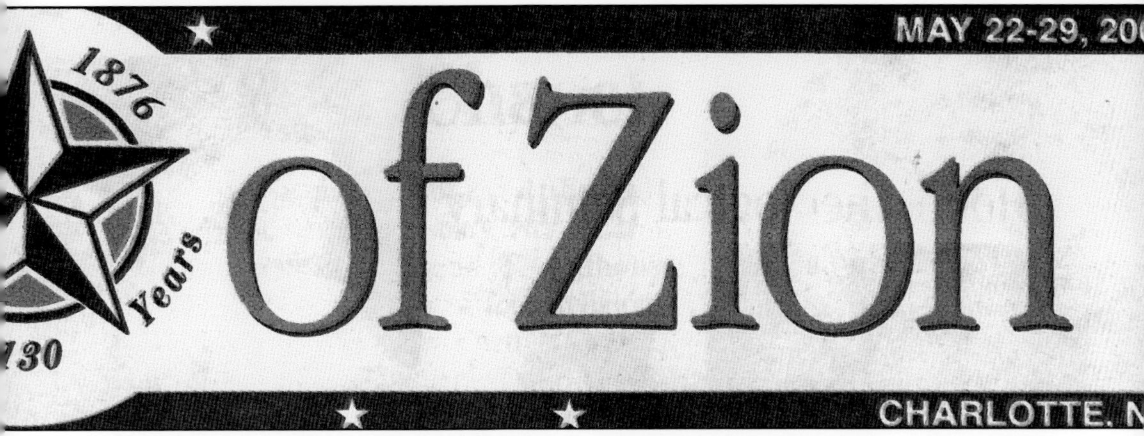

country roads remained unpaved. Delivery often took days or even weeks, so the church was the news center as well as the focus of all social activities.

Pictured below left is an article about the college in the November 15, 2001 edition of *The Star of Zion*. Below right is a collage of pictures from the same edition.

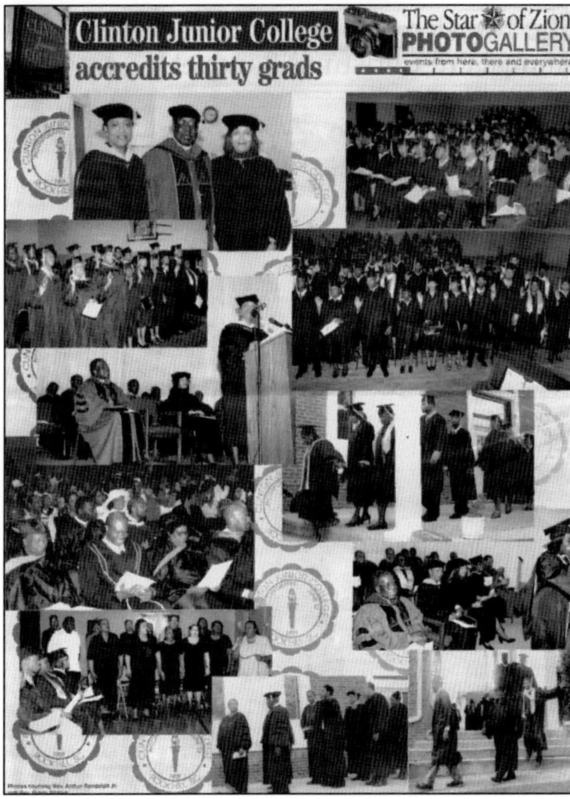

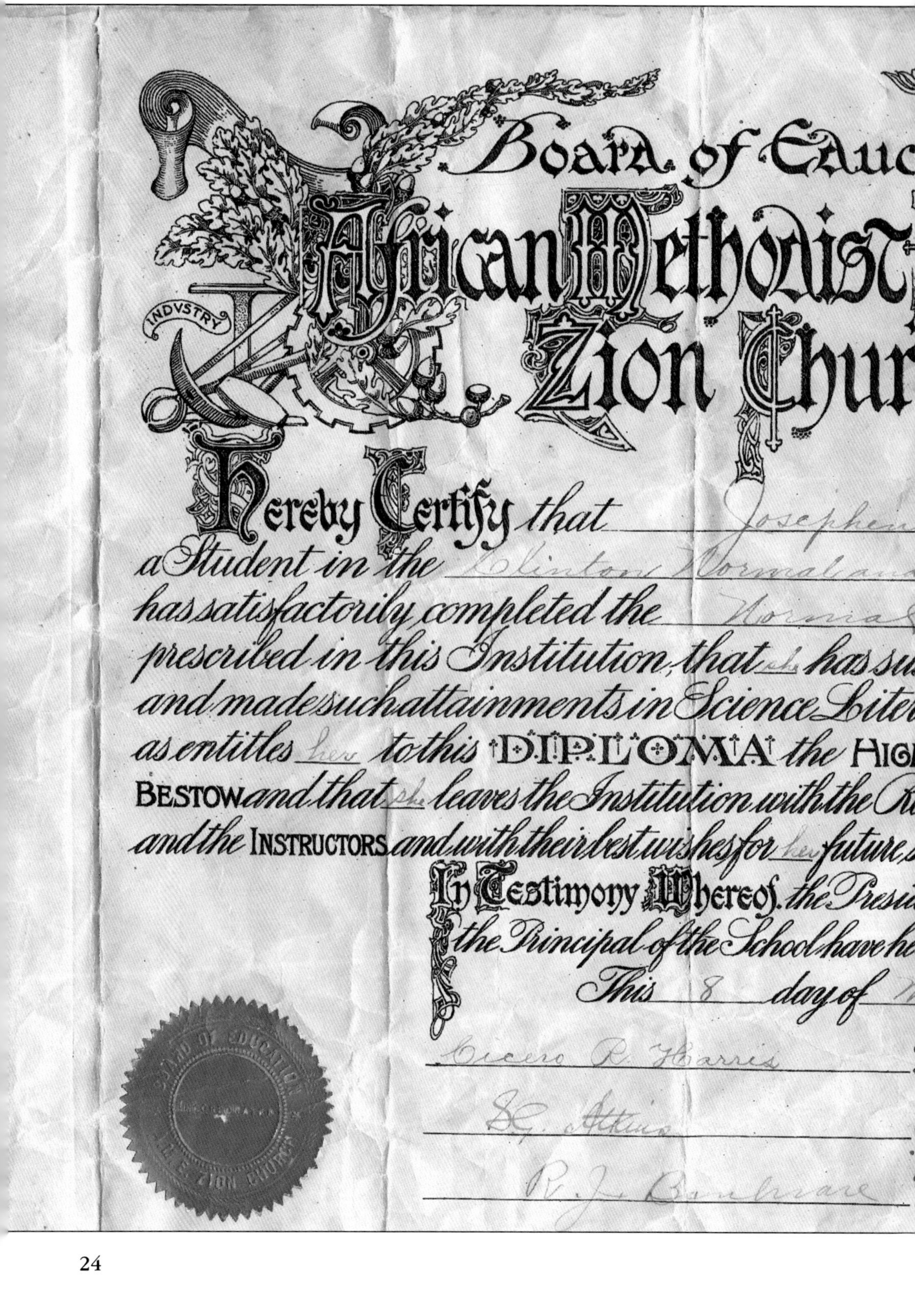

Board of Educ

African Methodist

Zion Chur

INDUSTRY

Hereby Certify that Josephin

a Student in the Clinton Normal and

has satisfactorily completed the Norma

prescribed in this Institution, that she has su

and made such attainments in Science Liter

as entitles her to this DIPLOMA the Hig

BESTOW and that she leaves the Institution with the Re

and the INSTRUCTORS and with their best wishes for her future,

In Testimony Whereof, the Presi

the Principal of the School have he

This 8 day of

Cicero R. Harris

S. G. Atkins

R. J. Buchanan

BOARD OF EDUCATION

INCORPORATED

A.M.E. ZION CHURCH

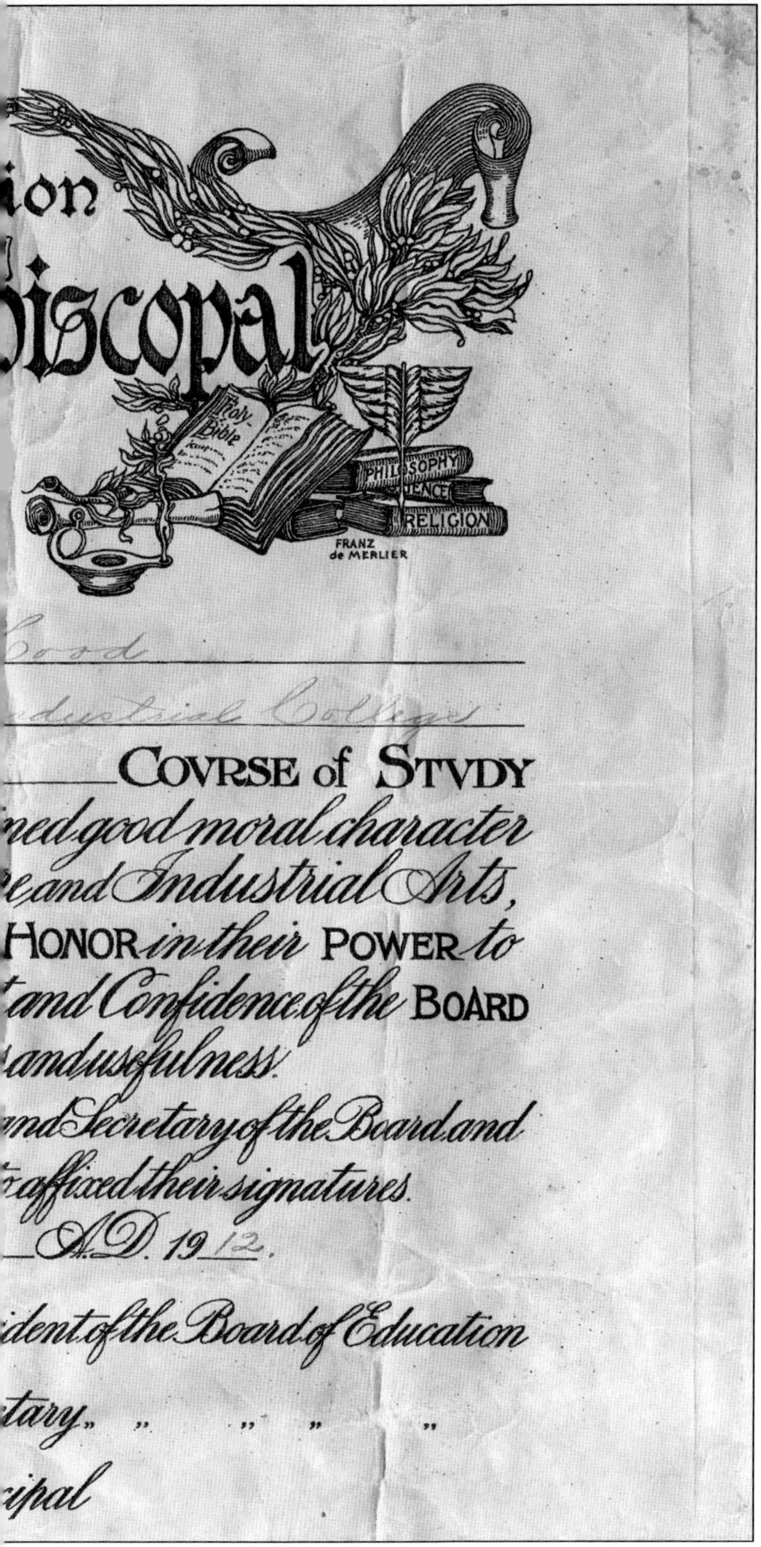

This diploma, sealed by the board of education of the A.M.E. Zion Church, was issued on May 8, 1912. The decorative document is more than 12 inches tall and almost 17 inches long.

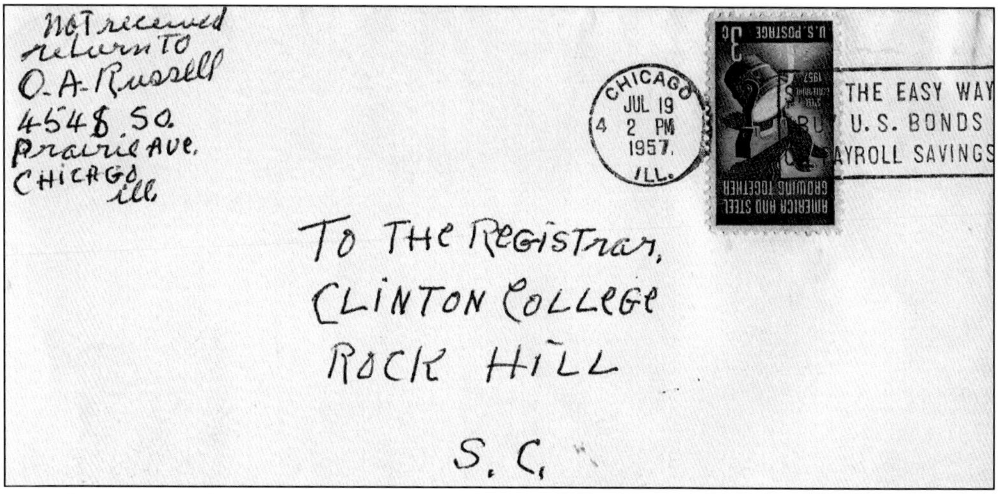
Not received return To
O. A. Russell
4548 So.
Prairie Ave.
Chicago
ill

CHICAGO
JUL 19
4 2 PM
1957
ILL.

U.S. POSTAGE 3¢
AMERICA AND STEEL GROWING TOGETHER

THE EASY WAY
BUY U.S. BONDS
PAYROLL SAVINGS

To The Registrar,
Clinton College
Rock Hill
S. C.

On July 19, 1957, this envelope was received by the registrar at Clinton Junior College from 4548 South Prairie Avenue in Chicago, Illinois. Such letters were commonplace as the 20th century progressed, and Clinton Junior College was an effective resource to its alumni, as the contents below can testify.

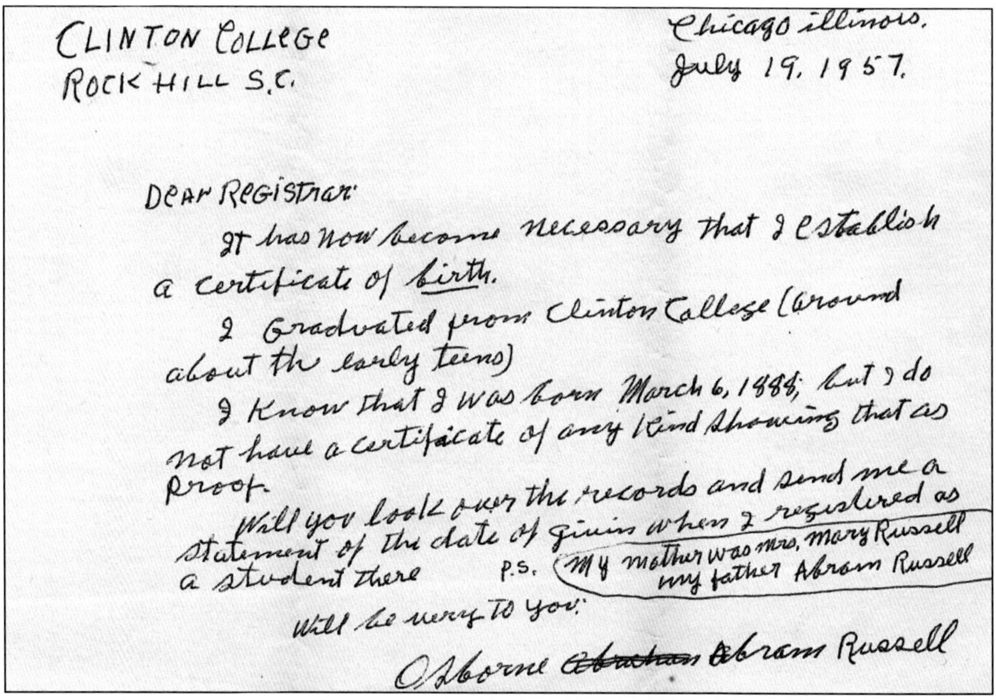
Clinton College
Rock Hill S.C.

Chicago illinois.
July 19, 1957.

Dear Registrar:
It has now become necessary that I establish a certificate of birth.
I Graduated from Clinton College (around about the early teens)
I Know that I was born March 6, 1888; but I do not have a certificate of any Kind Showing that as proof.
Will you look over the records and send me a statement of the date of givin when I registered as a student there
P.S. My mother was mrs. mary Russell my father Abram Russell
Will be very to you:
Osborne ~~Abraham~~ Abram Russell

Osborne Abram Russell was 69 years old when he requested from Clinton Junior College a letter testifying to the dates that he attended school there. He hoped to prove that he was born March 6, 1888, since he had no official birth certificate. Few Southern African Americans were born in hospitals or doctors' offices, and their births were either not recorded or were only recorded on paper, which many times were burned in the all-too-common fires in the poverty-stricken South. Many African Americans planted trees for such occasions. African Americans later realized that school records like those at Clinton Junior College proved invaluable when determining age to the federal government.

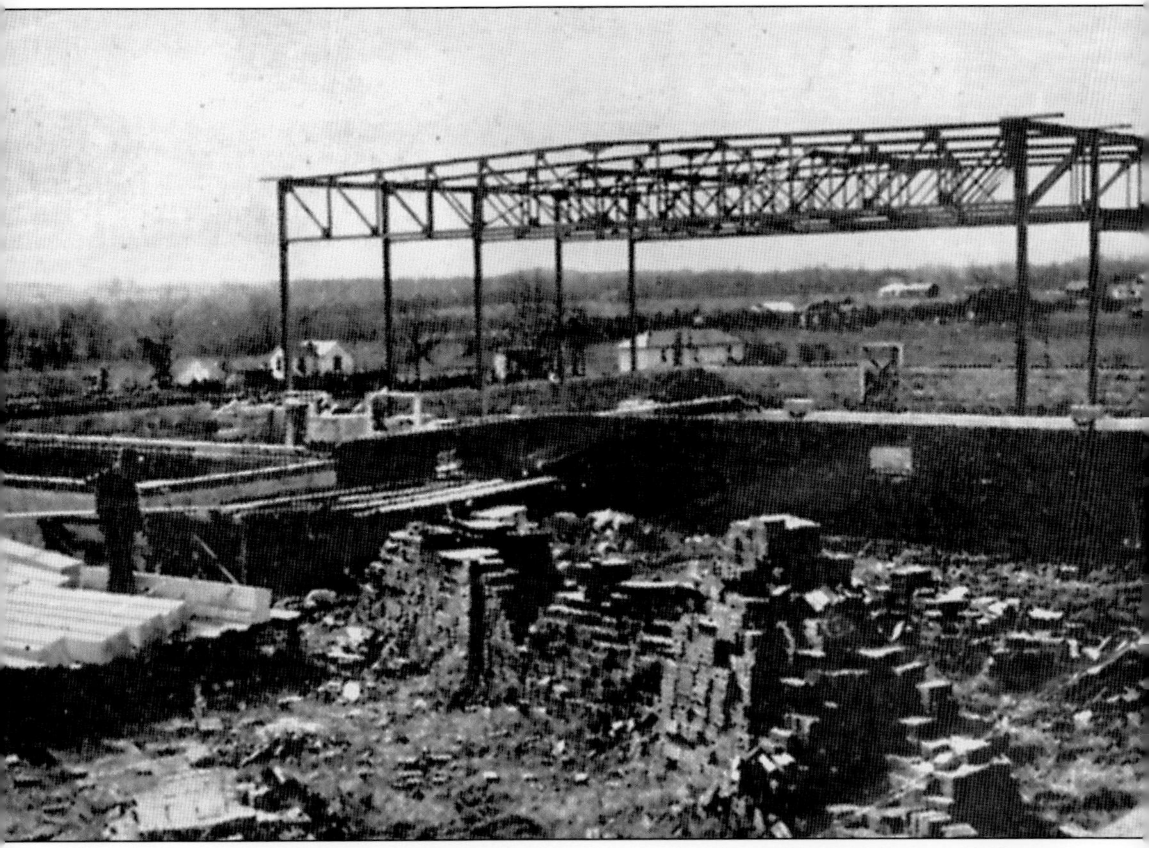

The image on the front of the college application is from the early 1950s. Notice the farms dotting the rolling hills surrounding Clinton Junior College as construction begins on a new administration building. Heckle Boulevard, or SC Highway 901, is a two-lane path, and Crawford Road is not visible from the campus at all.

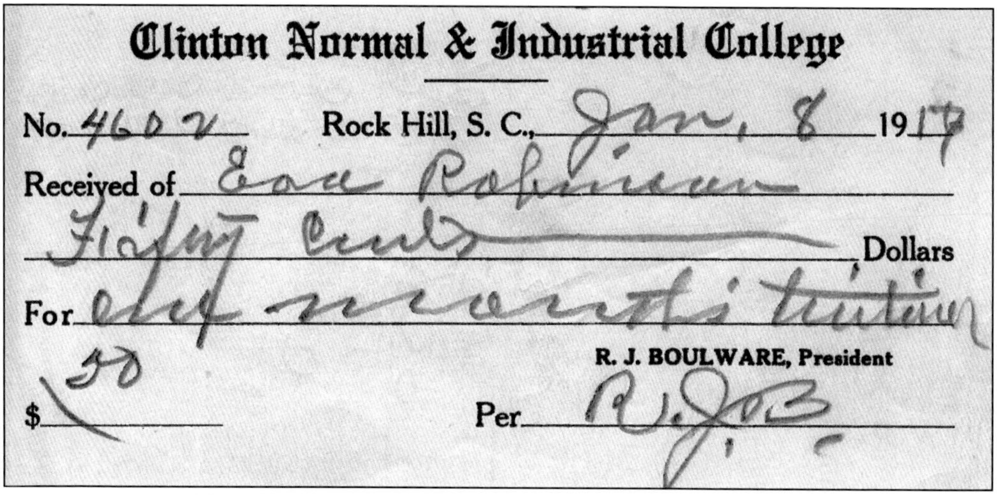

Clinton Normal & Industrial College

No. 4602 Rock Hill, S. C., Jan. 8 1917

Received of Eva Robinson

Fifty Cents Dollars

For one month's tuition

R. J. BOULWARE, President

$ .50 Per R.J.B.

Receipt number 4602 is dated January 8, 1917, from R.J. Boulware, president of Clinton Normal and Industrial College. It is for one month's tuition, or 50¢. Tuition is much higher in the 21st century.

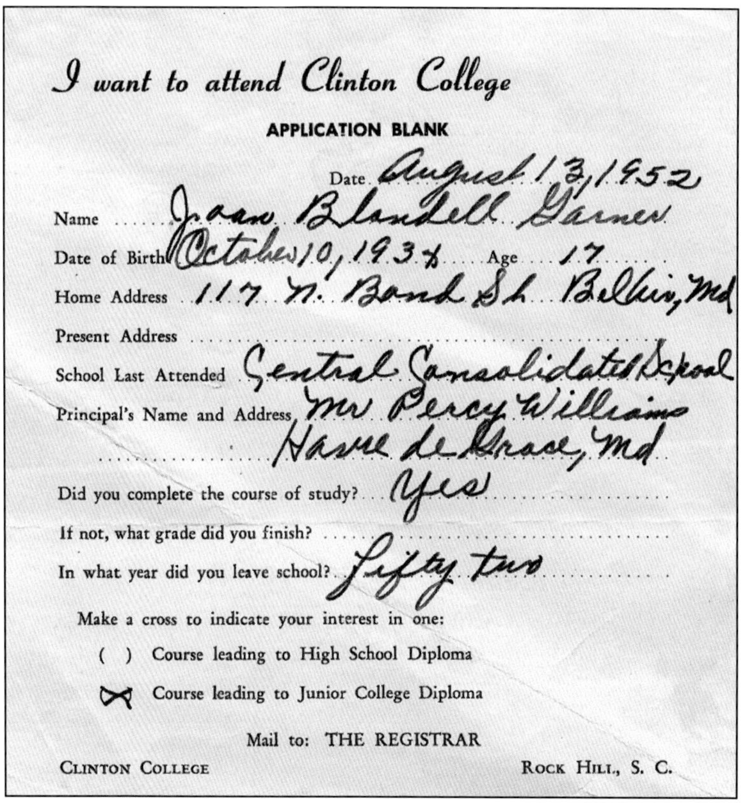

I want to attend Clinton College

APPLICATION BLANK

Date August 13, 1952

Name Joan Blandell Garner

Date of Birth October 10, 1934 Age 17

Home Address 117 N. Bond St. Belair, Md

Present Address

School Last Attended Central Consolidated School

Principal's Name and Address Mr Percy Williams Havre de Grace, Md

Did you complete the course of study? Yes

If not, what grade did you finish?

In what year did you leave school? Fifty two

Make a cross to indicate your interest in one:

( ) Course leading to High School Diploma

(X) Course leading to Junior College Diploma

Mail to: THE REGISTRAR

CLINTON COLLEGE ROCK HILL, S. C.

By the middle of the 20th century, registration at Clinton Junior College required an application such as this one from 1952. The student was from Maryland. Students come from all over the world to attend Clinton Junior College.

Three

EDUCATION

Inspire and Instruct

Education meant prosperity in the South. Tithes and special offerings from black Baptist Sunday schools purchased nine acres for Friendship College (founded 1891) on Allen Street. Friendship and Clinton Junior College (founded 1894) predate Winthrop's Rock Hill campus (founded 1895). Winthrop provided training for women, while Friendship College and Clinton educated both genders without prejudice. Friendship eventually closed in 1992, but Clinton Junior College continues to thrive. A new city hall was built during the 1930s, as well as a post office. Clinton Junior College also began expanding at this time.

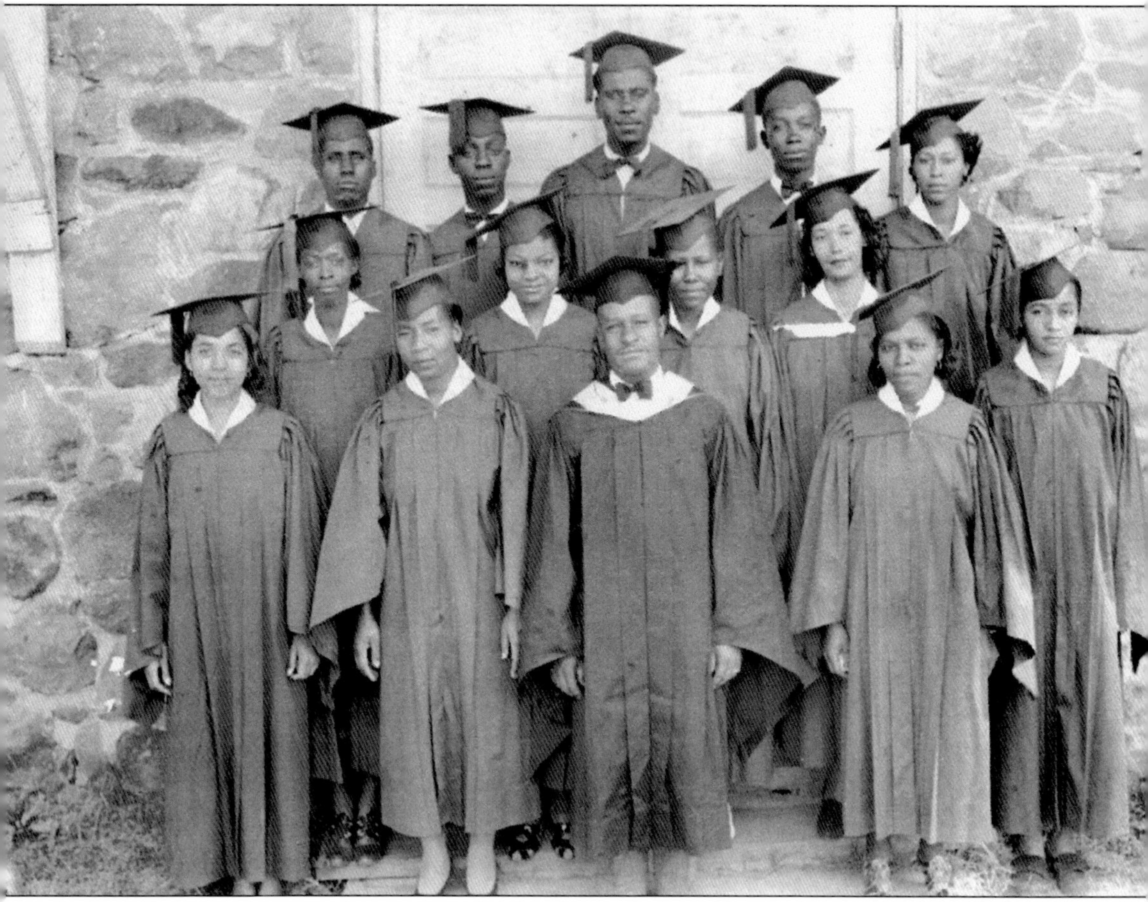

Pictured is the Class of 1938. Identified from left to right are (front row) Inez Meadow, Carrie Wade, C.H. Turner (class advisor), Martha Green, and Mae Rose Barber; (middle row) Laurado Barnett Patterson, Sallie Ann Edwards, Edith Cureton, and Florence Blake Burris; (back row) J.D. Gladden, David Moore, Alexander "Legs" Barnette, Robert Fuller, and Annell Reid.

Shown here is the 1942 commencement invitation. Approximately 30 students graduated that year.

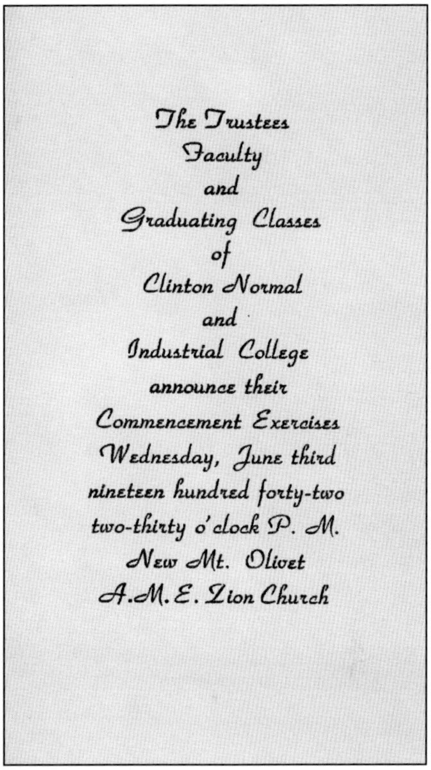

The Trustees
Faculty
and
Graduating Classes
of
Clinton Normal
and
Industrial College
announce their
Commencement Exercises
Wednesday, June third
nineteen hundred forty-two
two-thirty o'clock P. M.
New Mt. Olivet
A.M.E. Zion Church

Clinton Junior College was physically built one block at a time. Concrete and bricks compose the majority of the buildings. The campus architecture is generally mid-20th century contemporary designs, and function is primary while form is secondary. The W.W. Slade Hall is a dominant feature in the landscape. Presently, Clinton Junior College consists of seven brick buildings and four wooden structures. The brick buildings include the H.B. Shaw Dining Hall, the John W. Martin Gymnasium, W.W. Slade Hall, J.D. Cauthen and Arthur Marshall Residence Halls, the Student Center, and Fisher Memorial Library. The wooden structures consist of the Faculty Building, the Computer Laboratory, the Thomas Wilkes Bookstore, and the Weight Room.

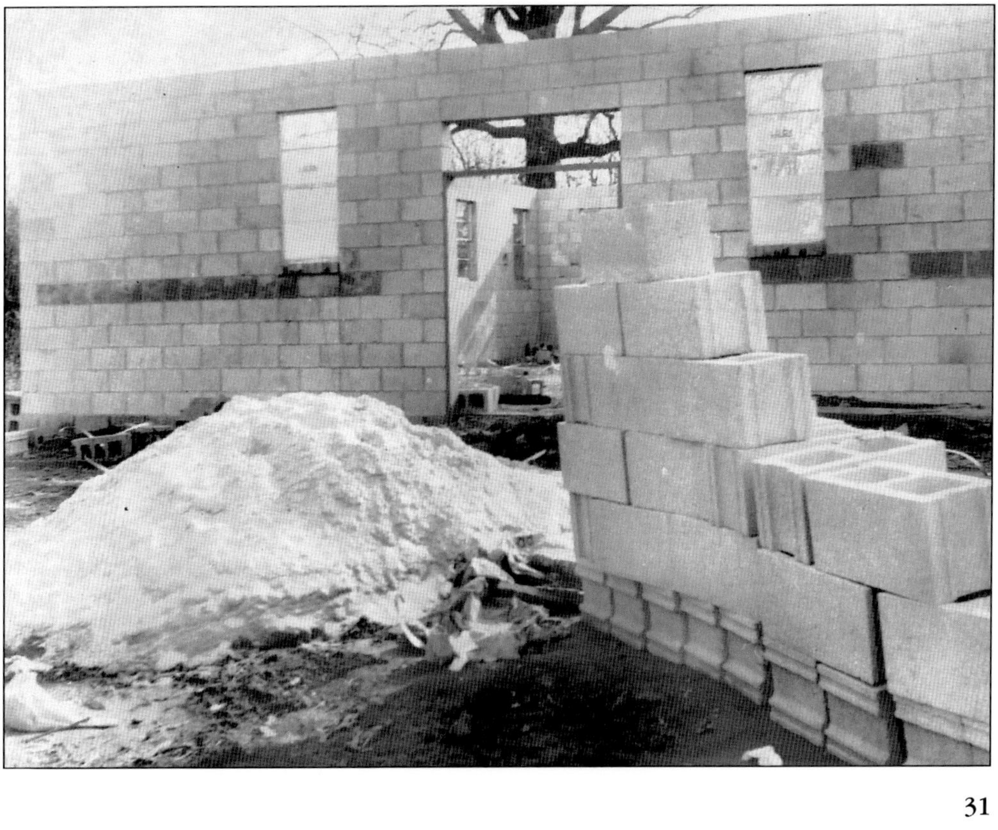

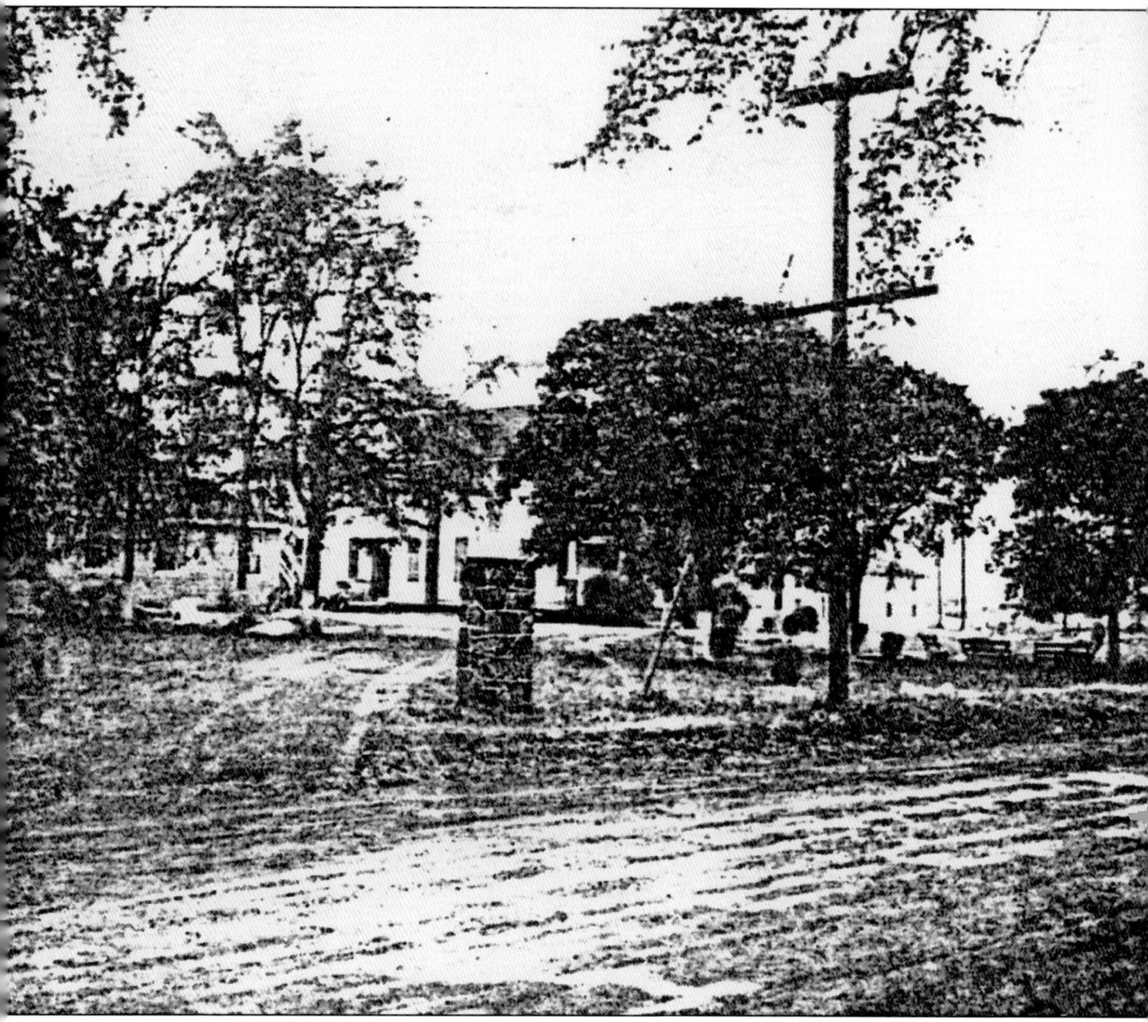

Pictured is the college campus facing what is now Crawford Road. In the 1930s, this road was not paved, and Heckle Boulevard did not run perpendicular to Crawford Road.

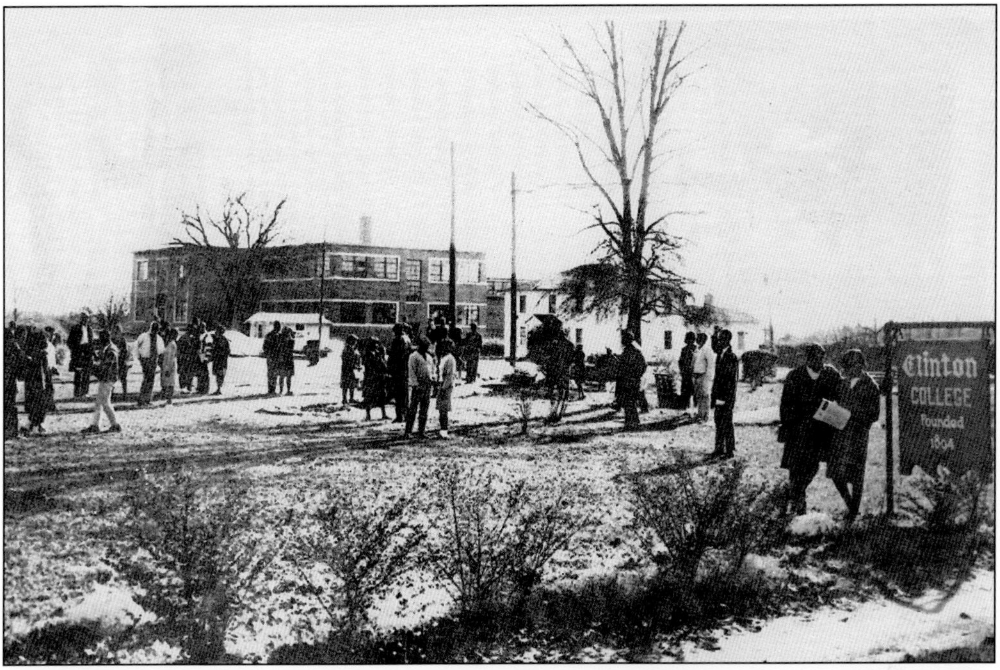

This image from a 1968 college announcement features the old and new buildings, which comprised the original campus. The white wooden structure no longer stands.

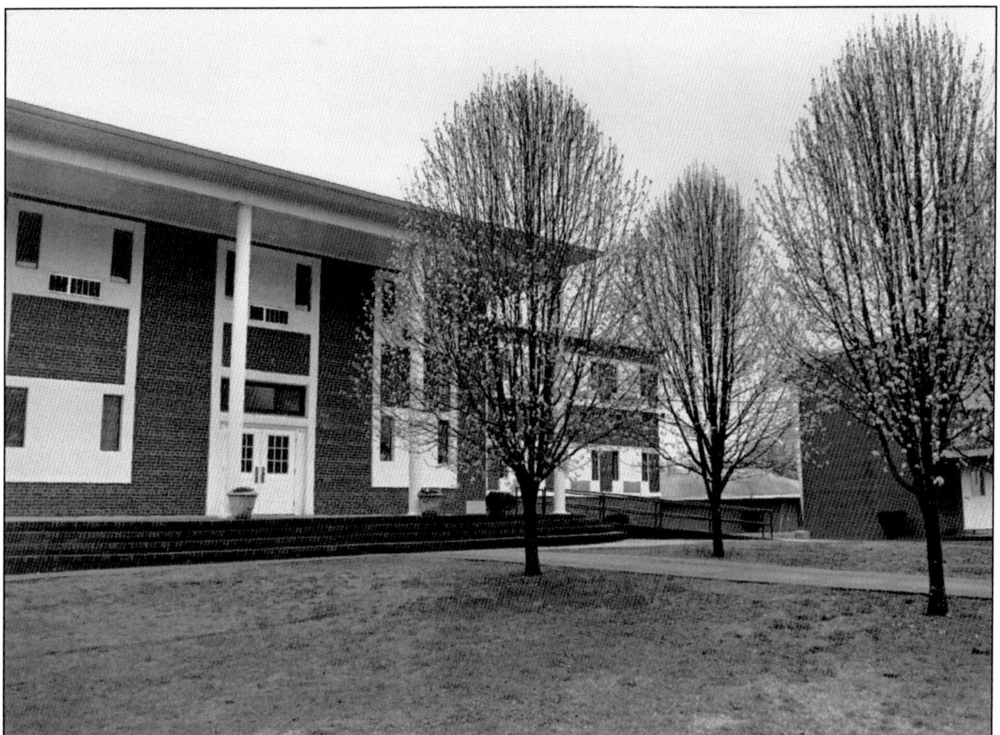

The sidewalk leading to the Administration Building is now lined with pear trees. The Administration Building was renovated in 1988.

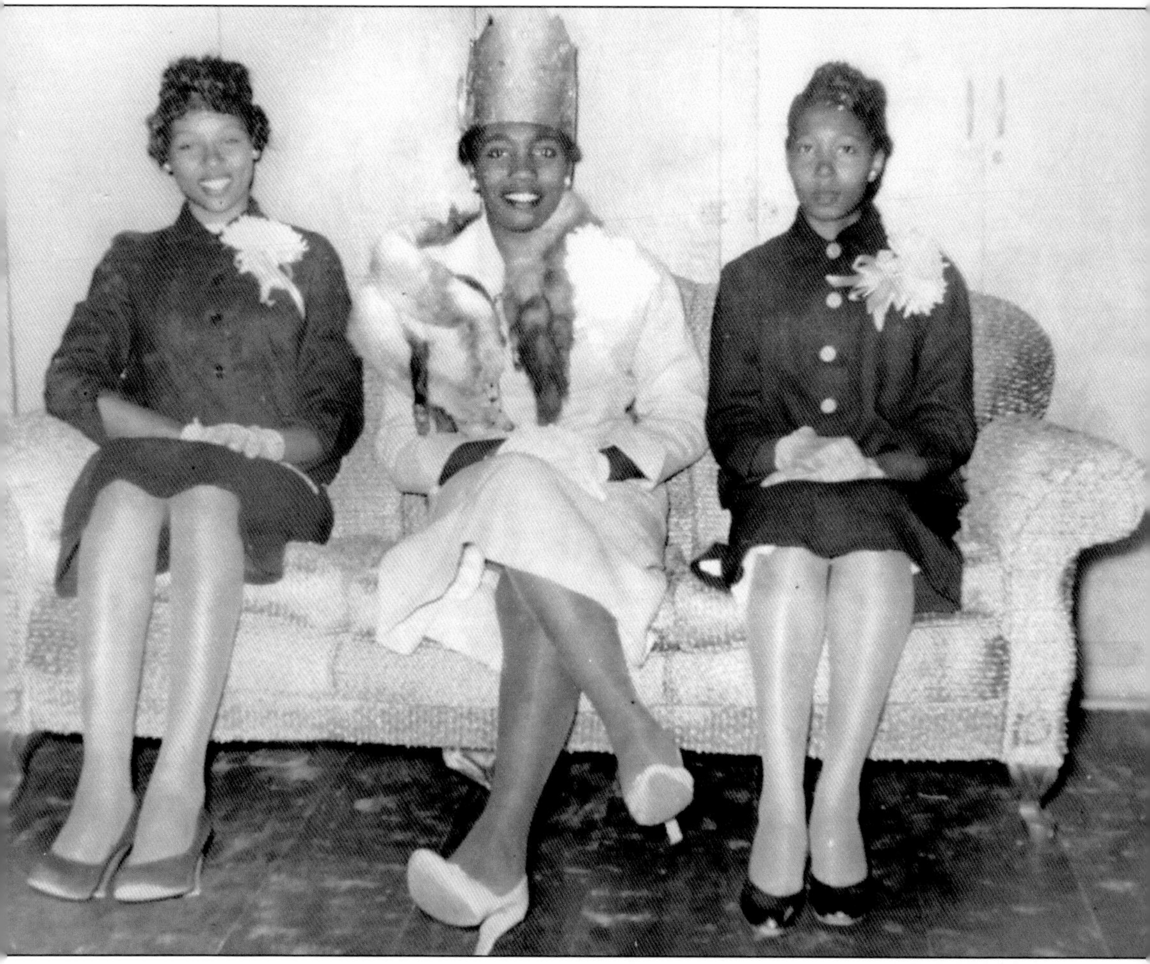

These young ladies were honored for their academic achievement, character, and beauty as part of a Clinton Junior College celebration during the mid-20th century. Clinton Junior College offers a variety of student contests and awards, and many students enjoy the extra-curricular events.

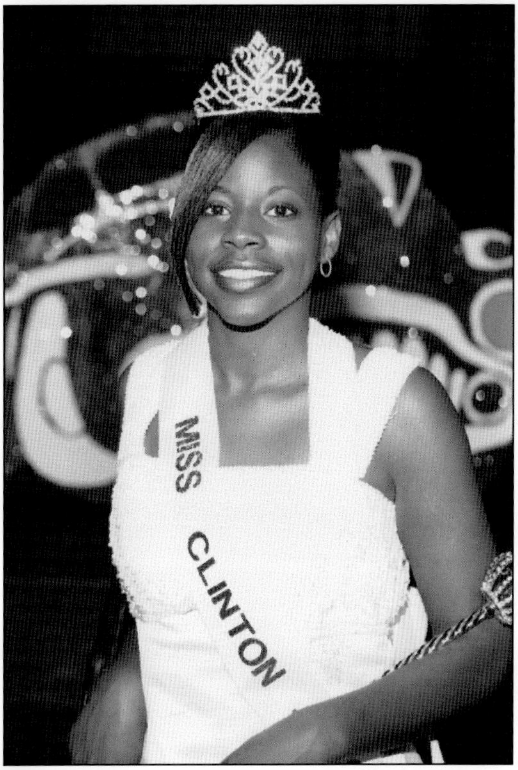

At right is Miss Clinton College 1998, Miss Taniel Tyson. Below is Miss Shirley Royal, Miss Clinton College 2002.

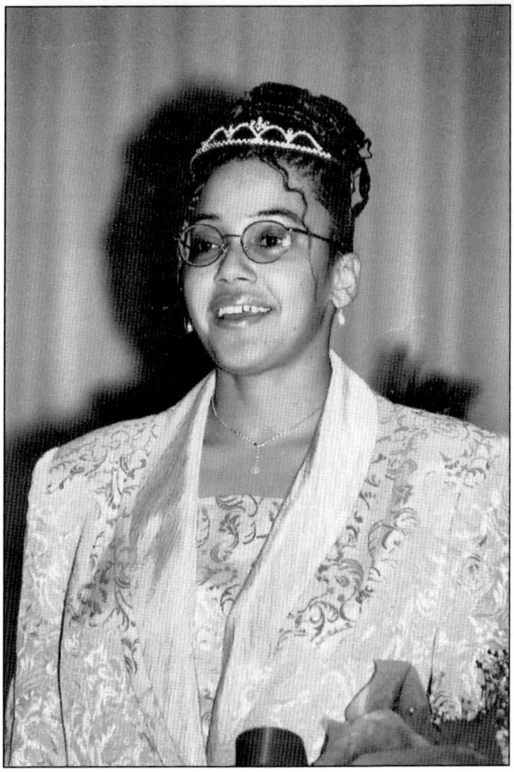

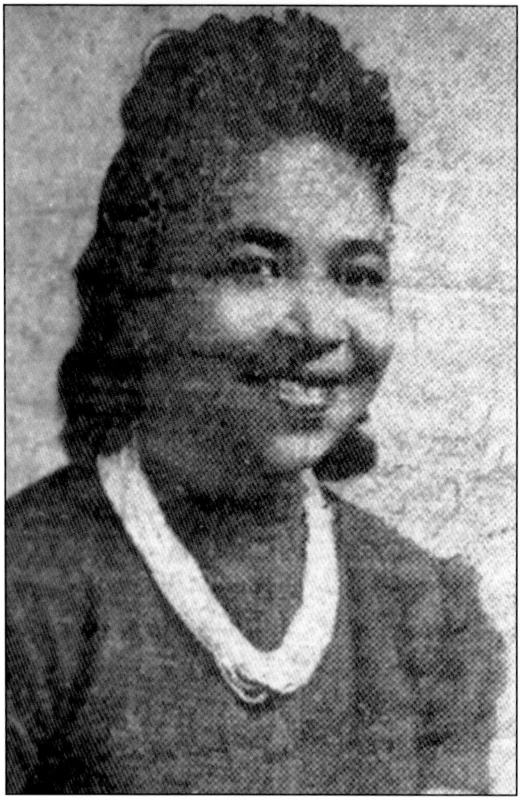

Miss Wilhemenia Peay (above) was Miss Clinton College in 1942 during the administration of Pres. Edward Warner Brice. This article from a newspaper (right) was in a scrapbook compiled by President Brice and written by Miss Peay.

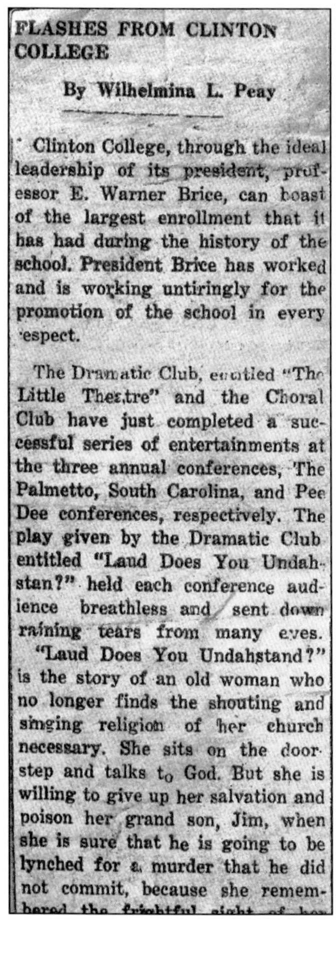

FLASHES FROM CLINTON COLLEGE

By Wilhelmina L. Peay

Clinton College, through the ideal leadership of its president, professor E. Warner Brice, can boast of the largest enrollment that it has had during the history of the school. President Brice has worked and is working untiringly for the promotion of the school in every respect.

The Dramatic Club, entitled "The Little Theatre" and the Choral Club have just completed a successful series of entertainments at the three annual conferences, The Palmetto, South Carolina, and Pee Dee conferences, respectively. The play given by the Dramatic Club entitled "Laud Does You Undahstan?" held each conference audience breathless and sent down raining tears from many eyes. "Laud Does You Undahstand?" is the story of an old woman who no longer finds the shouting and singing religion of her church necessary. She sits on the door-step and talks to God. But she is willing to give up her salvation and poison her grand son, Jim, when she is sure that he is going to be lynched for a murder that he did not commit, because she remembered the frightful sight of her

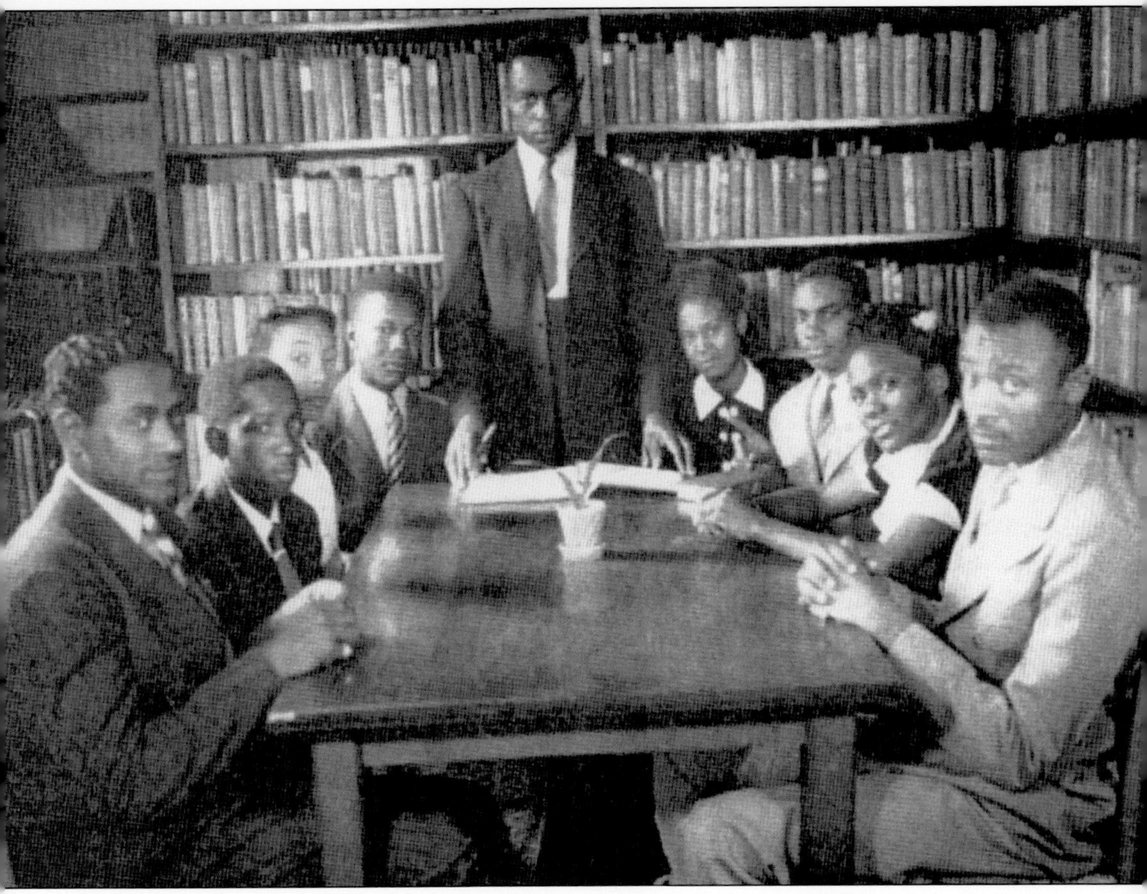

The 1942 student council meets in the college library. This was the predecessor of what is now the Student Government Association.

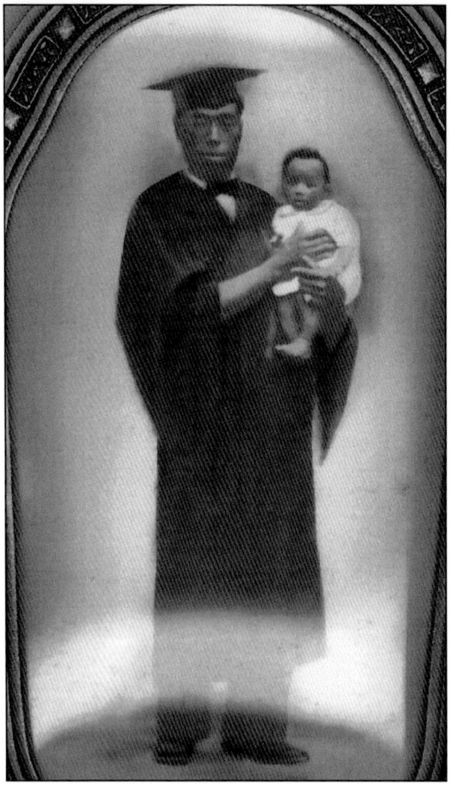

Mr. Thomas Wilkes, a 1940 graduate of Clinton, holds his daughter Elizabeth Ann Wilkes.

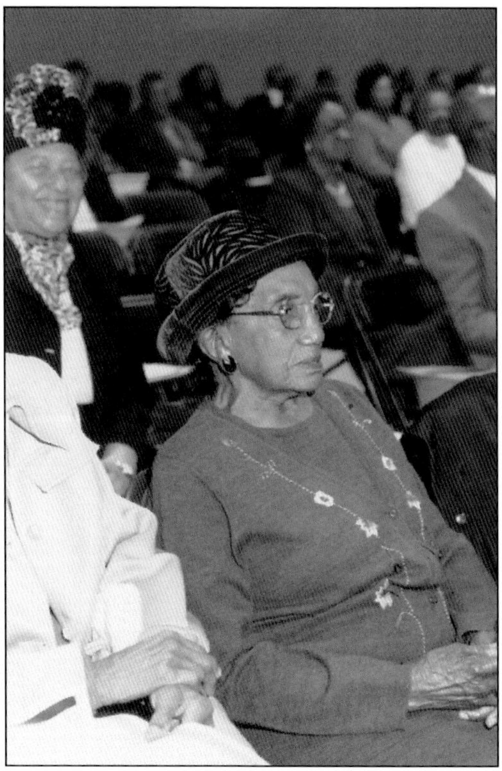

Mrs. Annie Bell Meeks is the oldest known living Clinton alum at the time of the writing of this book. She graduated in 1926 and is pictured here attending the college's 2004 Founders' Day celebration.

Elizabeth Ann Wilkes Reid taught biology and physics at Clinton in 1965. Both of her parents were graduates of Clinton.

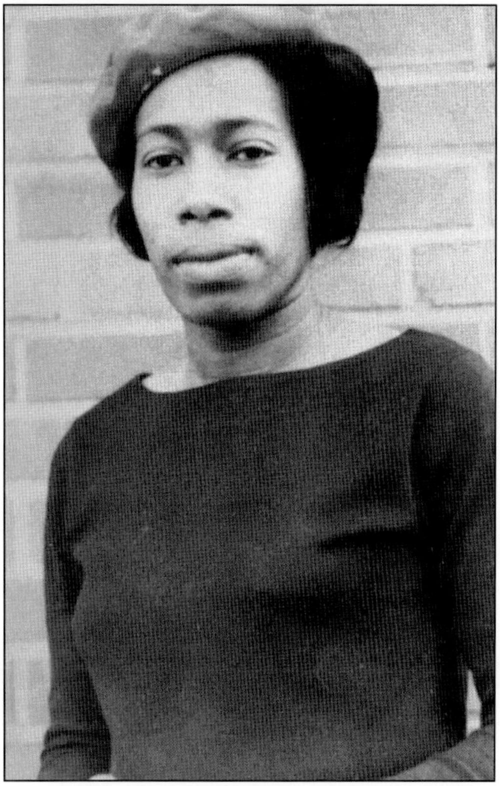

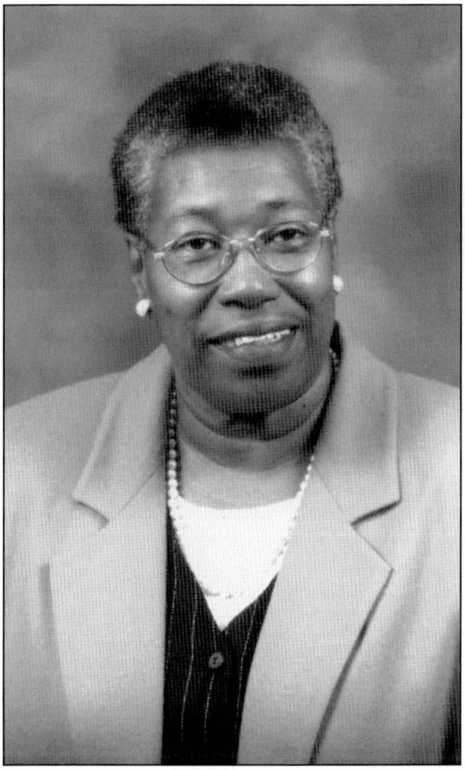

Elizabeth Ann Wilkes Reid is a great legacy of the college. After retiring from the public school system, she returned to teach biology and physical science.

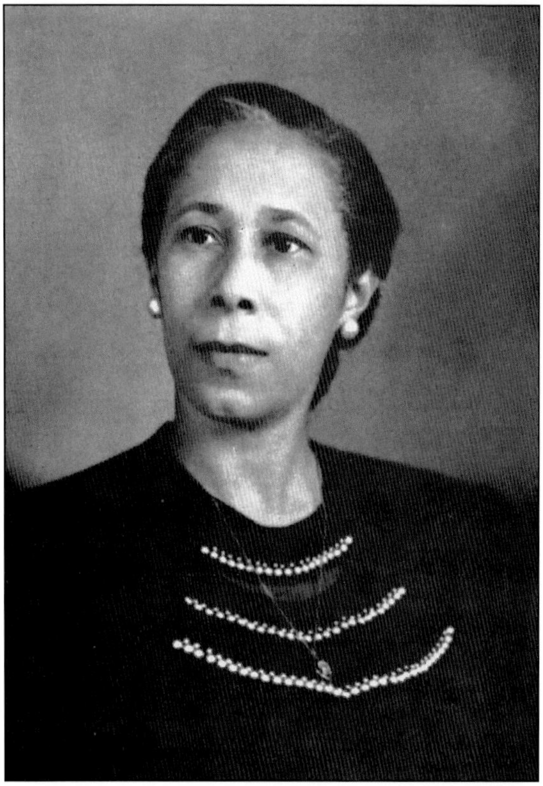

Dr. Sallie V. Moreland (*c.* 1898–2000) was a native of Greensboro, North Carolina, who provided leadership for Clinton Junior College for 48 years. She attended Livingstone College and was a graduate of Benedict College, Columbia University, and the University of Oregon. She began her tenure at Clinton Junior College as a social studies instructor and served in 1946 as acting president. By appointment of the board of trustees, she became the 10th president. The high school program was discontinued under her leadership. Then Clinton Junior College began awarding an associate's degree in liberal arts, an associate's degree in business, and certification in religious studies. Dr. Moreland retired in 1994 and resided in Rock Hill until her death.

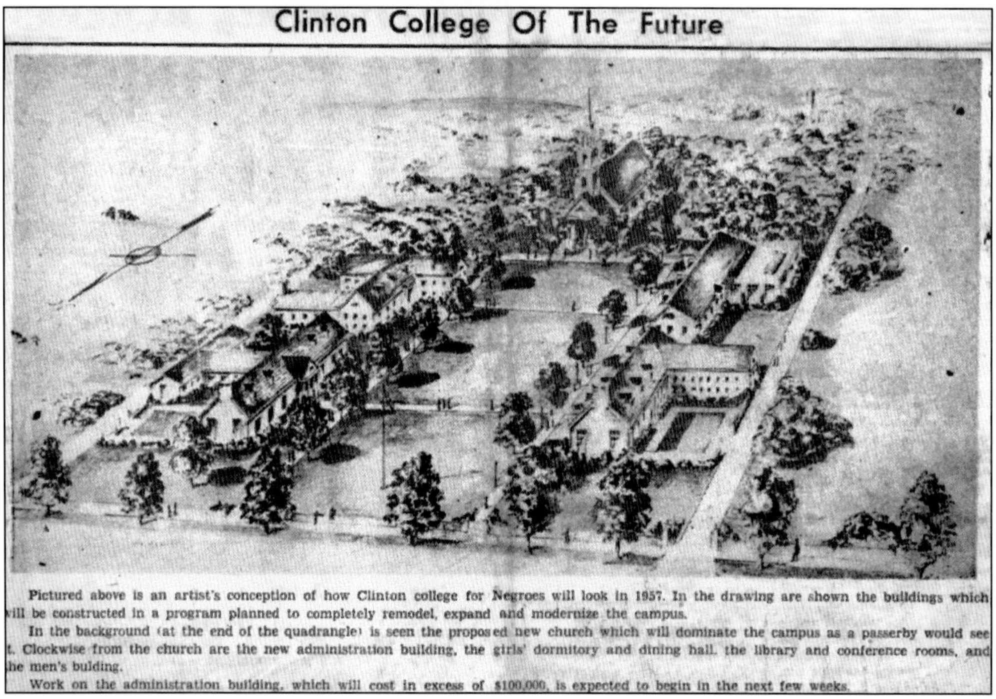

Clinton College Of The Future

Pictured above is an artist's conception of how Clinton college for Negroes will look in 1957. In the drawing are shown the buildings which will be constructed in a program planned to completely remodel, expand and modernize the campus.

In the background (at the end of the quadrangle) is seen the proposed new church which will dominate the campus as a passerby would see it. Clockwise from the church are the new administration building, the girls' dormitory and dining hall, the library and conference rooms, and the men's bulding.

Work on the administration building, which will cost in excess of $100,000, is expected to begin in the next few weeks.

In 1957, an artist drew this picture of the future Clinton Junior College. This particular plan did not come to fruition.

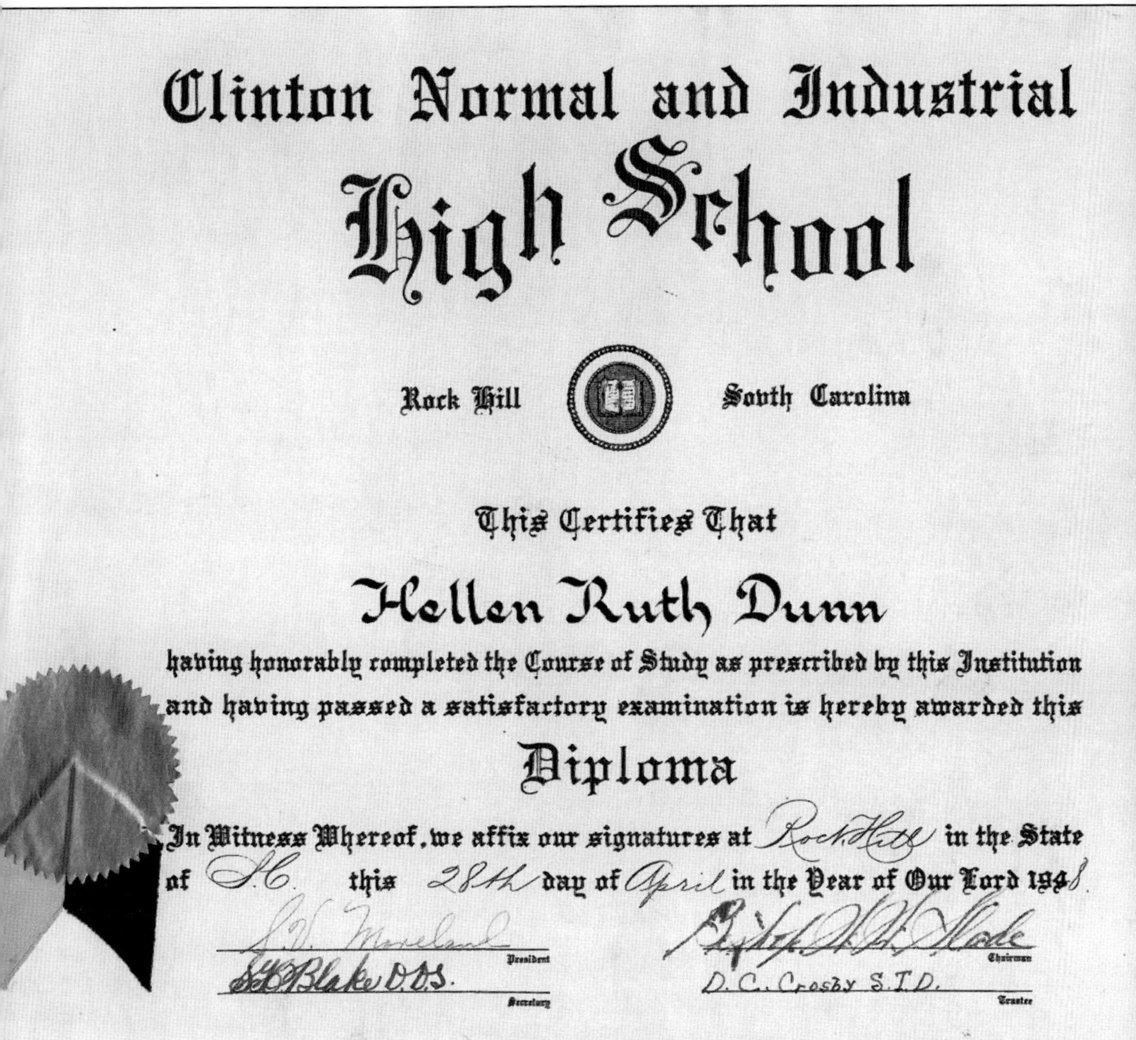

Clinton Normal and Industrial

High School

Rock Hill South Carolina

This Certifies That

Hellen Ruth Dunn

having honorably completed the Course of Study as prescribed by this Institution and having passed a satisfactory examination is hereby awarded this

Diploma

In Witness Whereof, we affix our signatures at Rock Hill in the State of S.C. this 28th day of April in the Year of Our Lord 1948.

S.V. Moreland, President

S.G. Blake D.D.S., Secretary

Bishop W. W. Slade, Chairman

D.C. Crosby S.T.D., Trustee

Until the early 1990s, Clinton College also had a high school program. This high school diploma dates from 1948 and is signed by Pres. Sallie V. Moreland.

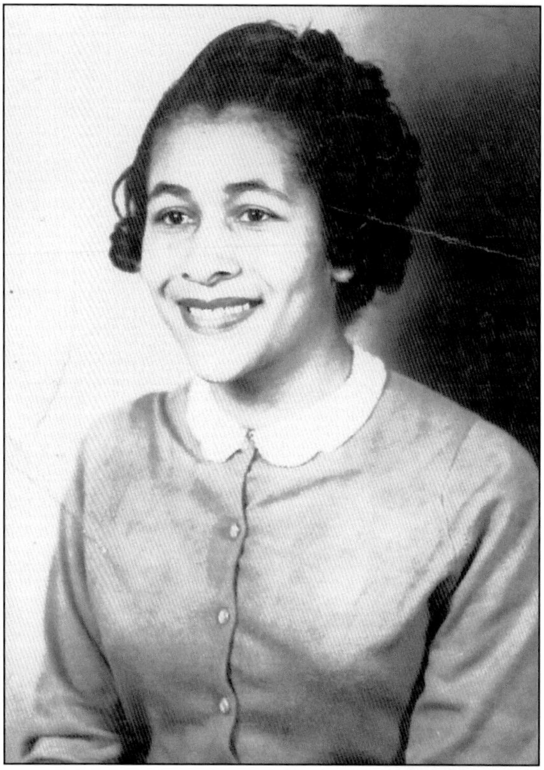

Juanita Simon Scott, Ph.D., a 1956 graduate of Clinton, transferred to Livingstone College after graduation from Clinton and eventually became a professor of biology and vice president for academic affairs at Benedict College.

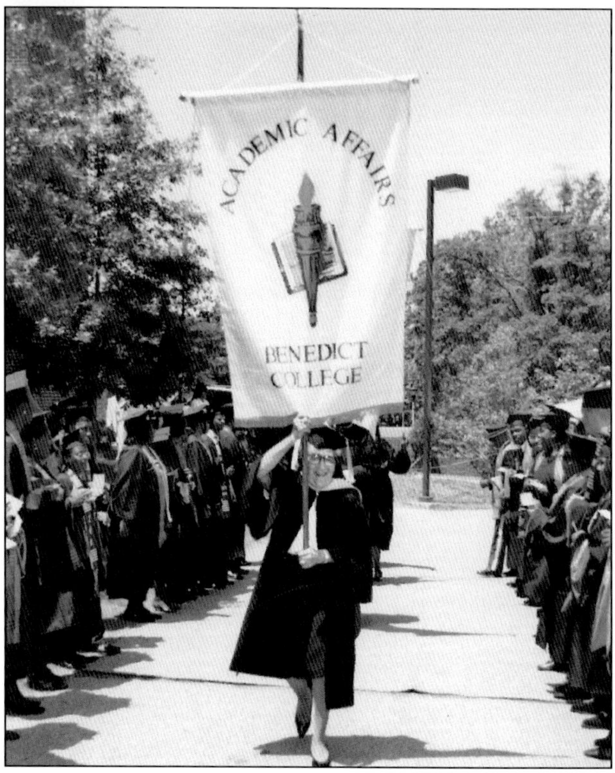

Dr. Scott served as a trustee of Clinton Junior College from 1993 to 2000.

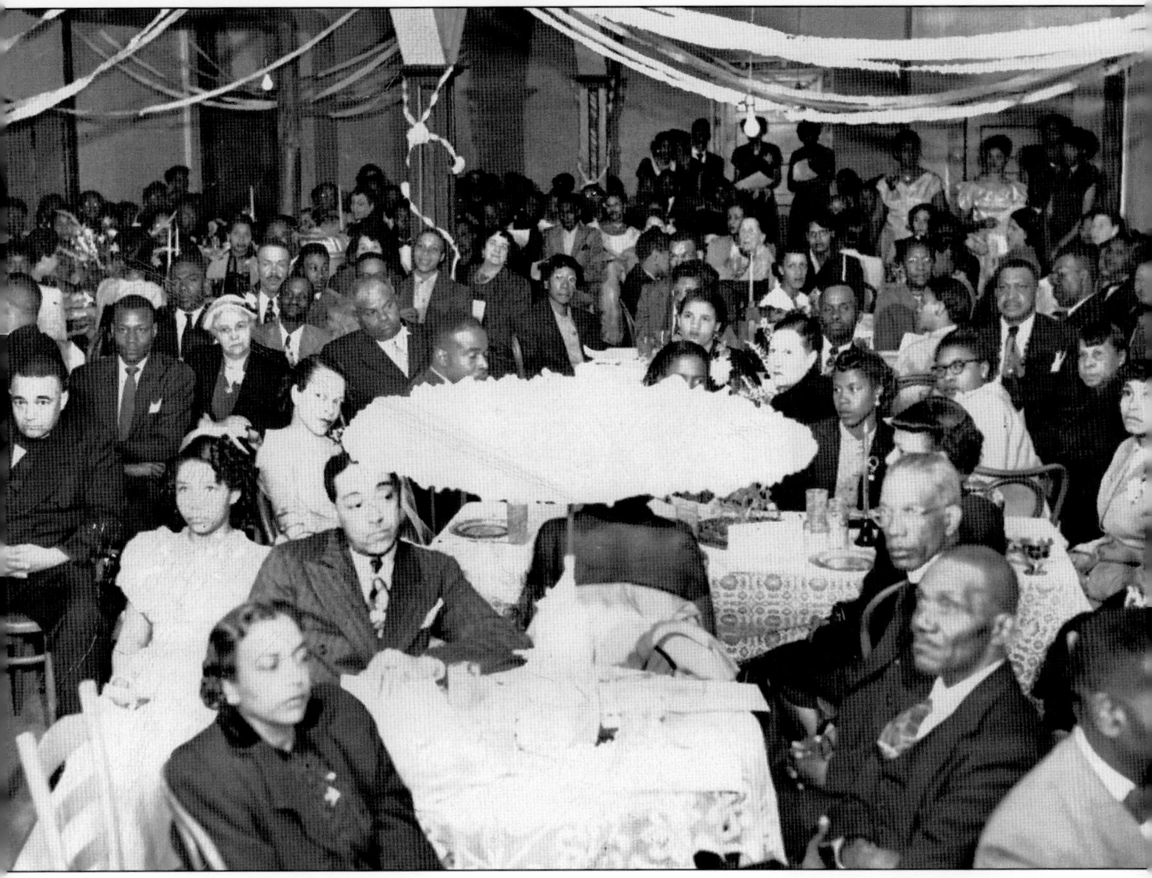

The Calendar Tea is an annual Clinton Junior College celebration begun in the 1950s. What appears to be a white blob in the middle of the image is actually a beautiful paper umbrella. The Calendar Tea offers an opportunity for alumni, students, and members of the A.M.E. Zion Church to enjoy fellowship at Clinton Junior College.

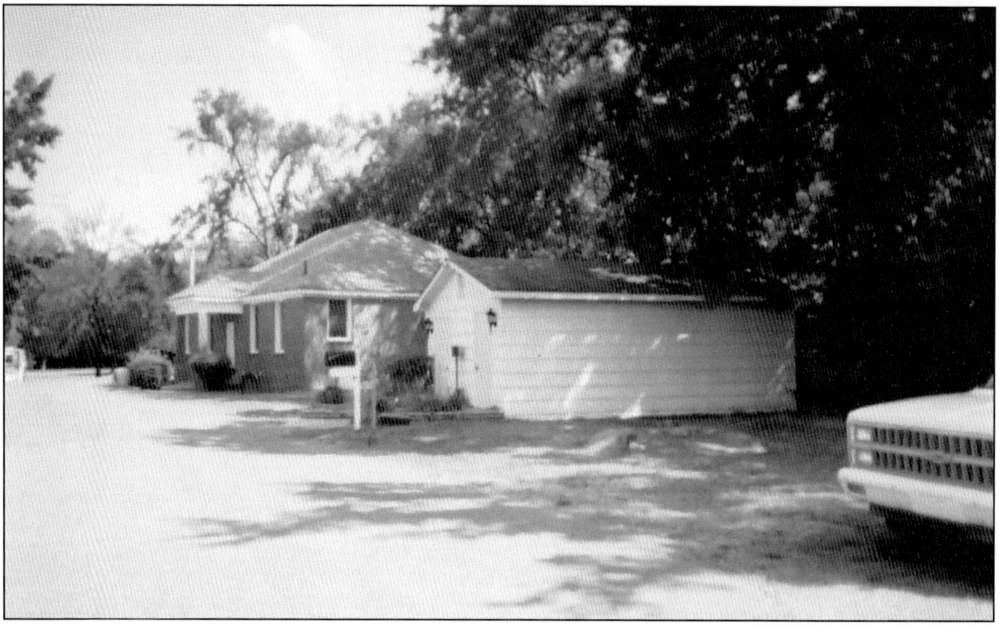

From 1894 until 1946, Clinton Junior College had six presidents. The campus expanded, and under Dr. Sallie Moreland's leadership, the student body averaged 225 in the mid-20th century. Growth continued, and the campus and its equipment obtained a value of $250,000 shortly after World War II ended. Pictured is the brick student center, which once served as the library, and the wood building that presently functions as the Thomas Wilkes Bookstore. These two structures on the campus have survived to serve the student body to this day.

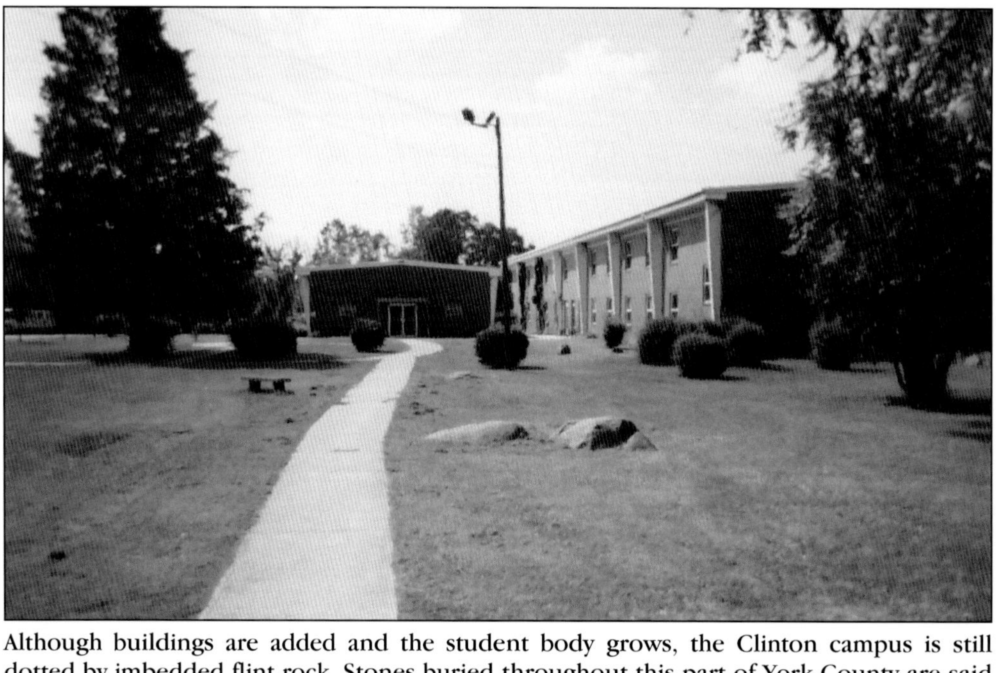

Although buildings are added and the student body grows, the Clinton campus is still dotted by imbedded flint rock. Stones buried throughout this part of York County are said to be the real reason why the city is named Rock Hill.

Rev. Lloyd Snipes has witnessed over 40 years of Clinton Junior College's growth as a student and an employee. He gives testimony to the prayers that changed history. Reverend Snipes presently serves Clinton College as the director of plant operations.

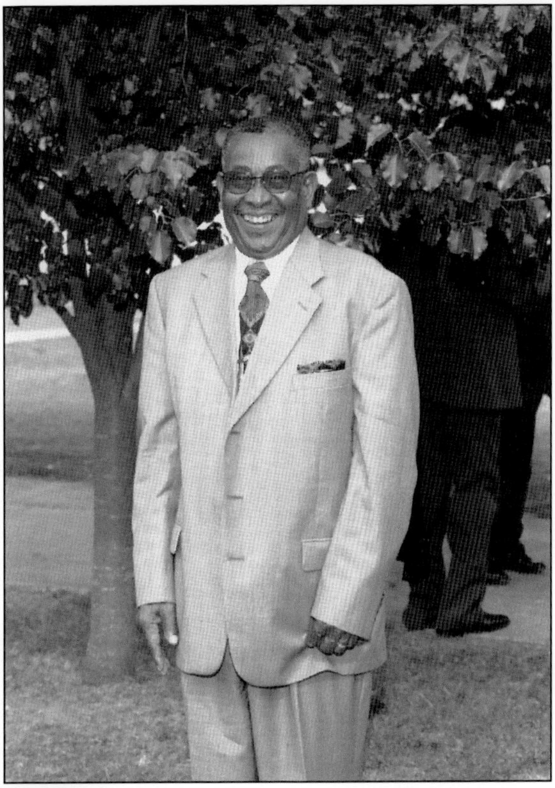

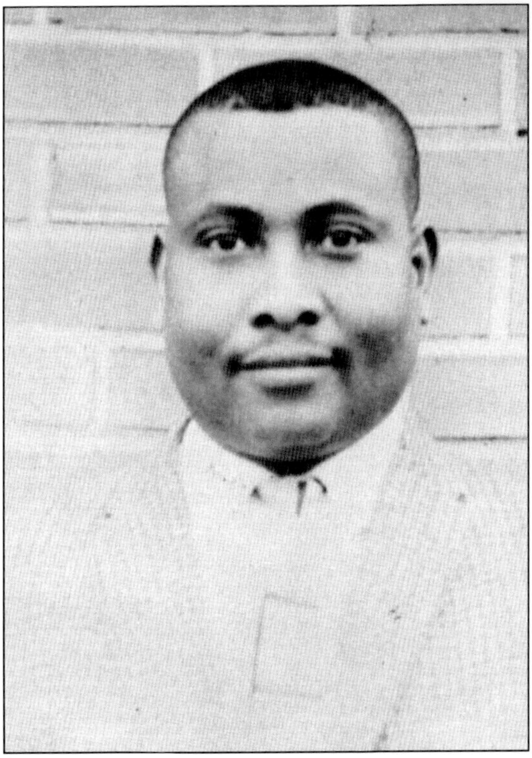

Reverend Snipes is pictured here in 1965. He was a student here from 1956 to 1958.

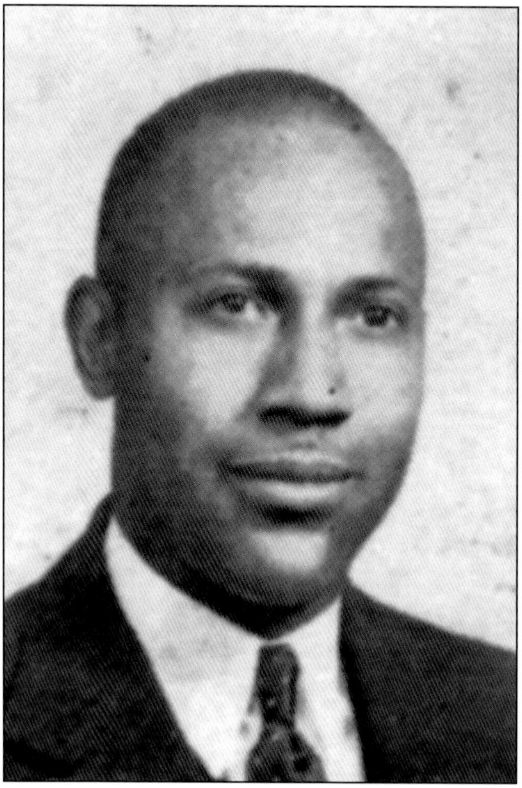

Pictured is Mr. A.J. Johnson, the father of Dr. Elaine Johnson Copeland, from a faculty photograph taken in 1942. Mr. Johnson met his wife, Lucille Hawkins Johnson, at Clinton Junior College while teaching there. A successful high school student at Clinton in the early 1920s, he graduated from Livingstone College in Salisbury, North Carolina, and received a master's degree from South Carolina State in Orangeburg. In addition to teaching mathematics and biology, he served as the football and basketball coach for Clinton Junior College from 1937 to 1942. Currently, Mr. Johnson's daughter is the president of Clinton Junior College. Other current faculty and staff with inter-generational ties are Elizabeth Ann Wilkes Reid, Sharon Browning Jenkins, Aaronita Johnson Belton, Alton Johnson, and Robert Copeland Jr., all who had parents or grandparents who were alumni and/or employees of the college.

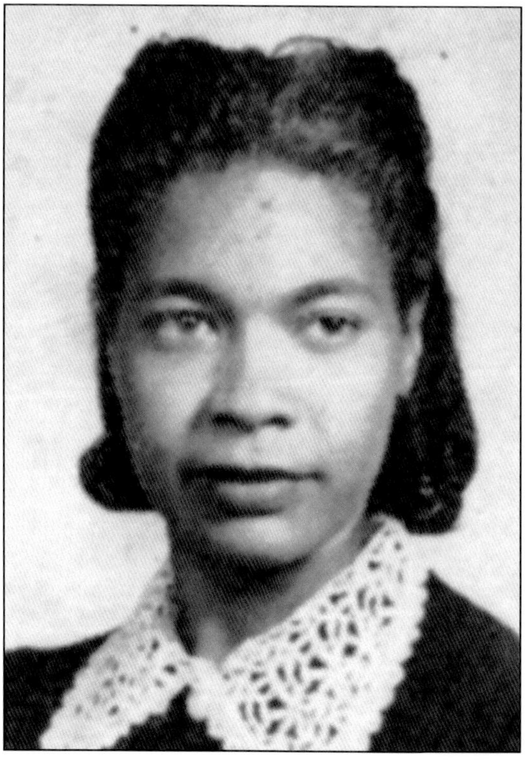

Mrs. Lucille Hawkins Johnson, the mother of Dr. Copeland, served as part of the faculty in 1942.

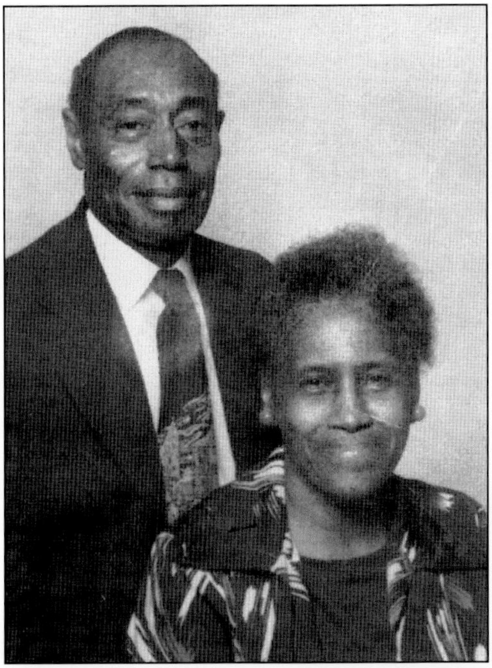

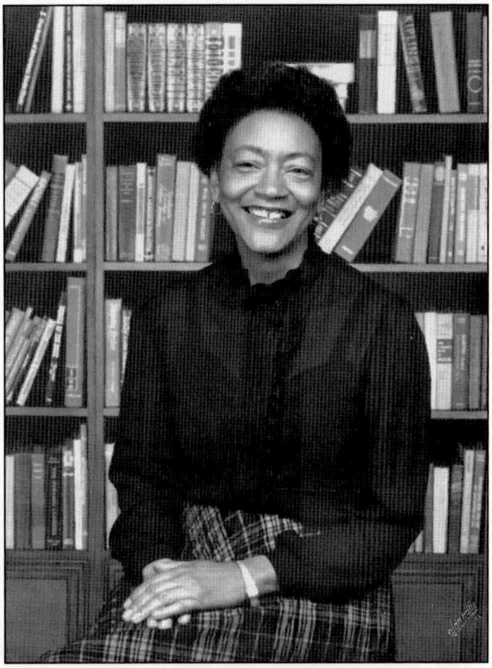

(Above left) Mr. Thomas Wilkes and Mrs. Henrietta Barber Wilkes met while they were students at Clinton in the 1940s. Mrs. Wilkes became the college librarian, and they both remained loyal to the college. The campus bookstore is names in honor of Mr. Wilkes. *(Above right)* Pictured is Bettye Crockett Gathings, the granddaughter of the founder Nero Crockett and grandniece of Robert Crockett, Clinton's first president. Mrs. Gathings taught English at Clinton in the 1990s. Her daughter, Stephanie Gathings Cain, is currently the college business manager.

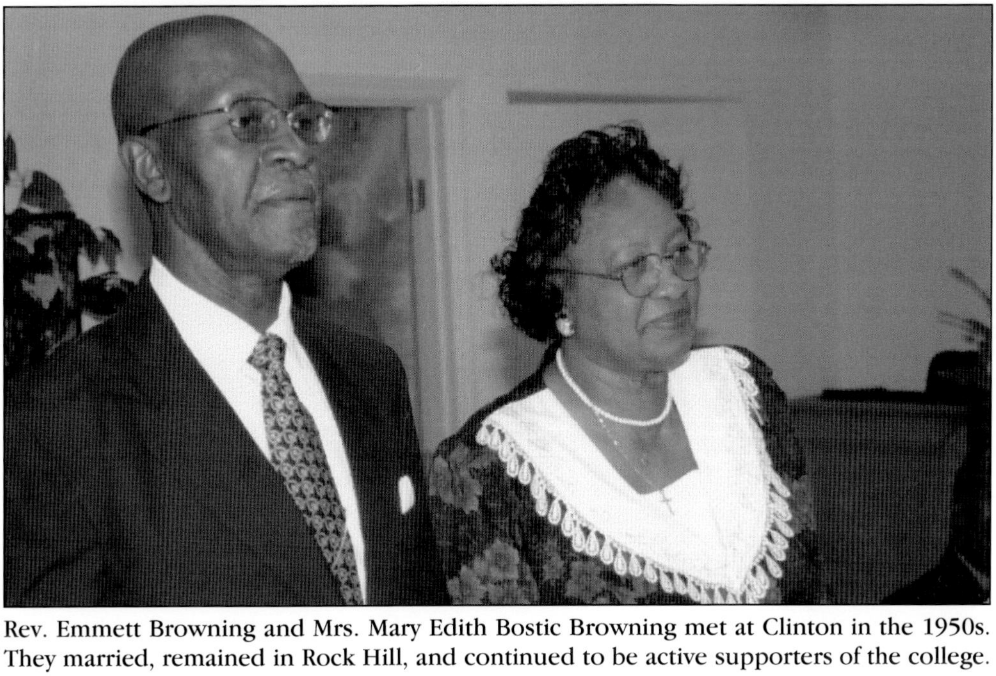

Rev. Emmett Browning and Mrs. Mary Edith Bostic Browning met at Clinton in the 1950s. They married, remained in Rock Hill, and continued to be active supporters of the college.

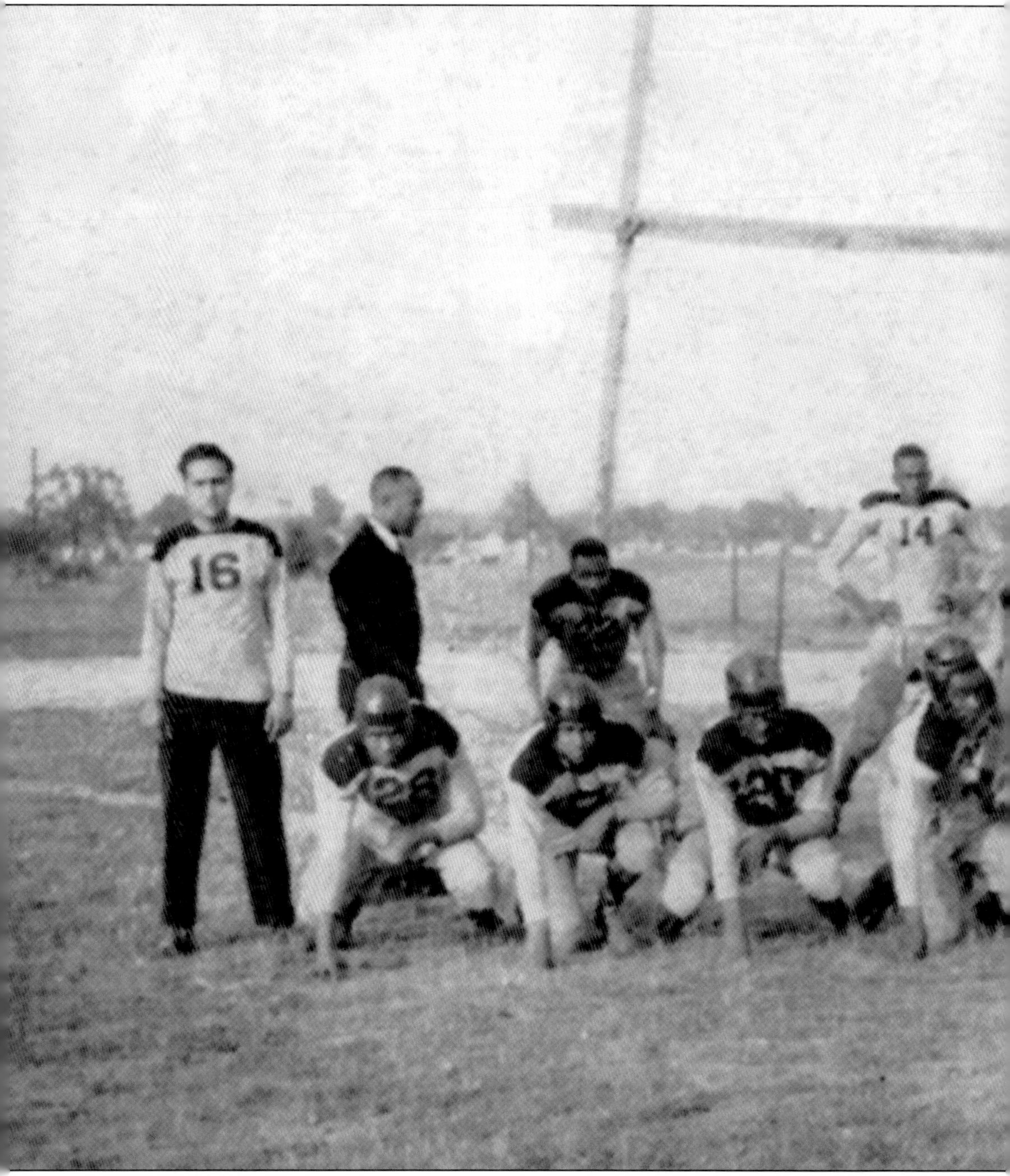

Clinton College Golden Bears football history can be traced to 1937 when Prof. Leon Stanback was head coach. The 1937 team consisted of John Murdock, right end and co-captain; David Moore, right tackle; Issac Banks, right guard; Alex "Legs" Barnette, center; Walter Culler, left guard; Thomas Wilkes, left tackle; Joseph Green, left end; Thedro Singleton, quarterback and punter; Willie Sawyer, left half back; Clinton Medlock, right half back; Robert "Bob" Stevenson, full back and captain; Jurden D. Gladden, end; C.L. (Cap) Knightner, lineman; L.A. Barber Jr., backfield; George McMurry, lineman; Thurma Sanders,

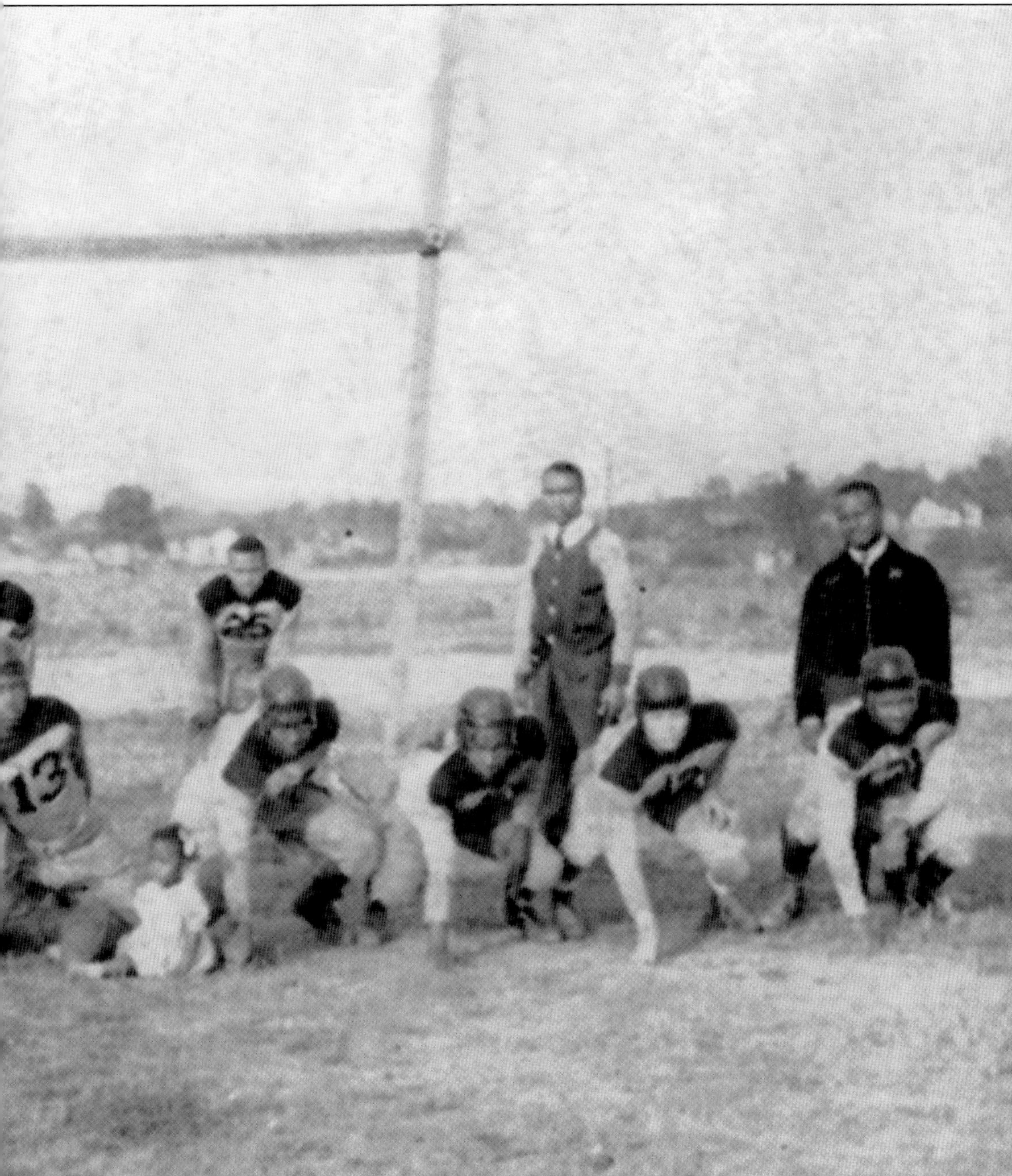

running back; Amos Ingram, running back; Walter Macon, lineman; Fred H. Thompson, end; and Robert G. Toatley, equipment manager. According to the writings of Alex "Legs" Barnette, the 1937 Golden Bears was called the "wonder squad" or "dream squad" because the team's many tricky formations kept the competition guessing. No known photographs of the 1937 Golden Bears team, when the assistant coach was Mr. A.J. Johnson, have survived. This photo shows a *c*. 1942 team.

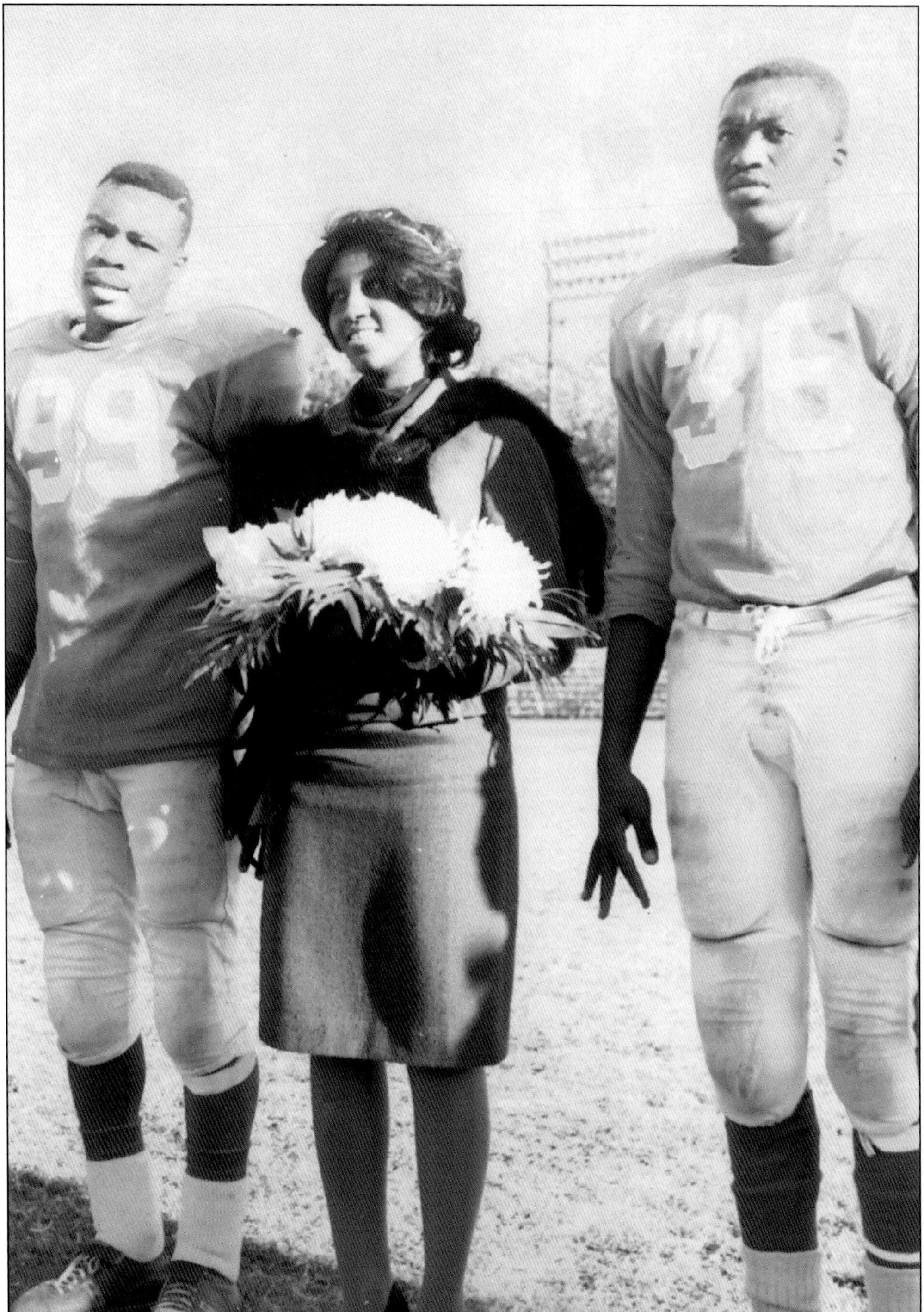

Alumni Alex Barnette also writes that the 1937 football team played all of its home games on the Clinton College field or at Highland Park Stadium. Pictured are a couple of Golden Bears escorting the homecoming queen. The photo is from the latter half of the 20th century.

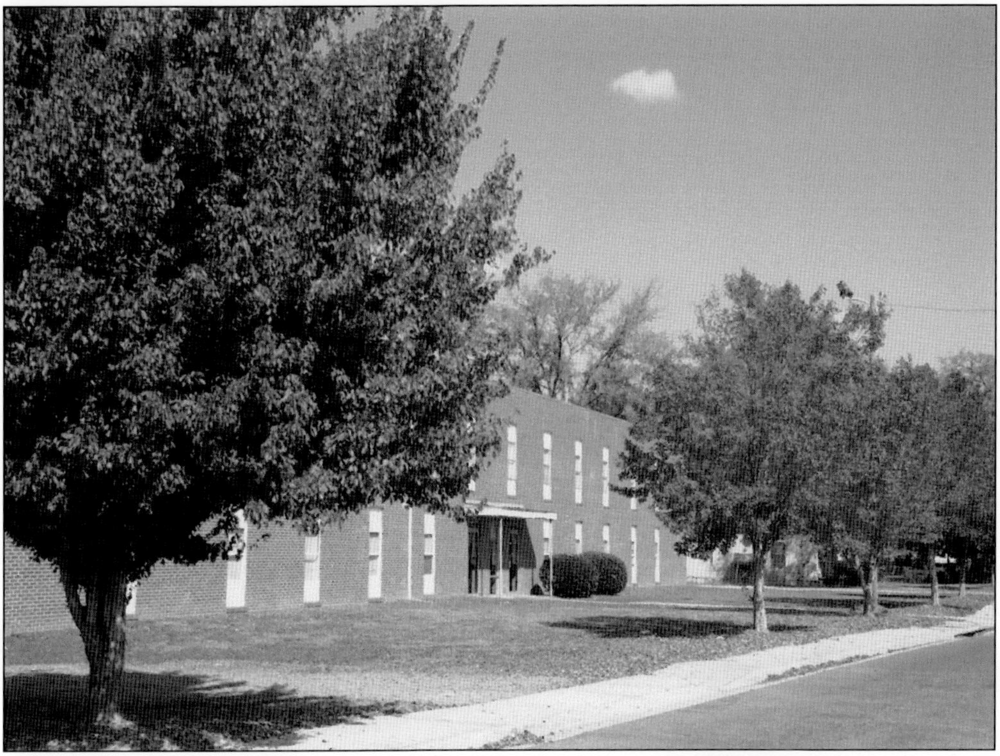

Crawford Road presently divides the campus. Pictured is the men's residence hall and Crawford Road in autumn. The trees surrounding the residence hall turn scarlet red and add to the beauty of the community.

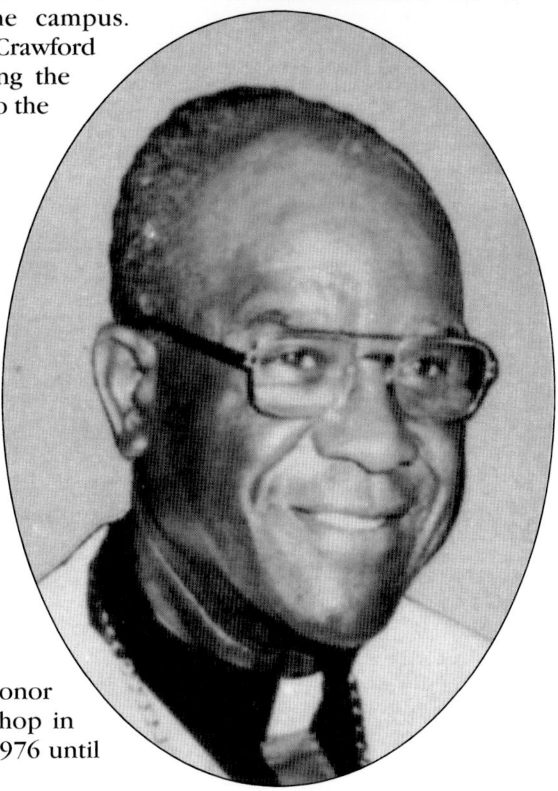

The men's residence hall is named in honor of Arthur Marshall. He was elected bishop in 1972 and served South Carolina from 1976 until his passing in 1987.

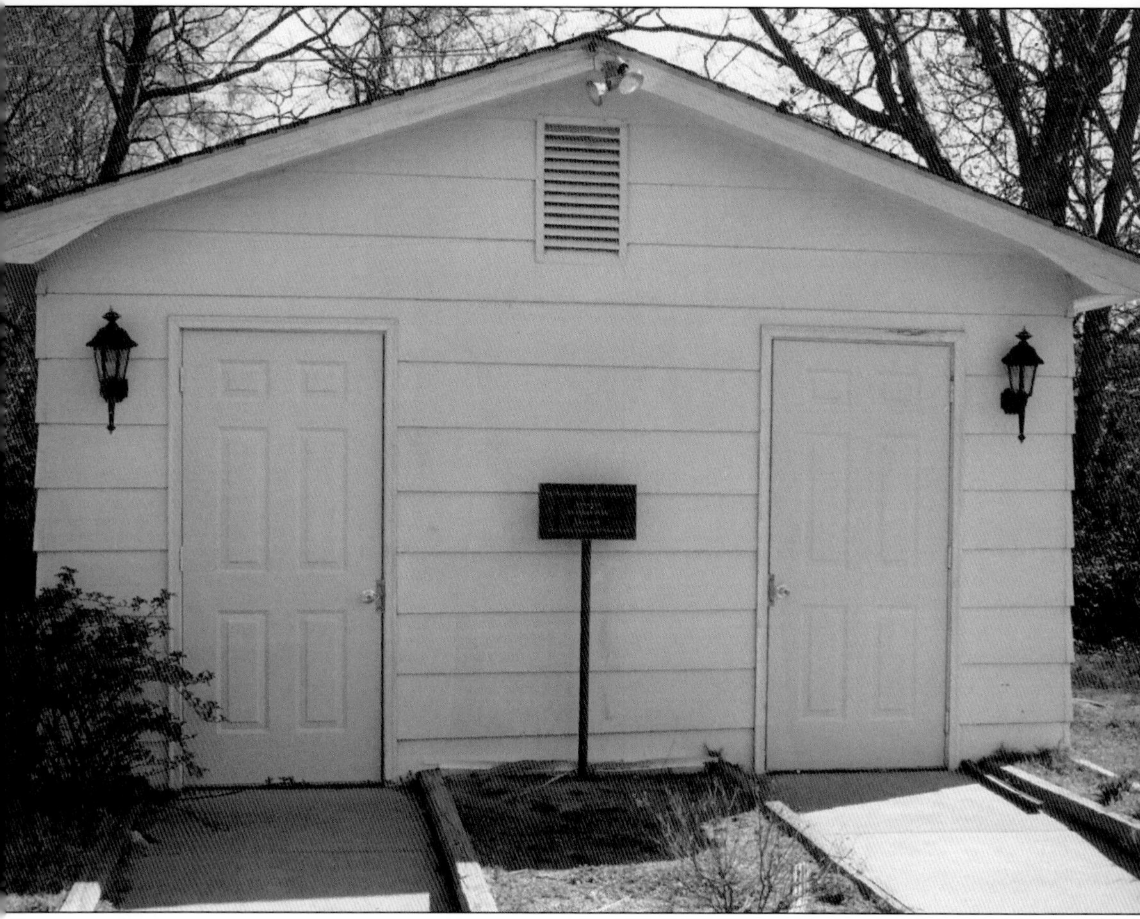

Buildings like the bookstore or the science hall can be restored when supporters work together and donate time, money, and energy to a project. This bookstore was renovated from a garage in 1996 with funds donated by the A.M.E. Zion Church Women's Home and Overseas Missionary Society. It is named Thomas Wilkes Bookstore.

CLINTON JUNIOR COLLEGE

UNDER SUPERVISION OF CHRISTIAN EDUCATION DEPARTMENT
AFRICAN METHODIST EPISCOPAL ZION CHURCH
ROCK HILL, SOUTH CAROLINA - 29730

OFFICE OF PRESIDENT

May 16, 1974

Mr. Charles L. Hunley, Director
The Belk Foundation
1103 Lakewood Drive
Monroe, North Carolina 28110

Dear Mr. Hunley:

This comes to acknowledge with deep gratitude the gift of $1,000.00 to the school for our science hall which must be equipped in order to meet the present educational requirements.

Your representative's were most gracious in their expression of your concern in our work here with students who without help, could not persue higher education.

Again, we are grateful to the organization.

Very truly yours,

S. V. Moreland (MRD)

S. V. Moreland, President

SVM/ppd

A letter from Dr. Moreland expresses gratitude to the Belk Foundation in Monroe, North Carolina, for a gift assisting in the purchasing of equipment for the science hall. The letter is dated 1974. Donations increased from the A.M.E.Z. Church and from the community at-large as Clinton Junior College grew throughout the 20th century. Recently, The Springs Close Foundation and the United Negro College Fund/NASA awarded Clinton Junior College significant grants that will further improve the campus and its curriculum for the 21st century.

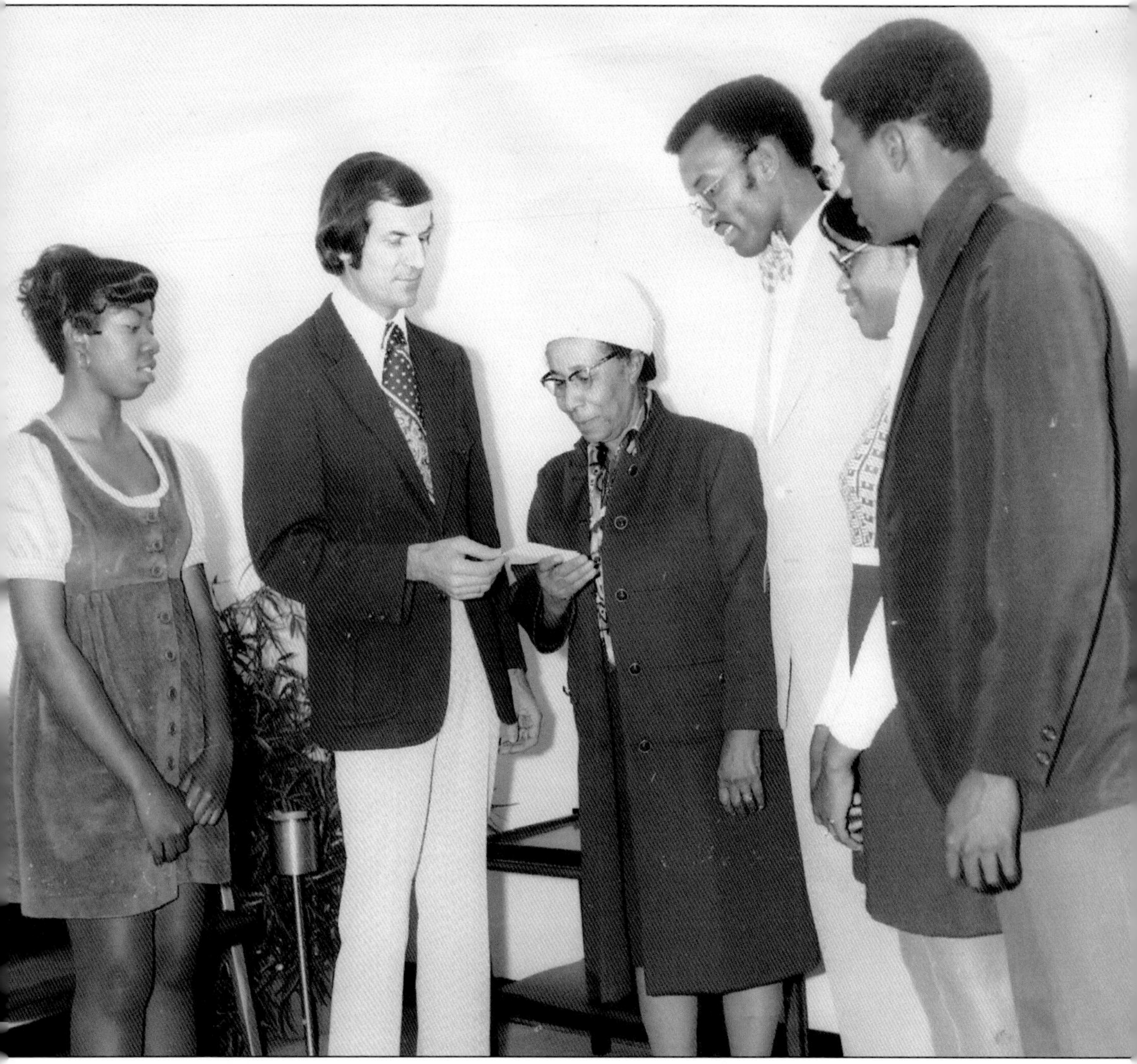

Depicted is a representative of the Belk Foundation presenting a financial contribution to Clinton Junior College. Students, faculty, and administrators express their appreciation with smiles, and the photographer records the event with film and flash bulb.

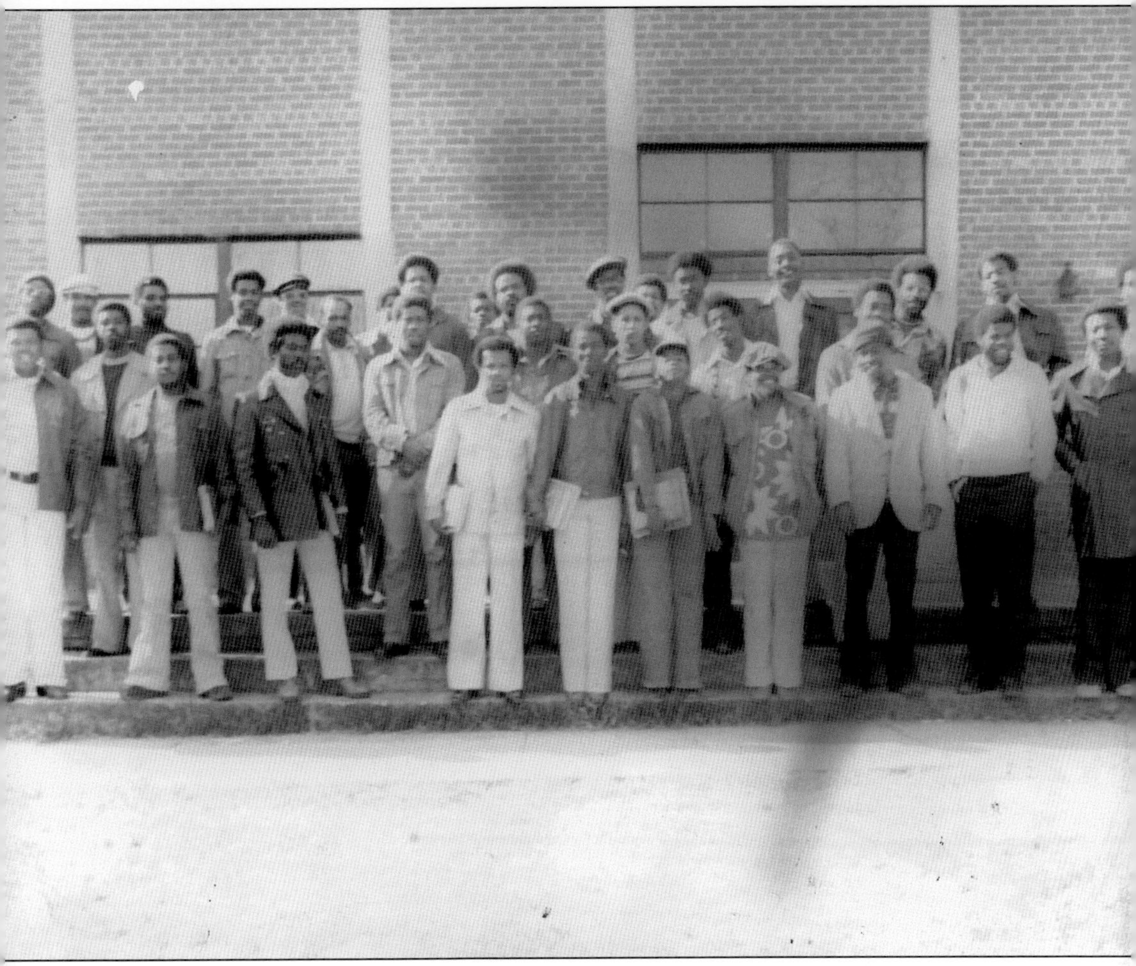

For 110 years, Clinton Junior College has worked to satisfy the needs of others. After World War II, the college implemented a program to benefit military servicemen and women. According to college documents labeled 1980–1981, Clinton Junior College worked in tandem with the Veterans Administration. The college curriculum presently gives veterans a 2-year liberal arts education or 64 hours of basic college work. It allows a veteran to transfer his or her credits at full value to other institutions of study. Pictured is a group of veterans who successfully participated in the curriculum in the 1960s.

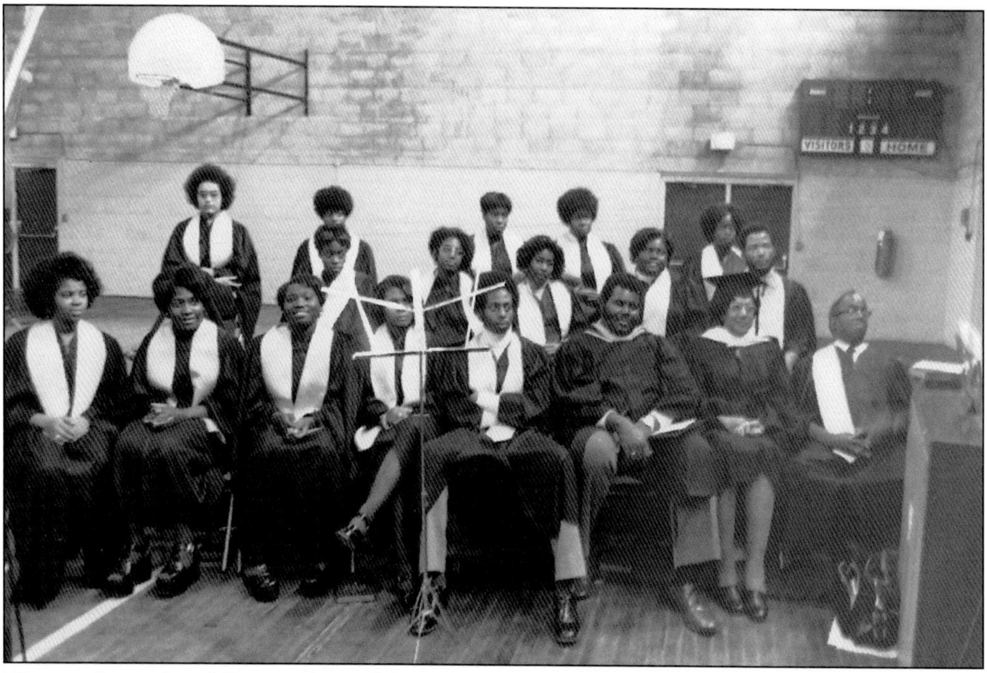

The arts have always been a part of the college curriculum. Music and choirs dominated this field of study in the 1960s. Pictured is an ensemble under the direction of Mr. Frontis Brooks.

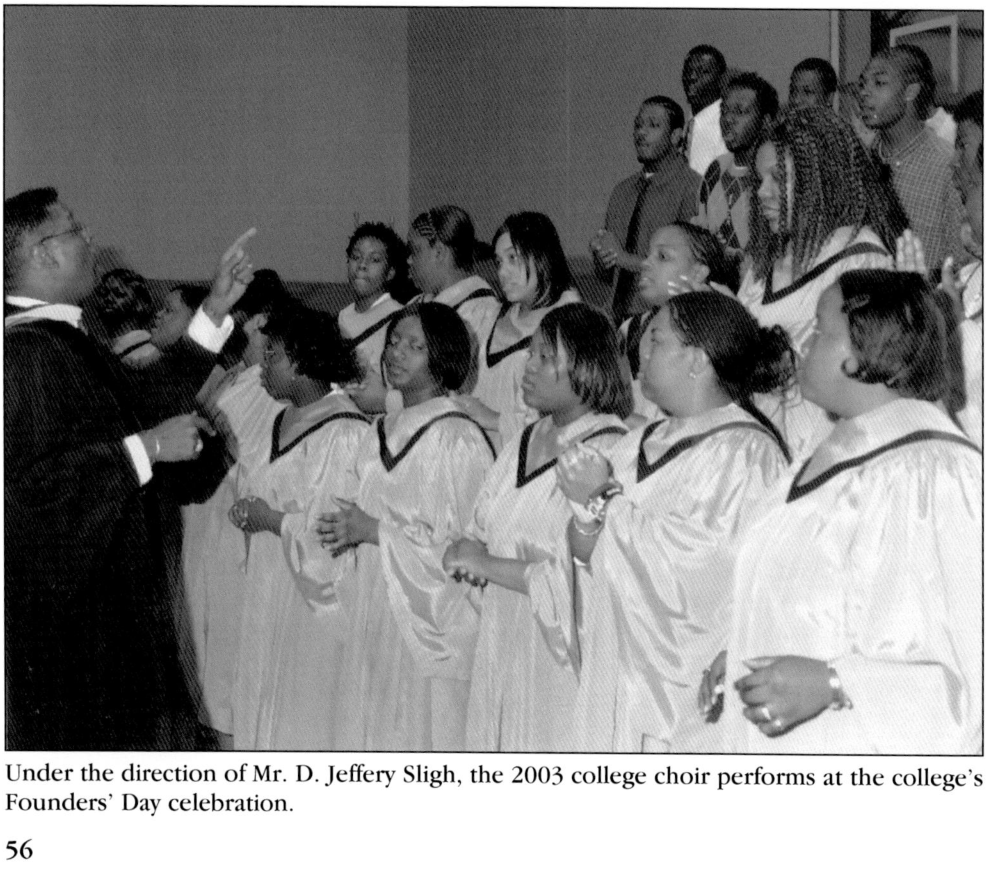
Under the direction of Mr. D. Jeffery Sligh, the 2003 college choir performs at the college's Founders' Day celebration.

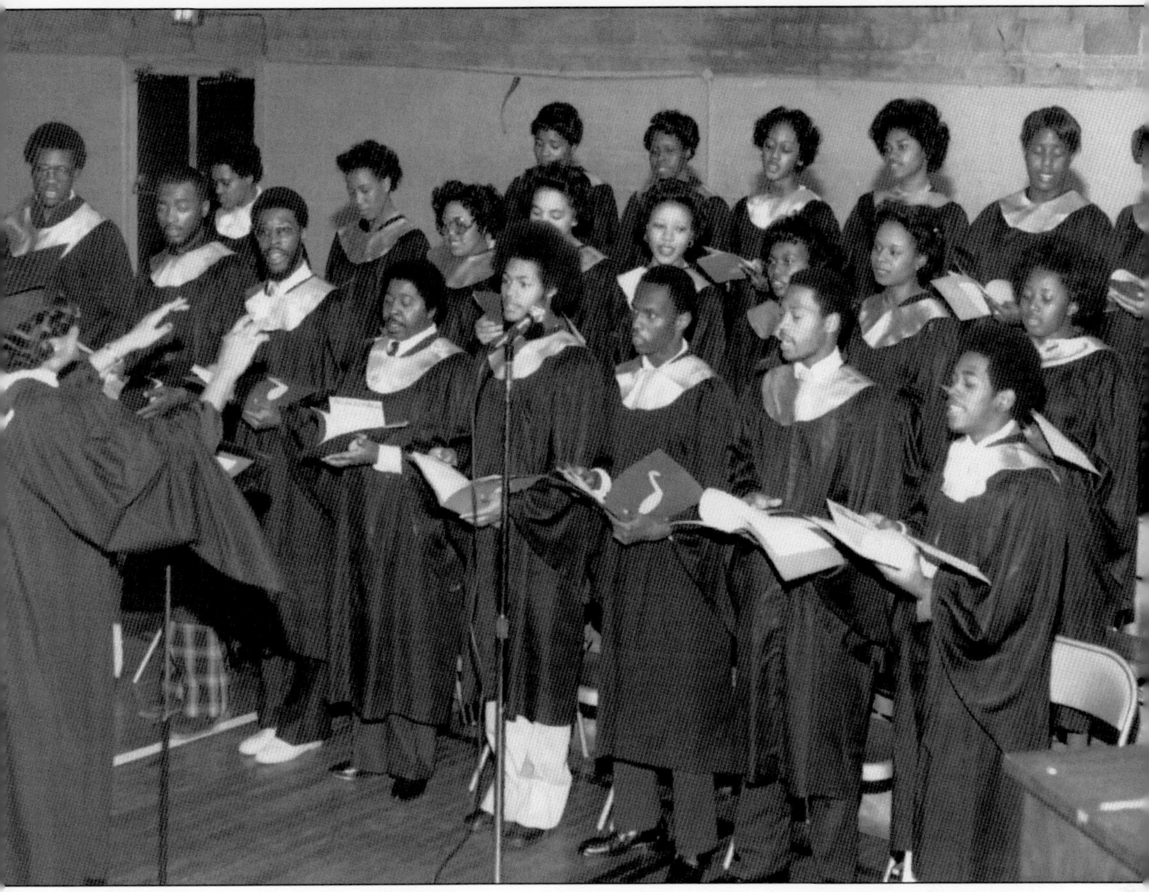

Student life on the Clinton campus is not all about study. Here, choir members prepare for worship and celebration ceremonies during the latter half of the 20th century. Clinton Junior College offered a variety of music courses, such as voice, piano, music appreciation, and music special topics classes. In the past, students participated in a simplified program that included choral union and the concert choir. The choral union stressed a good musical background and a creditable appearance for those who did not have the time or money to invest in special voice courses. The concert choir, also known as the "Singing Bears," toured churches and schools. Its membership was based on talent, classification, and scholarship.

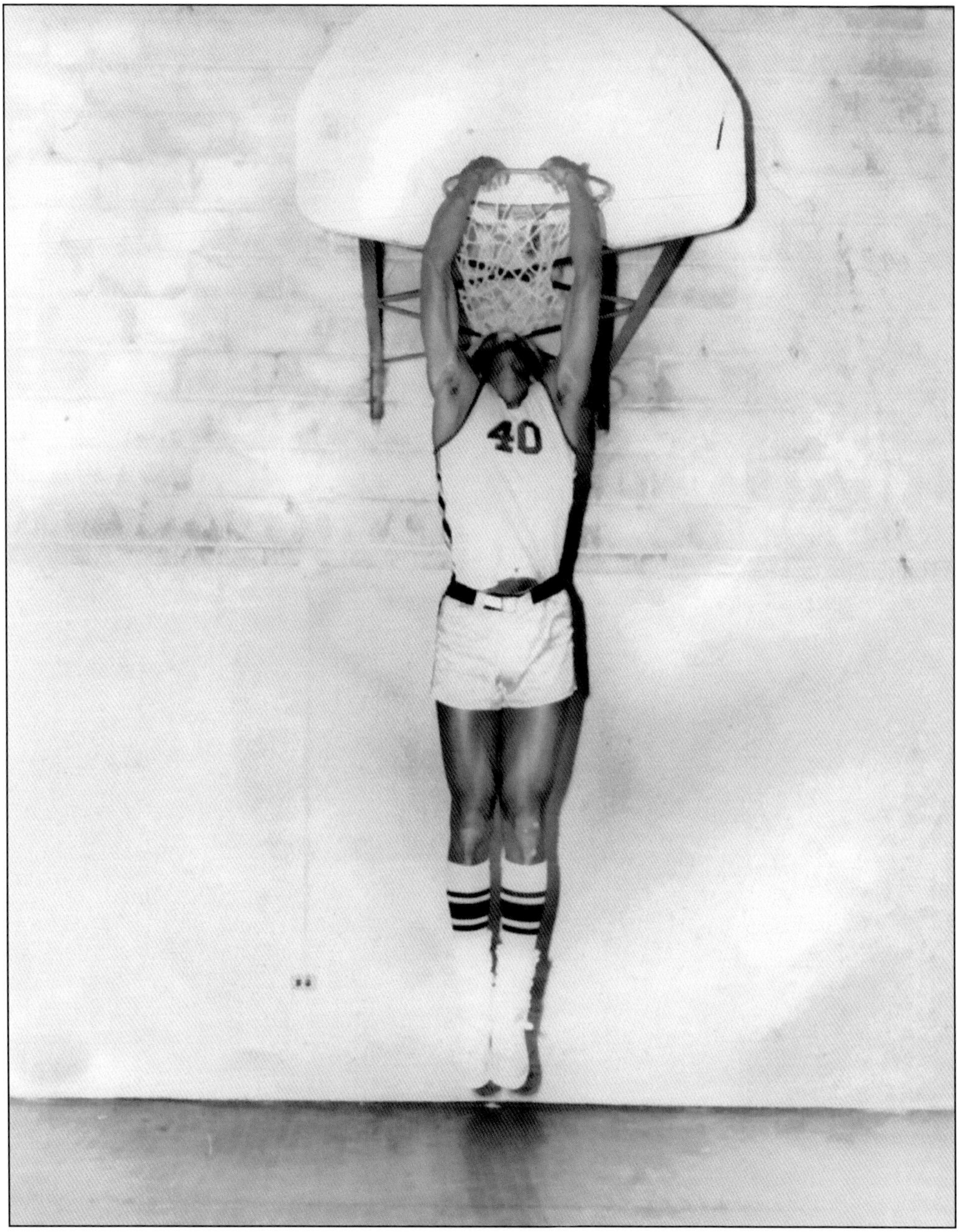

The mission of the Clinton Junior College athletic department is to promote excellence in both academics and athletics. Each student athlete is prepared to succeed beyond the college years. Clinton Junior College offers grants-in-aid to student athletes. Athletic awards are based on need. Murray Garvin, the present athletic director, received a bachelor's of science degree from Eastern Kentucky University in physical education. Pictured is a zealous student practicing a dunk shot in the 1970s.

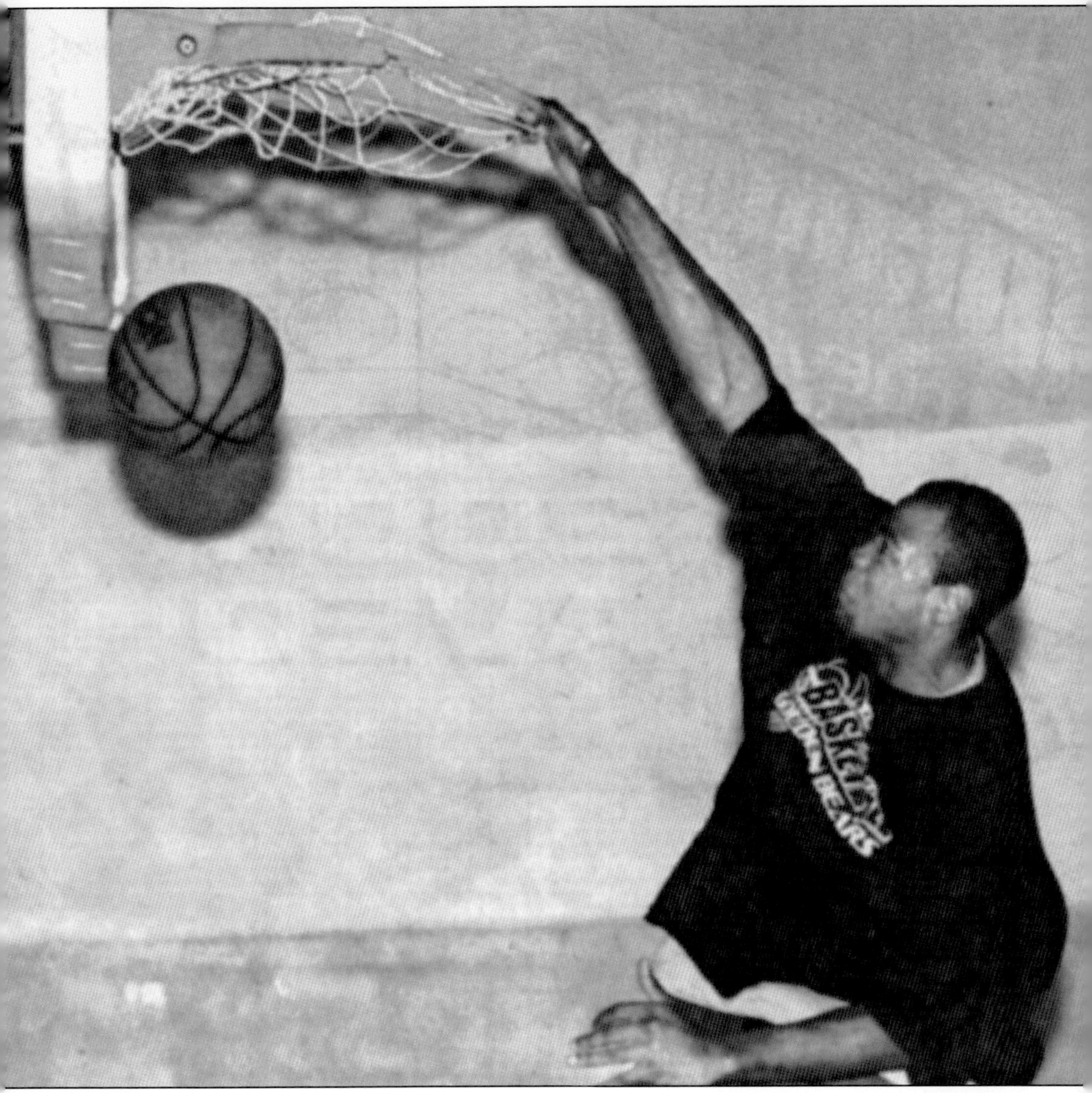

Clinton's David Johnson, a member of the 2003–2004 team, dunks in practice. (Courtesy of *The Herald*.)

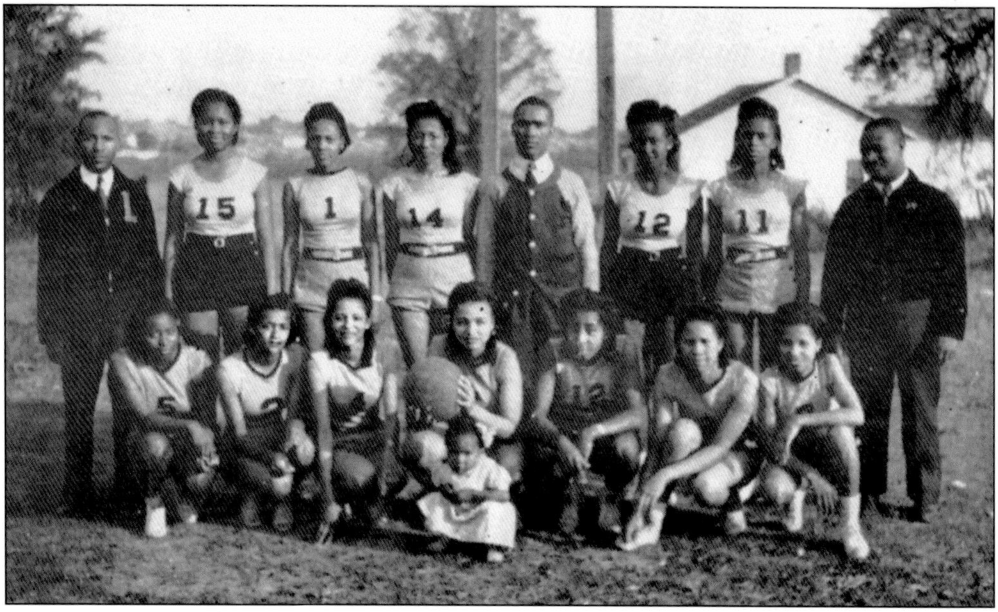

Pictured is the 1942 ladies' basketball team. Basketball for women has been a part of Clinton athletics for over 40 years.

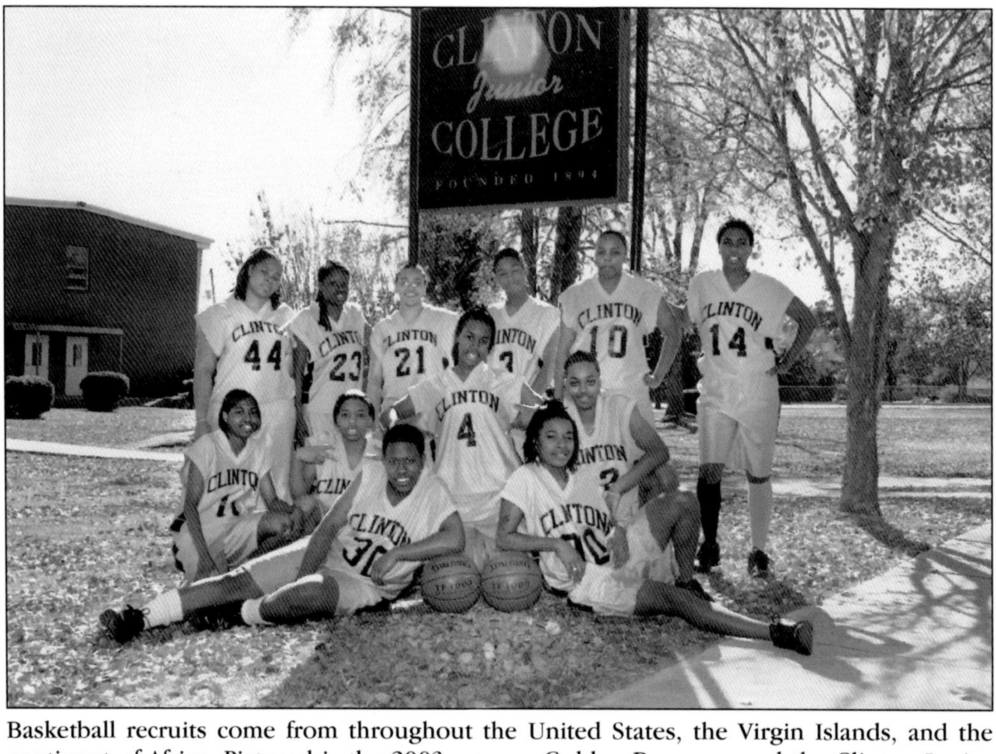

Basketball recruits come from throughout the United States, the Virgin Islands, and the continent of Africa. Pictured is the 2003 women Golden Bears around the Clinton Junior College sign. The college is a member of the National Junior Collegiate Athletic Association, Region 10 Division I.

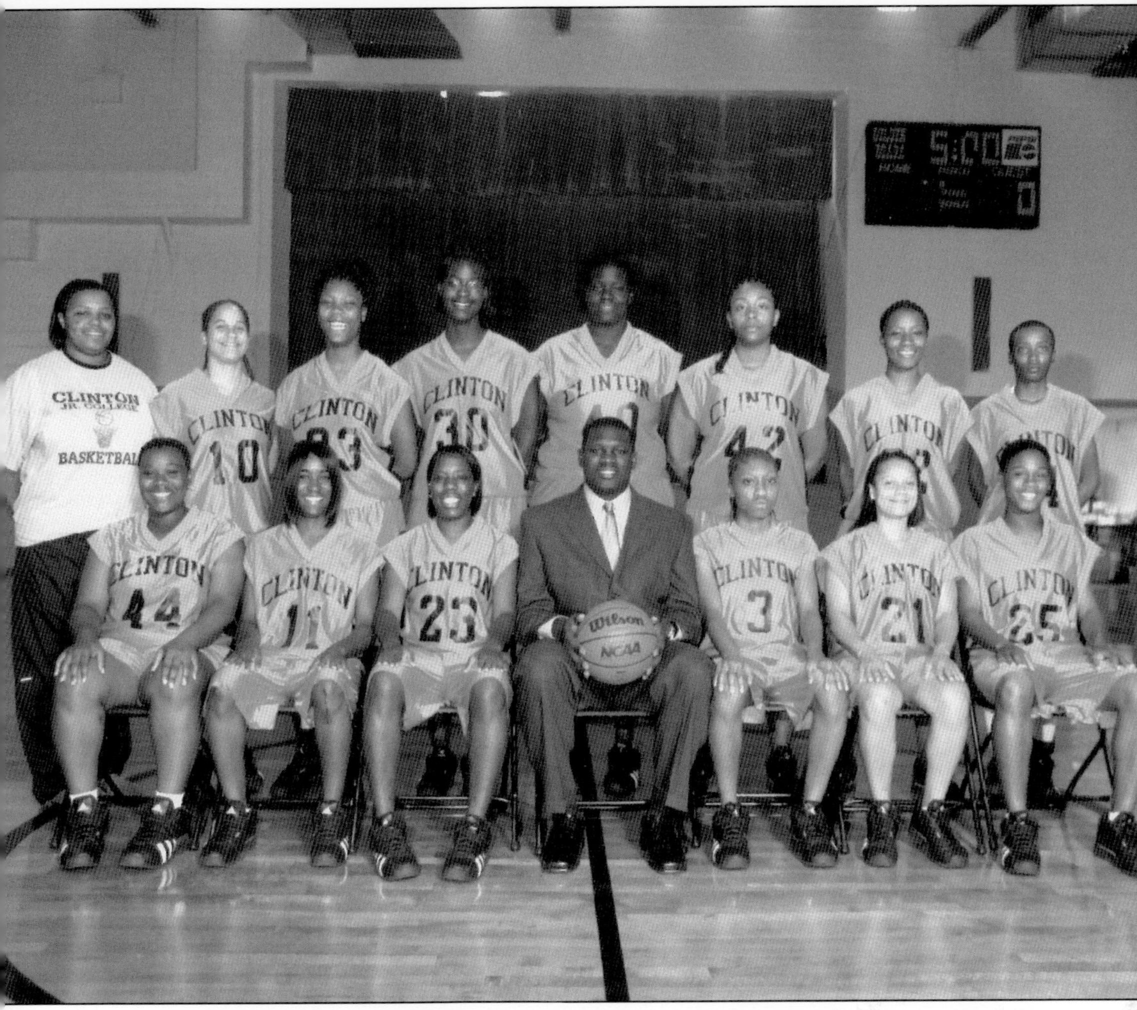

Pictured is the 2003–2004 basketball team with Coach Roderick Woods. Coach Woods is a graduate of Eastern Kentucky University, where he also played basketball.

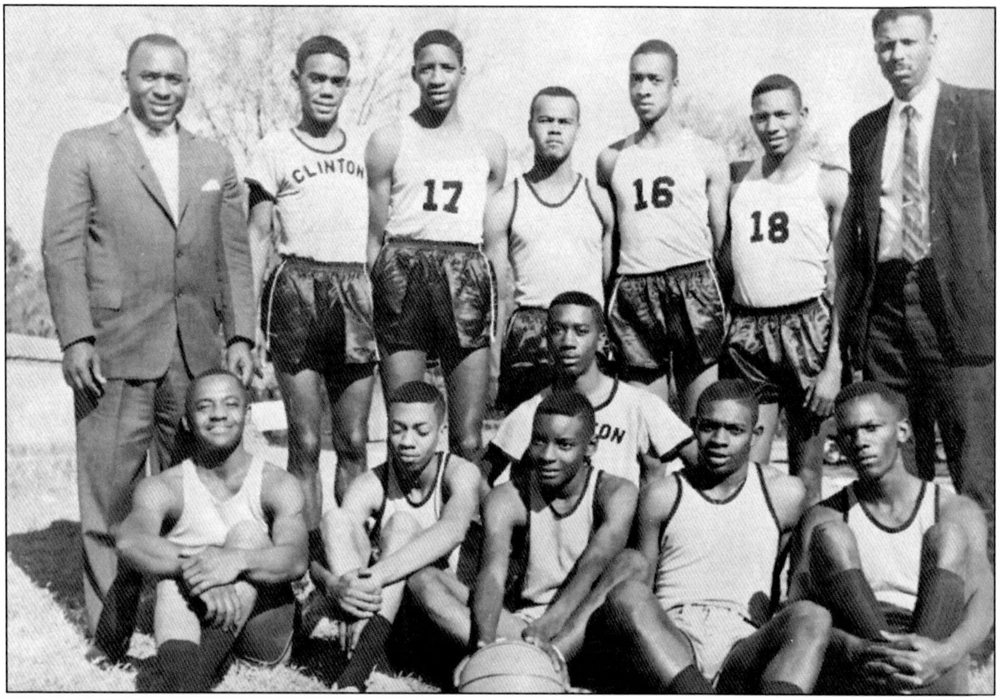

The 1964 men's basketball team and its coaches are pictured here.

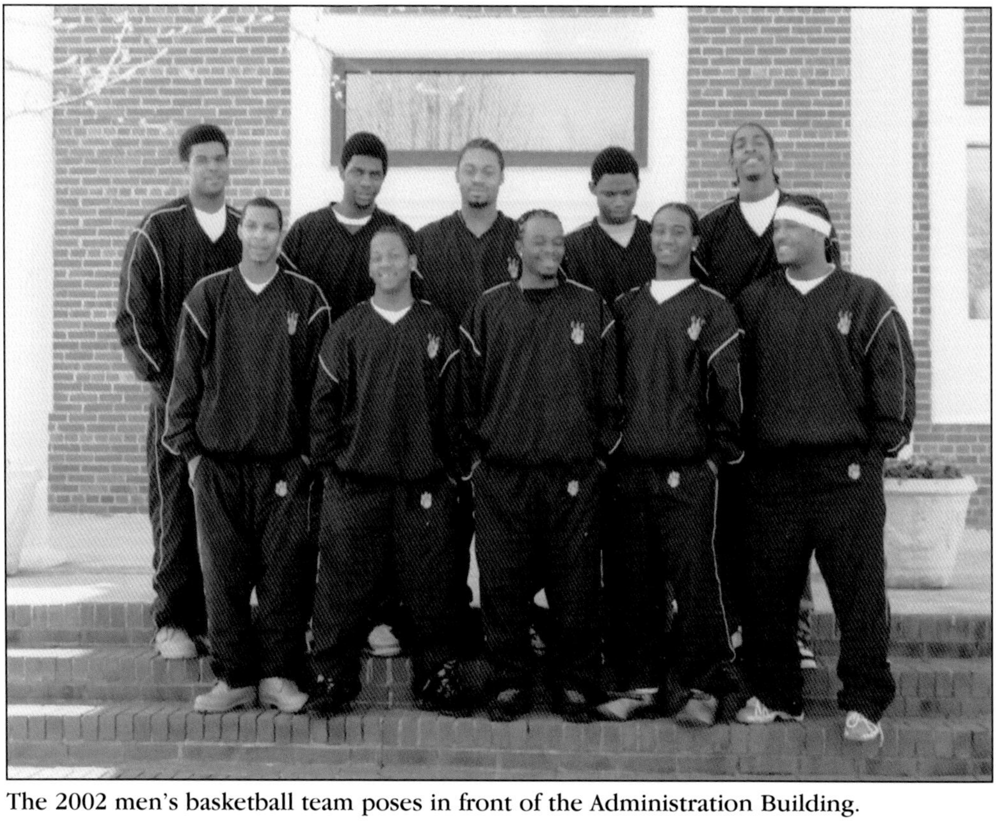

The 2002 men's basketball team poses in front of the Administration Building.

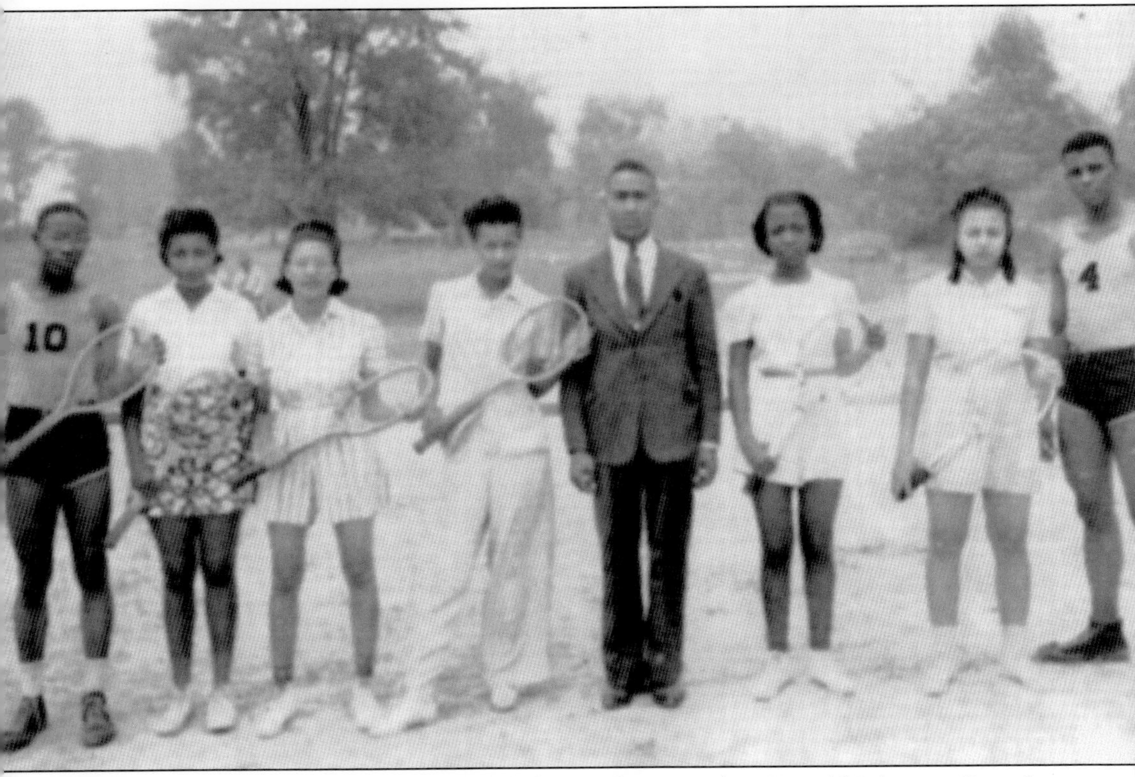

Pictured is the 1942 tennis squad. From left to right are Arthur Donald Johnson, Dorothy Walker, Thomy Lou Davis, Willa Mae Code, Coach David D. Ghist, Fairbee Sinclair, Alma Jimmelle Gladden, and Charlie Jones.

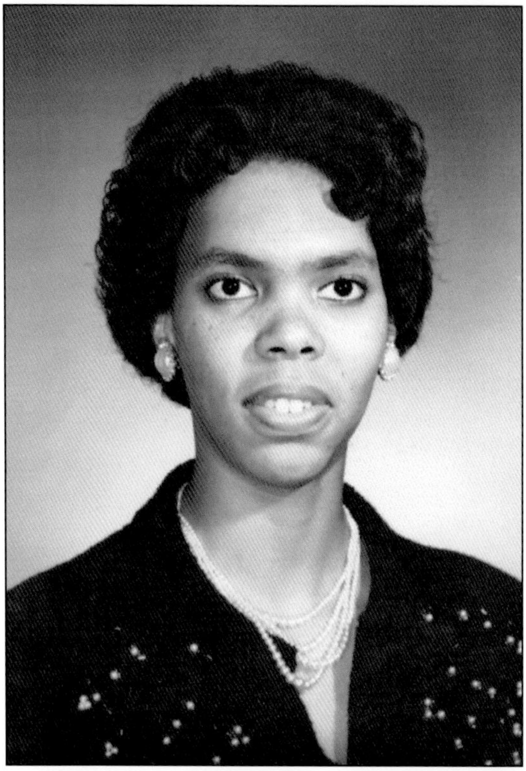

Winthrop University, an all-female training school until 1974, quietly integrated in 1964 when Cynthia Harriette Plair (Mrs. J.E.) Roddey slipped into a classroom and opened her books. She was 24 years old, a native of Rock Hill, and an educator at Emmett Scott High School. Cynthia's ambition included improving her teaching skills. She graduated cum laude in 1967 with a master's degree from Winthrop. Earlier, Cynthia had graduated from Johnson C. Smith University in Charlotte, North Carolina, with a bachelor of arts degree in English. She also holds a doctorate of ministries from Mid-Atlantic Seminary and presently serves as Clinton Junior College's director of informational services, librarian, and archivist at the Richard L. Fisher Memorial Library. The Fisher Memorial Library will be replaced in 2005 by a more modern facility. (From the Collections of Cynthia H. Plair Roddey and Winthrop University Archives, Dacus Library).

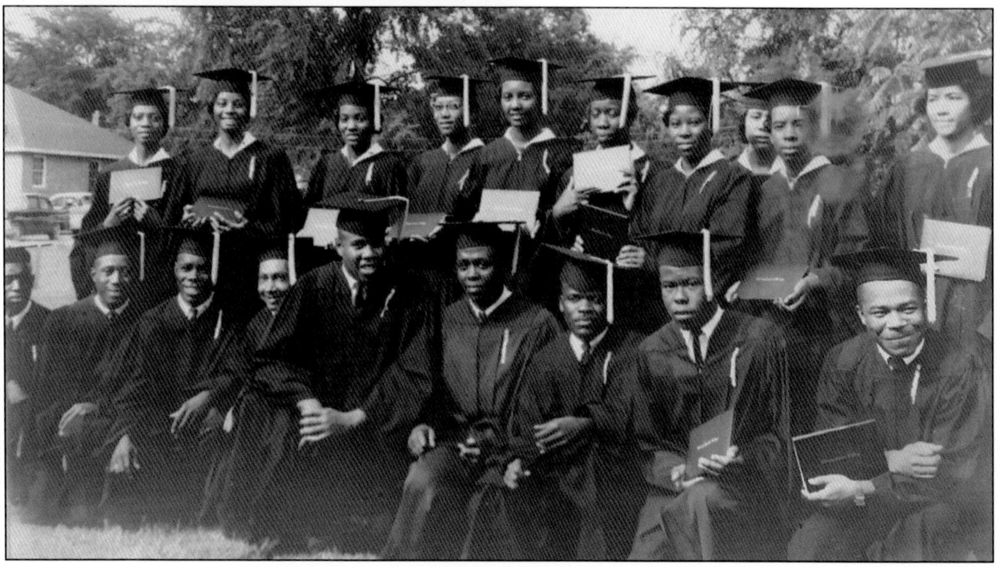

With the exception of the 1899 graduating class, no other group of Clinton graduates witnessed as many changes in America as the Class of 1964. The Civil Rights Act in 1964 passed, and segregated facilities in Rock Hill disappeared. In 1968, public schools integrated in Rock Hill. African-American registered voters doubled between 1968 and 1972. Juanita Goggins of Rock Hill became the first state legislator of African-American descent in 1974, and progress also continued as Clinton Junior College grew under the presidential leadership of Sallie Moreland.

Four

Progress

Keep the Light Shining

Clinton Junior College welcomes people without regard to race, religion, or national origin. It is primarily a residential institution with the majority of students living on campus. Residence hall coordinators and assistants are charged with the general responsibility for the welfare of the occupants of the halls. Students are urged to participate with staff in creating a nurturing atmosphere for living, learning, and studying within the residential halls. Students are encouraged to participate in extra-curricular activities such as choir, sports, student government, chess club, and the school newsletter. The Snipes Student Center offers recreation such as music, television, a pool, and ping-pong. A staff activities coordinator plans other events for students.

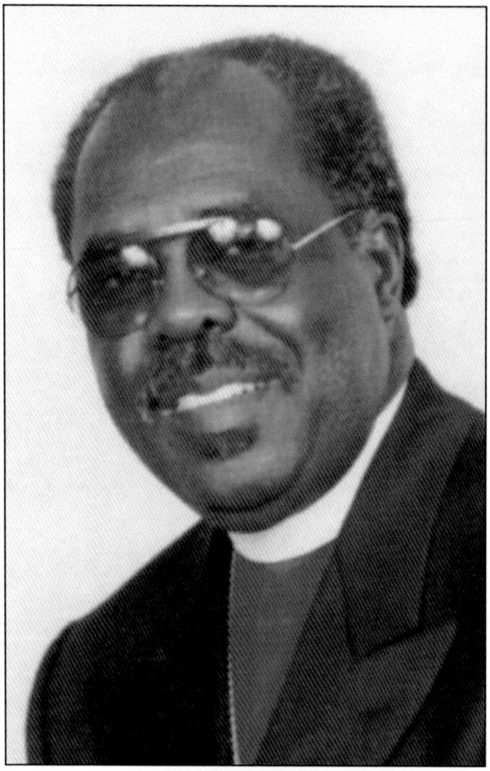

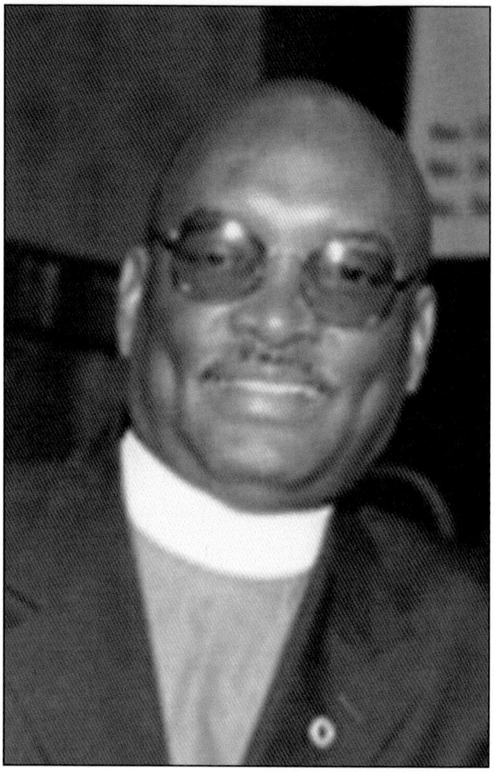

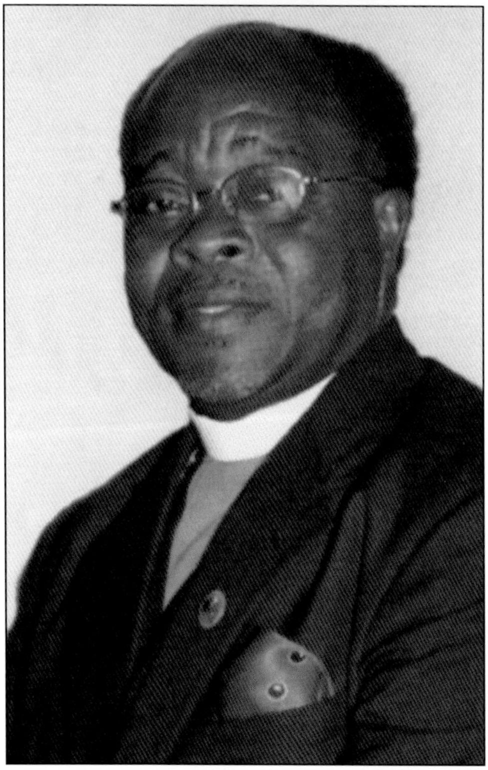

Three sitting bishops of the A.M.E. Zion Church are graduates of Clinton College. Above left is Bishop George W.C. Walker, who graduated in 1964. Above right is Bishop George E. Battle Jr., who graduated in 1968. At left is Bishop S. Chuka Ekemam, who also graduated in 1968.

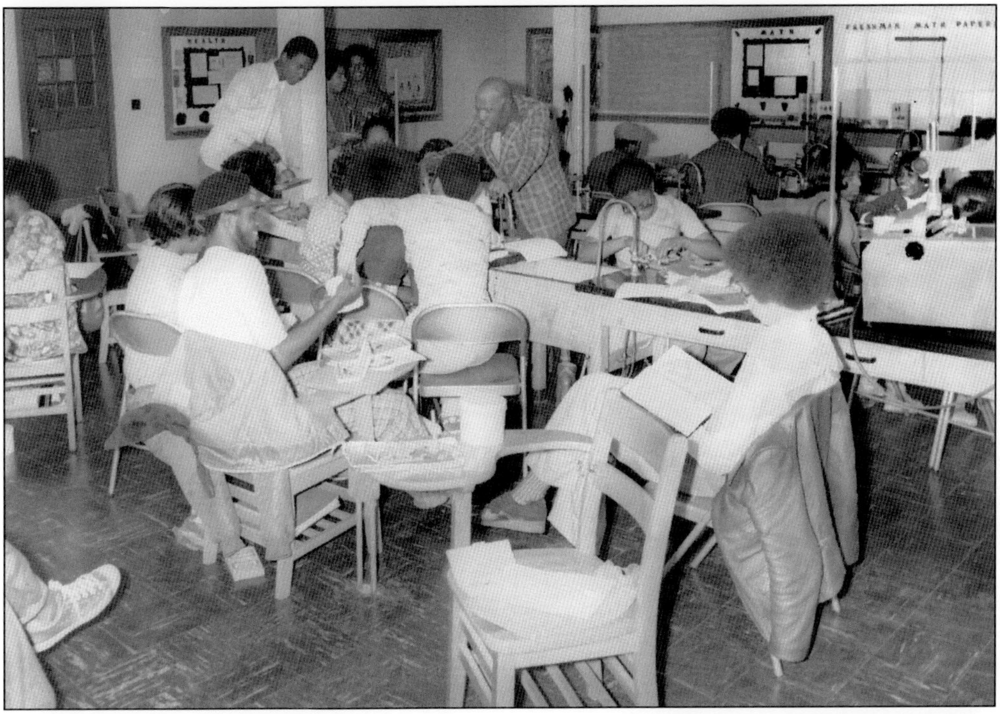

Pictured at center is Mr. A.J. Johnson, a former student at the college. He is teaching biology to eager scholars in the 1970s.

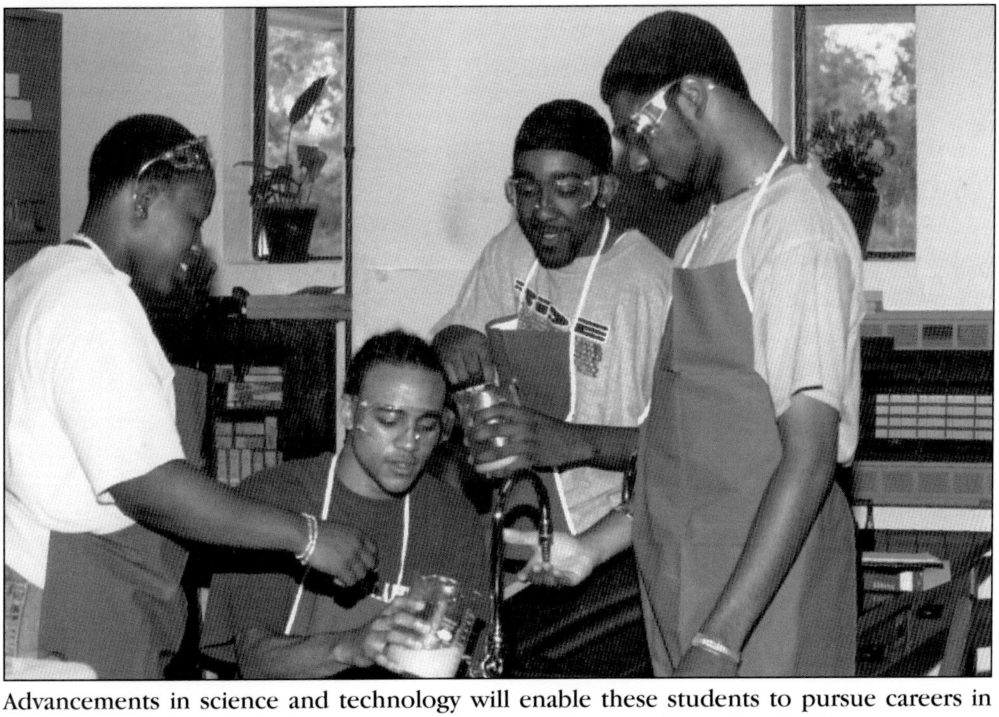

Advancements in science and technology will enable these students to pursue careers in science-related fields. In 2003, the college received a grant from CIPA/NASA to encourage more students to explore opportunities in scientific areas.

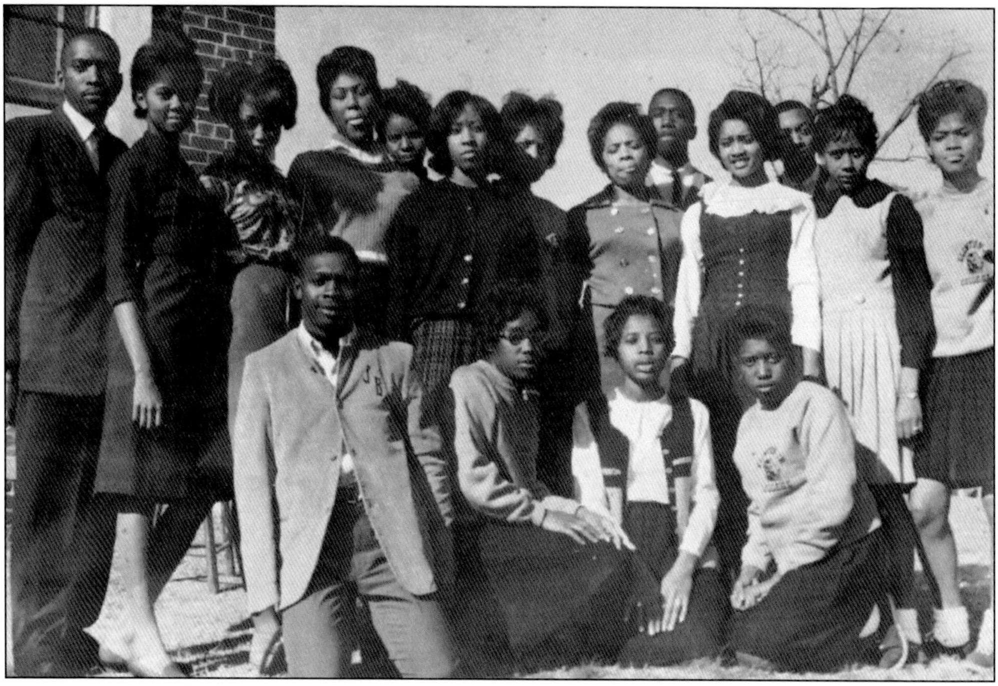

In the 1960s, French was taught at Clinton, and the French Club enabled students who were proficient in the language to spend additional time studying and conversing.

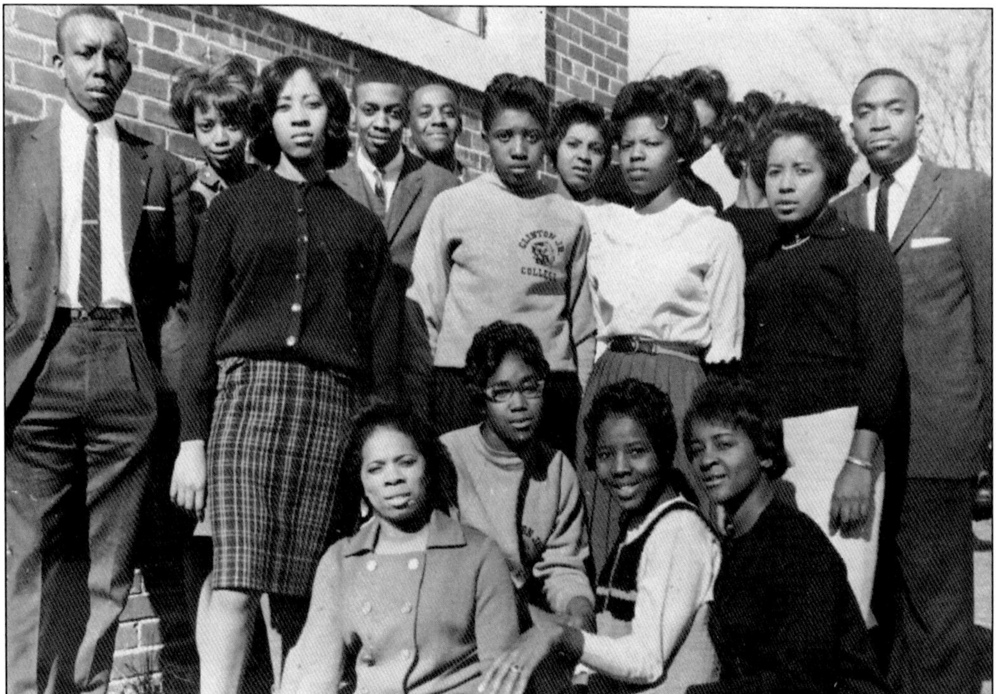

Another extra-curricular activity in the 1960s was the Speech Club. This club allowed students to practice public speaking and learn to prepare speeches.

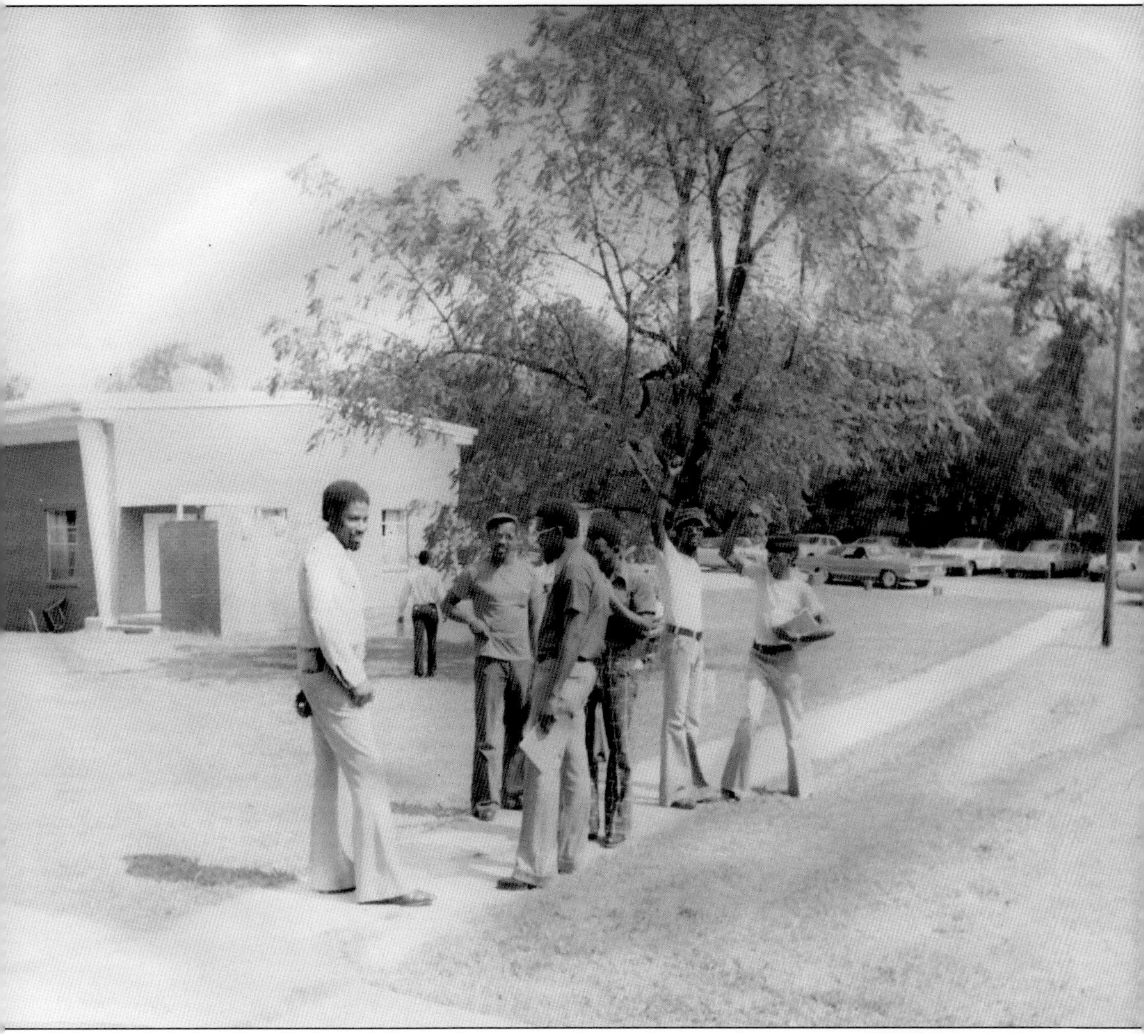

Veterans enjoy the sunshine in the 1970s. More than 75 percent of the student body resides on the coed campus according to 2003 statistics. The residential halls are within walking distance of a recreational center, located at the site of the former Emmett Scott High School. It includes a swimming pool, basketball courts, tennis courts, and softball fields. Eight churches of various dominations are also in the area.

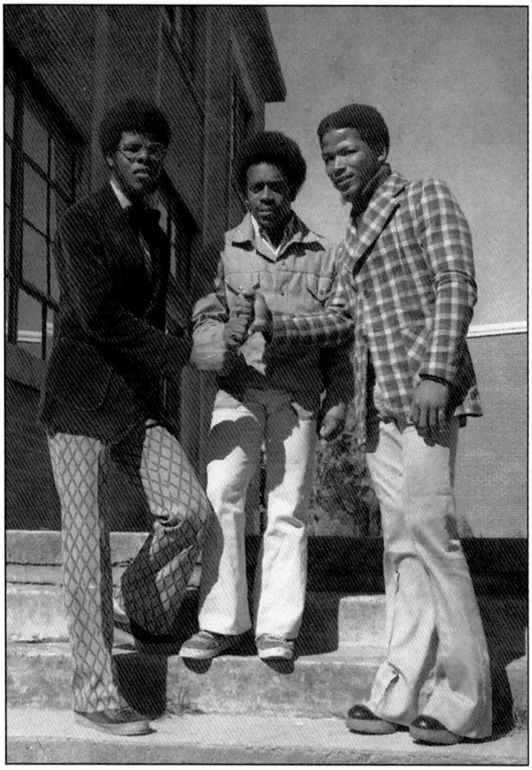

Clinton Junior College has a beautiful campus within the city limits of Rock Hill. It is 72 miles north of Columbia, South Carolina, and 25 miles south of Charlotte, North Carolina. Pictured are three students exhibiting expressions of solidarity at Clinton Junior College in the 1970s.

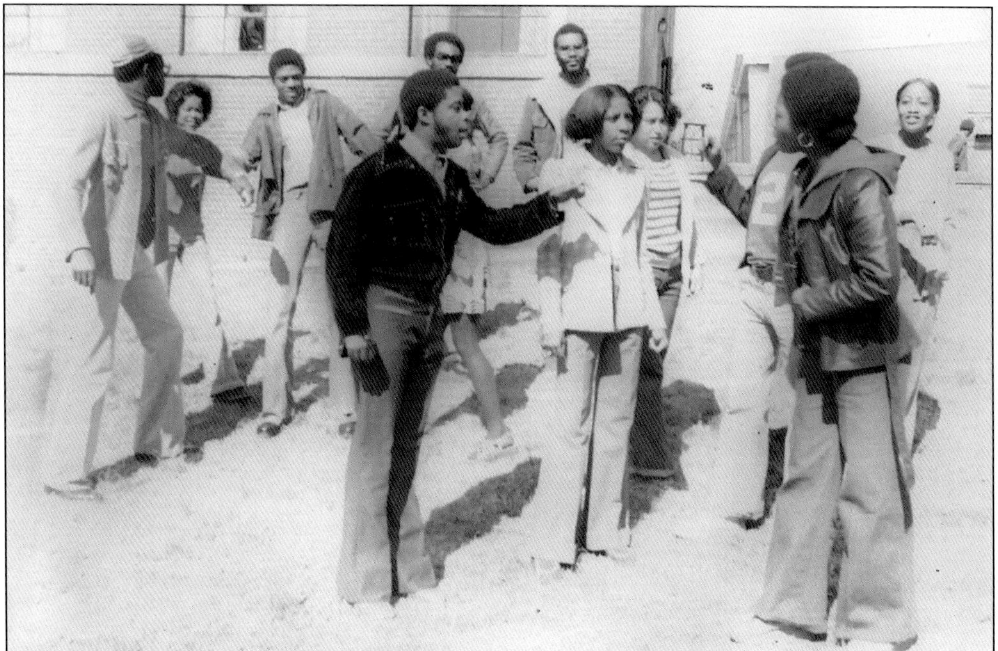

Throughout its 110 years of history, Clinton Junior College has made every effort to educate the whole person—mind, spirit, and body. Pictured here are students from a drama class in the 1970s discussing the day's events.

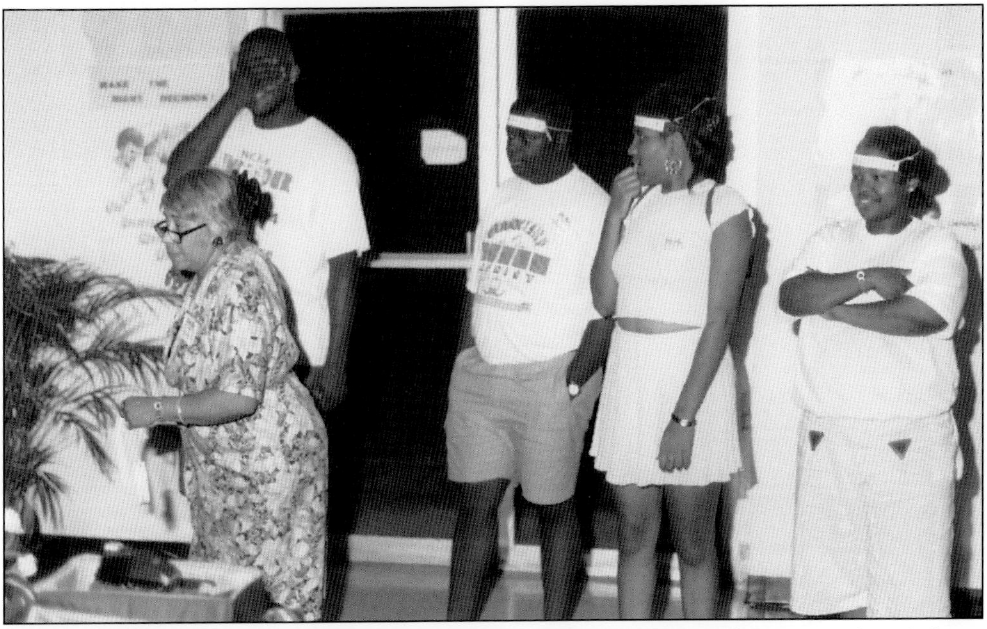

Throughout its history, Clinton Junior College has offered a variety of classes and workshops to help participants develop better stress management or business skills. Pictured is an anger management workshop. The participants are learning better communication techniques in order to disengage inappropriate behavior that might intensify conflict in an office situation or relationship. Cyphese Ramseur Redfern also conducted a team building workshop with students in the 1990s. The workshop helps promote good communication skills.

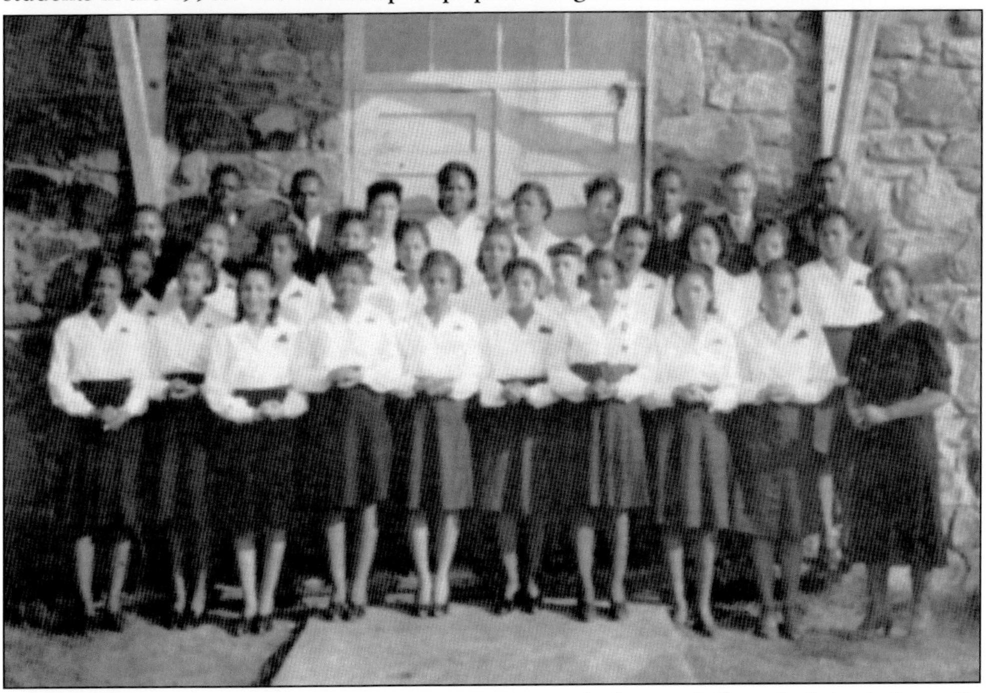

In the 1960s, singing without music was popular, and Clinton College had the A Cappella Choir. This choir entertained at college and community events.

CAP AND GOWN PROGRAM
CLINTON JUNIOR COLLEGE
ROCK HILL, SOUTH CAROLINA
MAY 17TH, 1984
2:00 P.M.

Prelude:

Entrance: Graduates 1. Preparatory 2. Sophomores

Invocation:

Music Battle Hymn of the Republic 549 __Audience

Scripture:

Prayer:

Selection: Hymn 251 __Audience

Presentation Of Speaker: Rev. A.N. David

Speaker: Rev. Kenneth Q. James
Pastor, Pierce's Chapel AME Zion Church
Clarkton, North Carolina

Acceptance: Aloysius Maduforo

Remarks:

Alma Mater:

ADVISORS: REV. A.N. DAVID
MRS. E.E. WALKER

PRESIDENT: DR. S.V. MORELAND

Pictured is a cap and gown ceremony program. The cap and gown ceremony was the predecessor to what are now the commencement exercises.

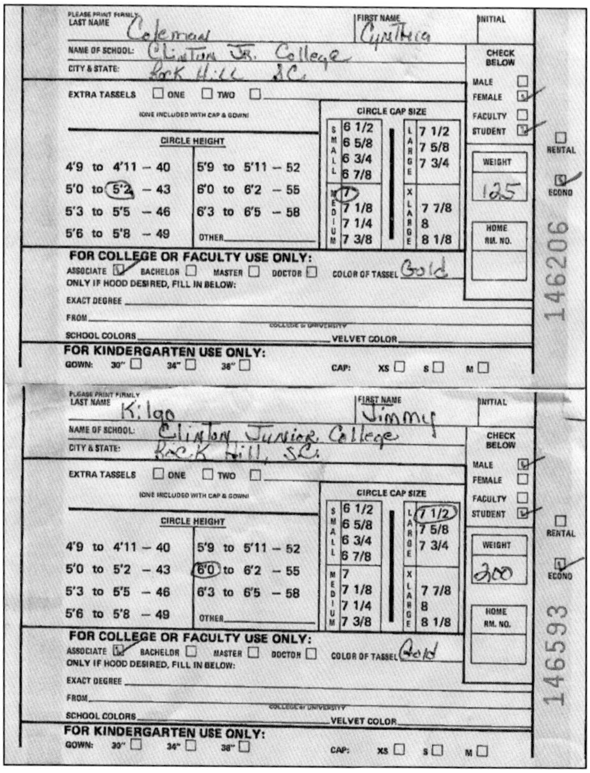

PLEASE PRINT FIRMLY LAST NAME Coleman FIRST NAME Cynthia INITIAL
NAME OF SCHOOL: Clinton Jr. College
CITY & STATE: Rock Hill SC
EXTRA TASSELS ☐ ONE ☐ TWO ☐
(ONE INCLUDED WITH CAP & GOWN)
CIRCLE HEIGHT: 4'9 to 4'11 – 40; 5'0 to 5'2 – 43; 5'3 to 5'5 – 46; 5'6 to 5'8 – 49; 5'9 to 5'11 – 52; 6'0 to 6'2 – 55; 6'3 to 6'5 – 58; OTHER
CIRCLE CAP SIZE: SMALL 6 1/2, 6 5/8, 6 3/4, 6 7/8; MEDIUM 7, 7 1/8, 7 1/4, 7 3/8; LARGE 7 1/2, 7 5/8, 7 3/4; X LARGE 7 7/8, 8, 8 1/8
CHECK BELOW: MALE ☐ FEMALE ☑ FACULTY ☐ STUDENT ☑
WEIGHT 125
HOME RM. NO.
☐ RENTAL ☑ ECONO
FOR COLLEGE OR FACULTY USE ONLY: ASSOCIATE ☑ BACHELOR ☐ MASTER ☐ DOCTOR ☐ COLOR OF TASSEL Gold
ONLY IF HOOD DESIRED, FILL IN BELOW:
EXACT DEGREE
FROM (COLLEGE or UNIVERSITY)
SCHOOL COLORS VELVET COLOR
FOR KINDERGARTEN USE ONLY: GOWN: 30" ☐ 34" ☐ 36" ☐ CAP: XS ☐ S ☐ M ☐
146206

PLEASE PRINT FIRMLY LAST NAME Kilgo FIRST NAME Jimmy INITIAL
NAME OF SCHOOL: Clinton Junior College
CITY & STATE: Rock Hill, SC
EXTRA TASSELS ☐ ONE ☐ TWO ☐
(ONE INCLUDED WITH CAP & GOWN)
CIRCLE HEIGHT: 4'9 to 4'11 – 40; 5'0 to 5'2 – 43; 5'3 to 5'5 – 46; 5'6 to 5'8 – 49; 5'9 to 5'11 – 52; 6'0 to 6'2 – 55; 6'3 to 6'5 – 58; OTHER
CIRCLE CAP SIZE: SMALL 6 1/2, 6 5/8, 6 3/4, 6 7/8; MEDIUM 7, 7 1/8, 7 1/4, 7 3/8; LARGE 7 1/2, 7 5/8, 7 3/4; X LARGE 7 7/8, 8, 8 1/8
CHECK BELOW: MALE ☑ FEMALE ☐ FACULTY ☐ STUDENT ☑
WEIGHT 200
HOME RM. NO.
☐ RENTAL ☑ ECONO
FOR COLLEGE OR FACULTY USE ONLY: ASSOCIATE ☑ BACHELOR ☐ MASTER ☐ DOCTOR ☐ COLOR OF TASSEL Gold
ONLY IF HOOD DESIRED, FILL IN BELOW:
EXACT DEGREE
FROM (COLLEGE or UNIVERSITY)
SCHOOL COLORS VELVET COLOR
FOR KINDERGARTEN USE ONLY: GOWN: 30" ☐ 34" ☐ 36" ☐ CAP: XS ☐ S ☐ M ☐
146593

Pictured are actual cap and gown order forms from 1964.

Five

GROWTH AND DEVELOPMENT

Using a holistic approach to growth and development, the college's student affairs/residence life program has the following five major objectives: to provide assistance for retention, to provide cultural enrichment, to foster positive spiritual and ethical development, to provide social development opportunities, and to provide physical conditioning. This well-planned and comprehensive series includes the mandatory lyceum/chapel series, an integral part of every student's college experience. Each student can rely on the staff and administrators to provide opportunities for creativity, innovation, and accomplishment. Special services are available to scholars who may experience academic or personal difficulties. These services may be obtained from the offices of academic dean, the college chaplain, and the director of student affairs, or through an appropriate community referral.

Disclaimer: This history contains gaps. Unfortunately, there are very few pictorial records for the 1950s and 1970s.

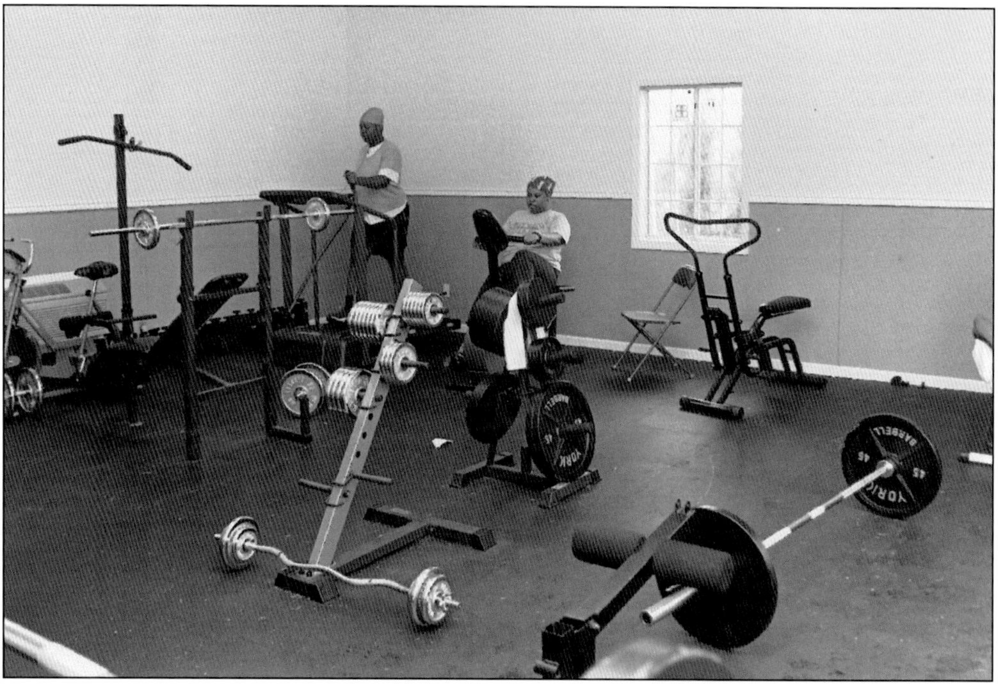

Exercise is vital to human health, and Clinton Junior College offers state-of-the-art fitness equipment for students. Physical education courses feature activities like basketball, volleyball, calisthenics, and aerobics.

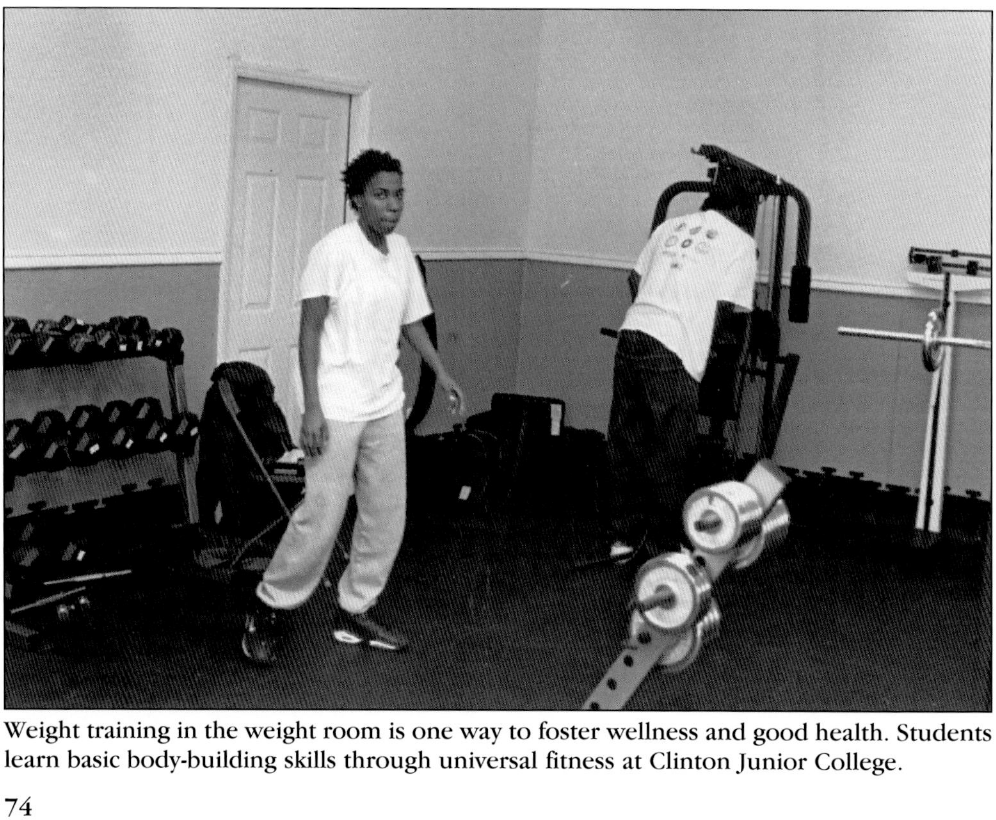

Weight training in the weight room is one way to foster wellness and good health. Students learn basic body-building skills through universal fitness at Clinton Junior College.

Clinton our dear old school
For thee; we'll reign and rule,
For thee we'll take our stand,
To honor thee.
We'll honor and cherish thee,
As down life's path we flee
Clinton our dear old school
We love you so.

When we enter her gates,
When we our classes take,
We pledge allegiance true
To old Clinton College.
We'll honor and cherish thee,
As down life's path we flee
Clinton our dear old school
We love you so.

Pictured here are the words to the Clinton Junior College alma mater. Although the writer of the alma mater is unknown, the song has been sung at Founders' Day, Commencement, and other special programs as far back as anyone remembers.

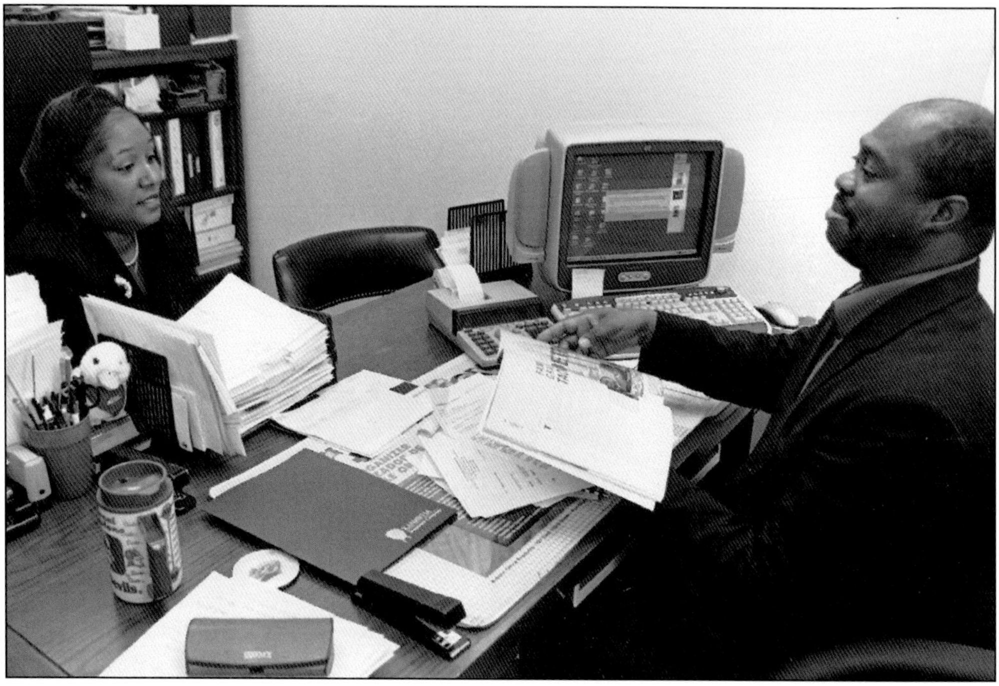

A dedicated group of educators and administrators, such as Cheryl McCullough and Willie Graham, shown here, work as a team to provide students with the best education possible. The college offers associate's degrees of business, liberal arts, and religious studies.

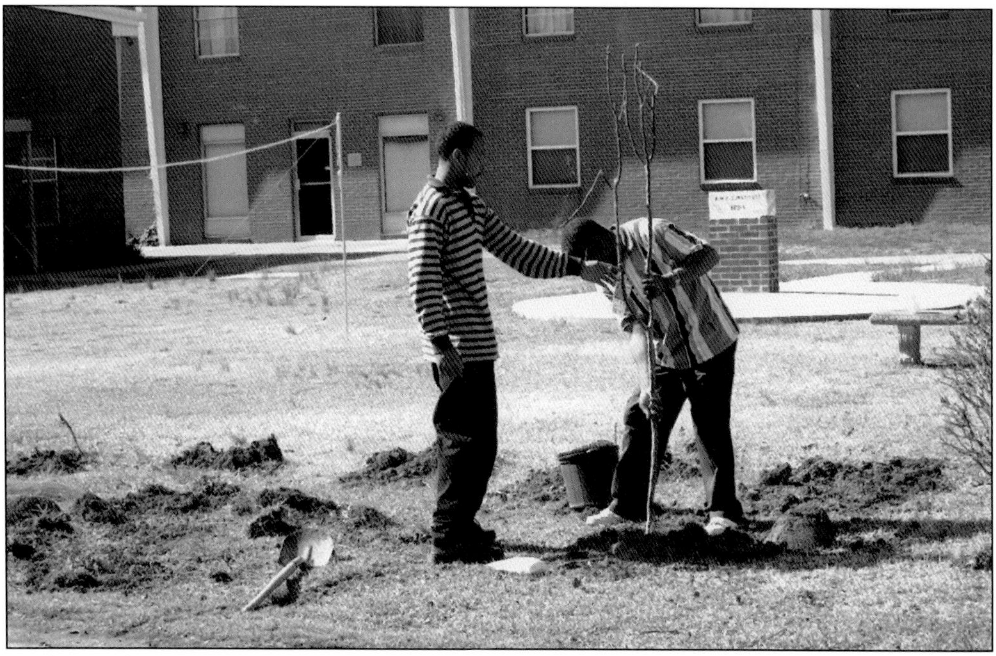

Student volunteers plant trees in memory of those people stricken with Acquired Immune Deficiency Syndrome (AIDS). Volunteerism is strongly encouraged at Clinton, and service to the community is deeply felt as well as appreciated. Notice the cornerstone monument behind the young men that earmarks the founding dates of Clinton Junior College.

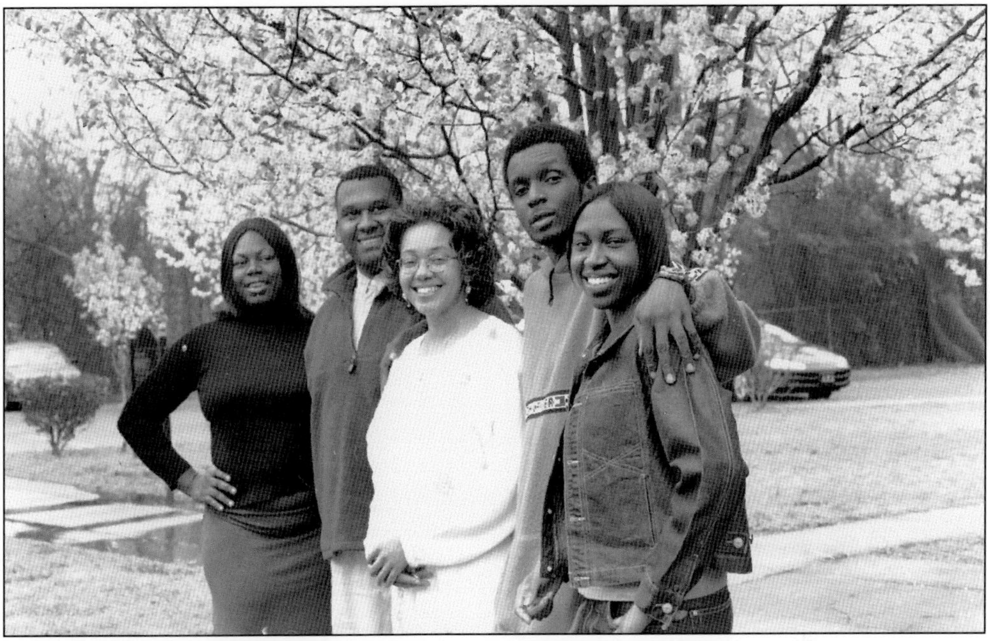

Students from all parts of the world attend Clinton Junior College. Although most are from the United States, a few young scholars leave their homelands—places like the Grand Bahamas, the British and U.S. Virgin Islands, or Africa—so they can learn Christian values at Clinton Junior College. Pictured is a group of students enjoying the sunshine during the spring semester.

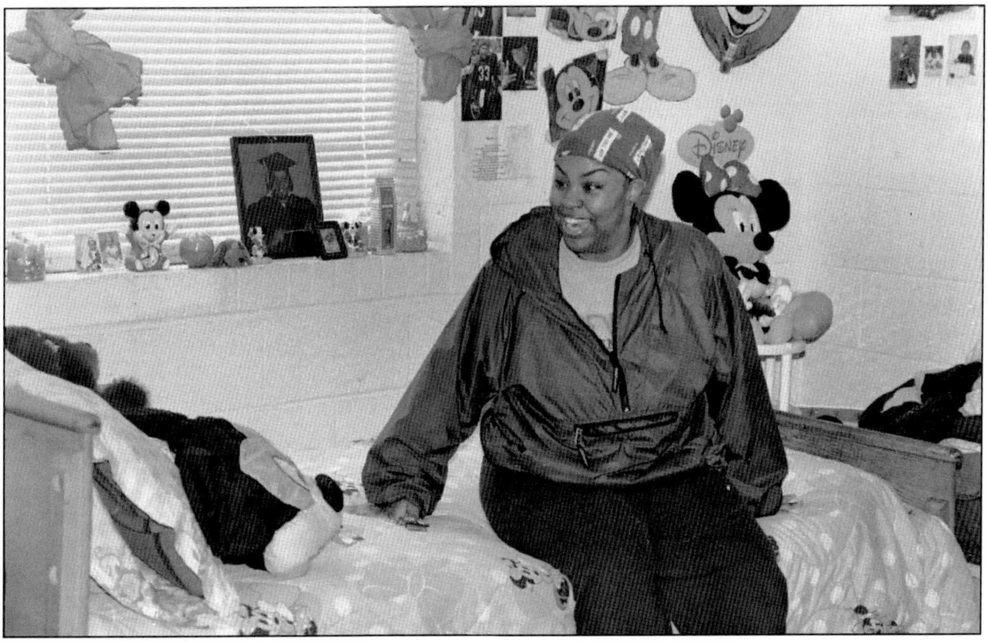

Each residence hall room is furnished with basic items, but students may choose linens, blankets, bedspreads, rugs, and other decorative items to bring to school from their homes. Small appliances such as lamps, radios, stereos, hair dryers, and electric razors are also permitted in the residential halls. Lori Davis likes Mickey Mouse.

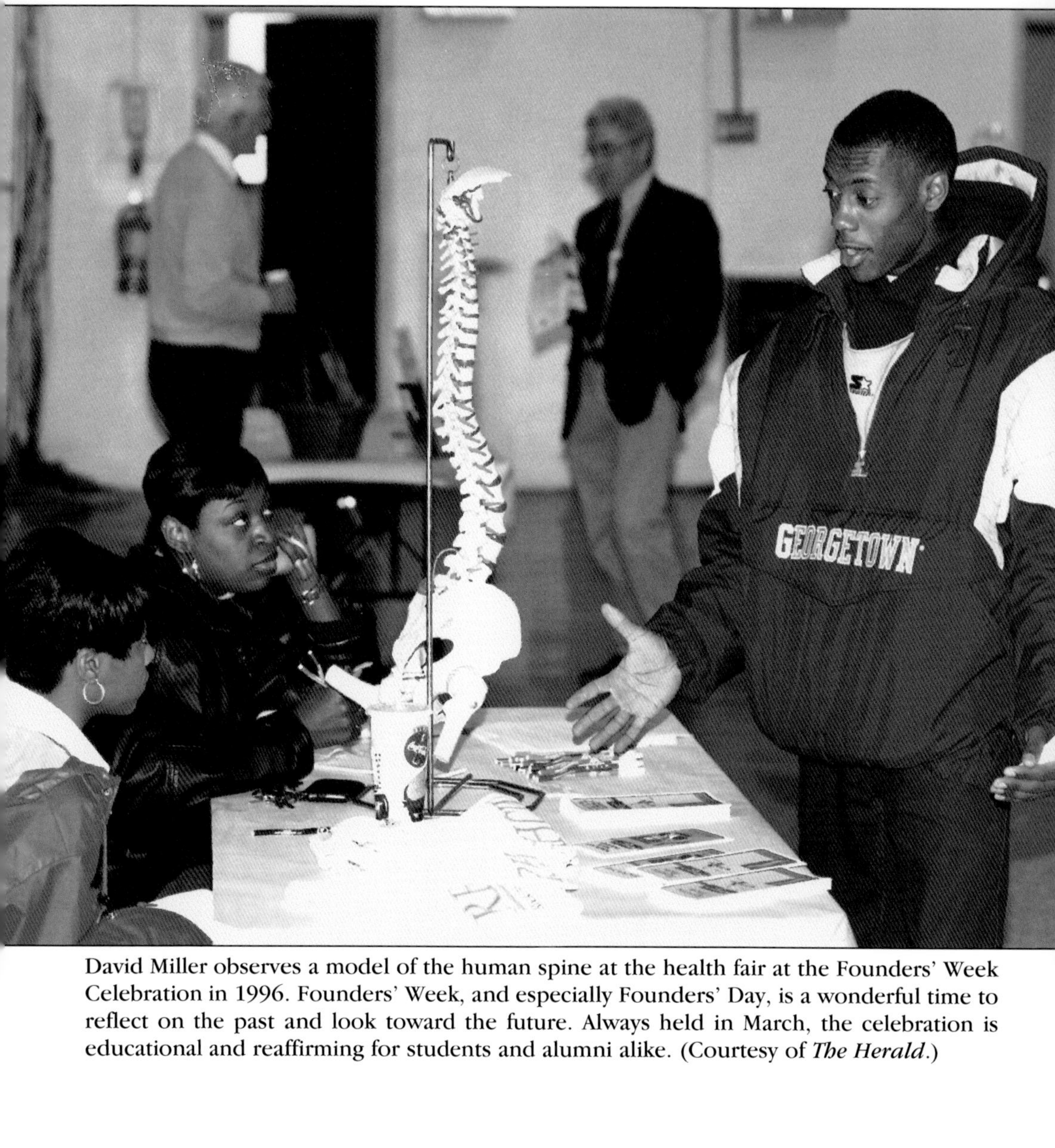

David Miller observes a model of the human spine at the health fair at the Founders' Week Celebration in 1996. Founders' Week, and especially Founders' Day, is a wonderful time to reflect on the past and look toward the future. Always held in March, the celebration is educational and reaffirming for students and alumni alike. (Courtesy of *The Herald*.)

THE WHITE HOUSE

WASHINGTON

February 22, 1995

Greetings to all those gathered to celebrate the 100th anniversary of Clinton Junior College.

Excellence in education is the key to our future. For 100 years, the faculty and staff of Clinton have been offering an ideal learning opportunity for their students and preparing them for the responsibilities that lie ahead. Our nation relies on schools such as yours to supply the knowledge and skills necessary to compete in the twenty-first century. I am confident that Clinton Junior College will continue to endow future generations with expertise and guidance.

Best wishes for a memorable celebration.

Bill Clinton

President William Jefferson ("Bill") Clinton sent his greetings in honor of Clinton Junior College's 100th anniversary. Local leaders and politicians also sent letters congratulating the educators and administrators for doing a fine job in the face of many hardships and challenges.

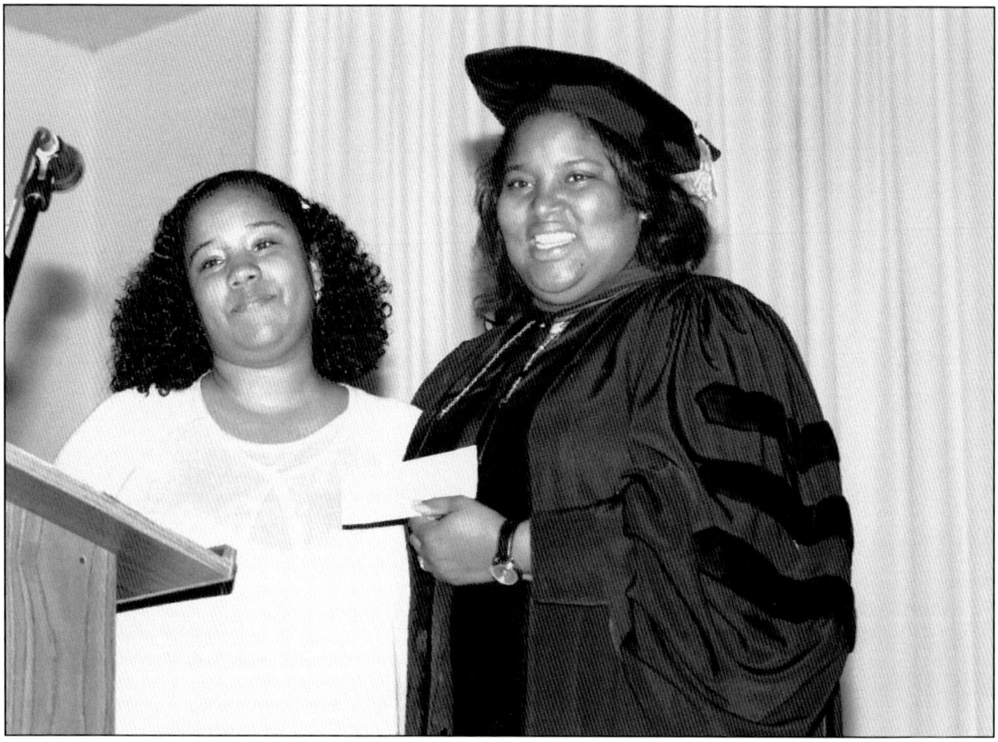

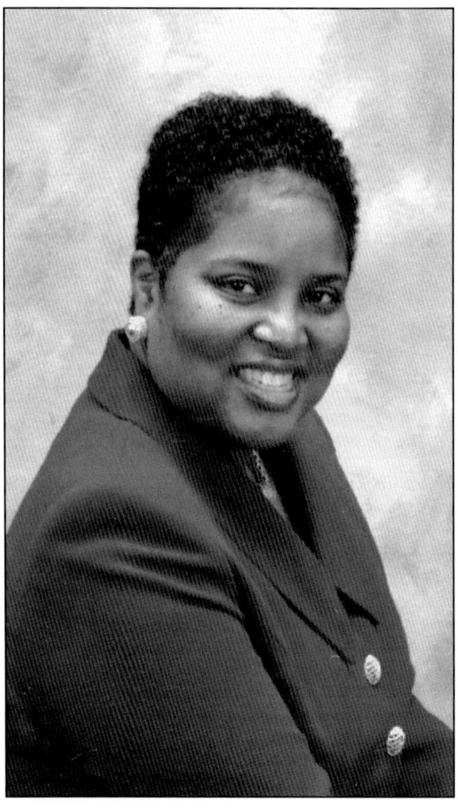

Dr. Sallie V. Moreland retired as college president in 1994. Pictured is Mrs. Gina Murray (left), speaking before presenting a $5,000 check from the estate of her grandmother Dr. Sallie V. Moreland to Clinton Junior College. Accepting is Pres. Cynthia McCullough Russell.

Dr. Cynthia L. McCullough Russell, an instructor at Clinton, became the college's 11th president in 1994. A Charlotte native, Dr. Russell graduated from Furman University, Southeastern Baptist Seminary, and Drew University. Following in the footsteps of her father, Rev. Fred McCullough, she became a minister in the A.M.E. Zion Church and served as pastor of North Corner A.M.E. Zion Church in Lancaster, South Carolina. Dr. Russell prepared the college for accreditation, and for three years, she and the committee formulated a plan of action. In August 1998, Dr. Russell and Dr. Russell Fitzgerald, executive director of Transnational Association of Christian Colleges and Schools met to discuss candidacy. New goals were set for the college to meet the educational challenges of the 21st century.

Six

Challenges

A Legacy of Liberation

From November 1998 to March 2001, Clinton Junior College aggressively pursued compliance with the recommendations of the Transnational Association of Christian Colleges and Schools (TRACS). Dr. Russell oversaw a massive expansion of facilities, staff, and curriculum development while Dr. Elaine Johnson Copeland directed the self-study. Most of the buildings were renovated and then formally dedicated. TRACS granted the college candidacy on March 3, 2001. Dr. Russell's tenure ended in May 2001. Candidacy status allowed the college to receive federal funds such as Pell Grants, student loans, and Title III funding. Title III is a grant from the U.S. Department of Education for "strengthening historically black colleges and universities."

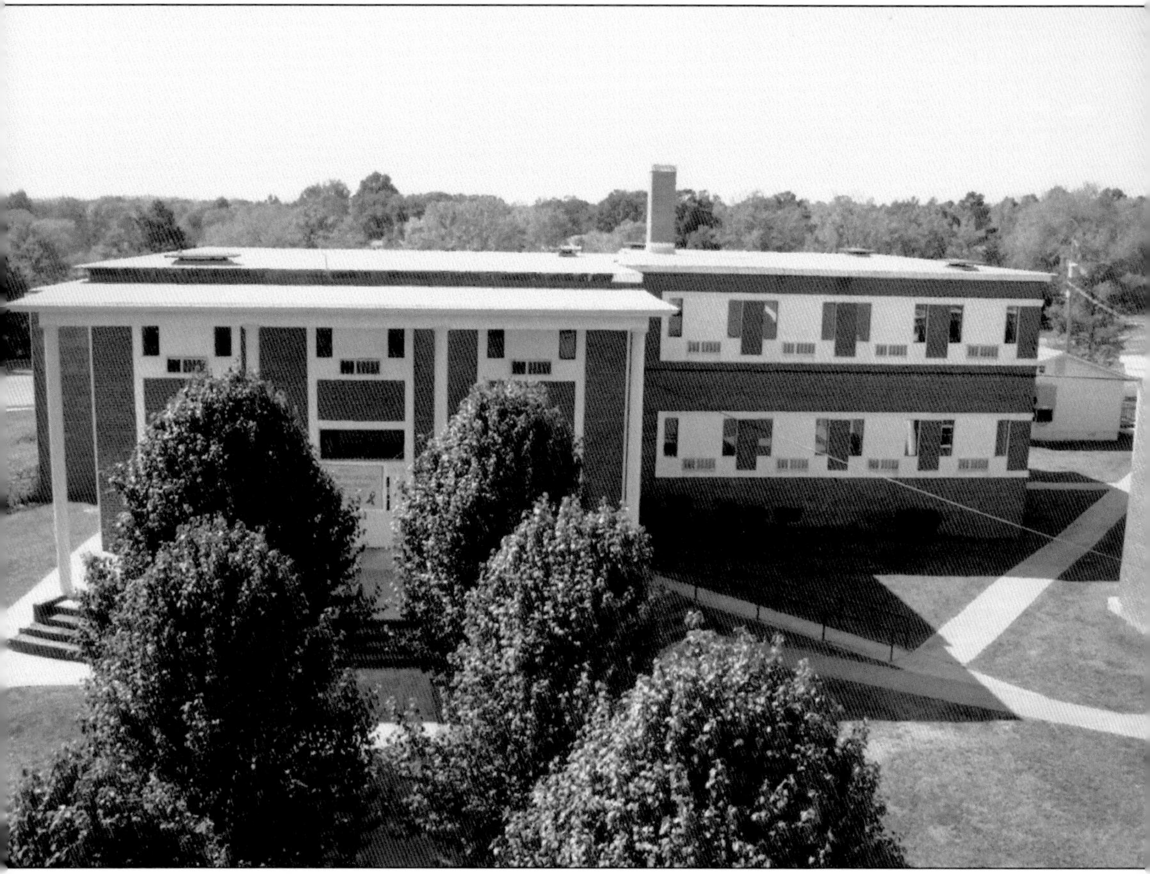

Pictured is an aerial view of the current administration and classroom building.

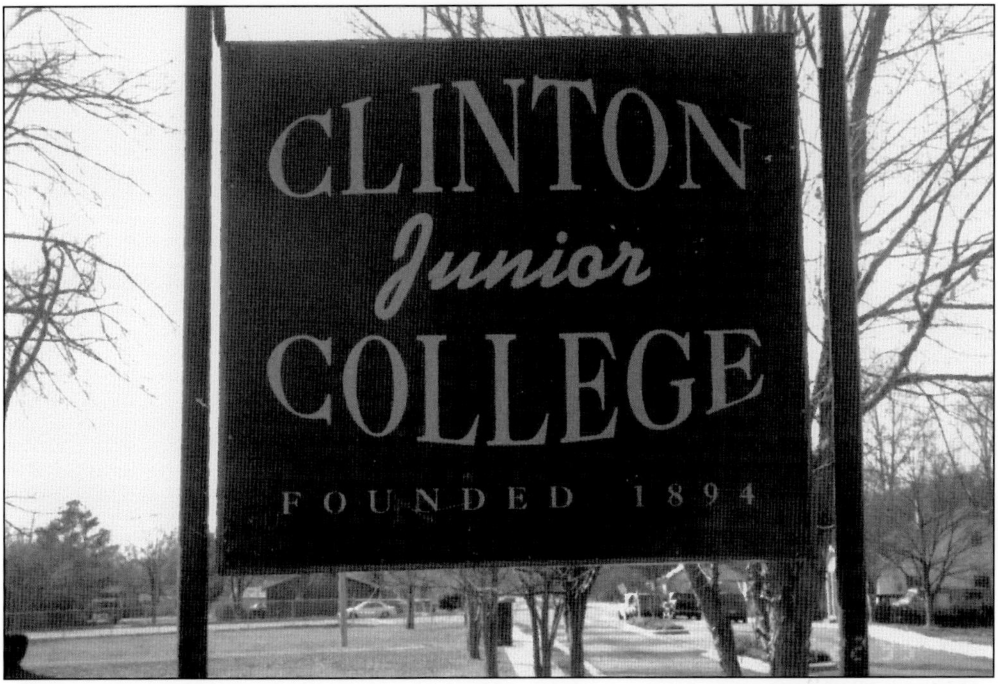

The second sign erected at the college is pictured here. It replaced the first sign in the 1960s.

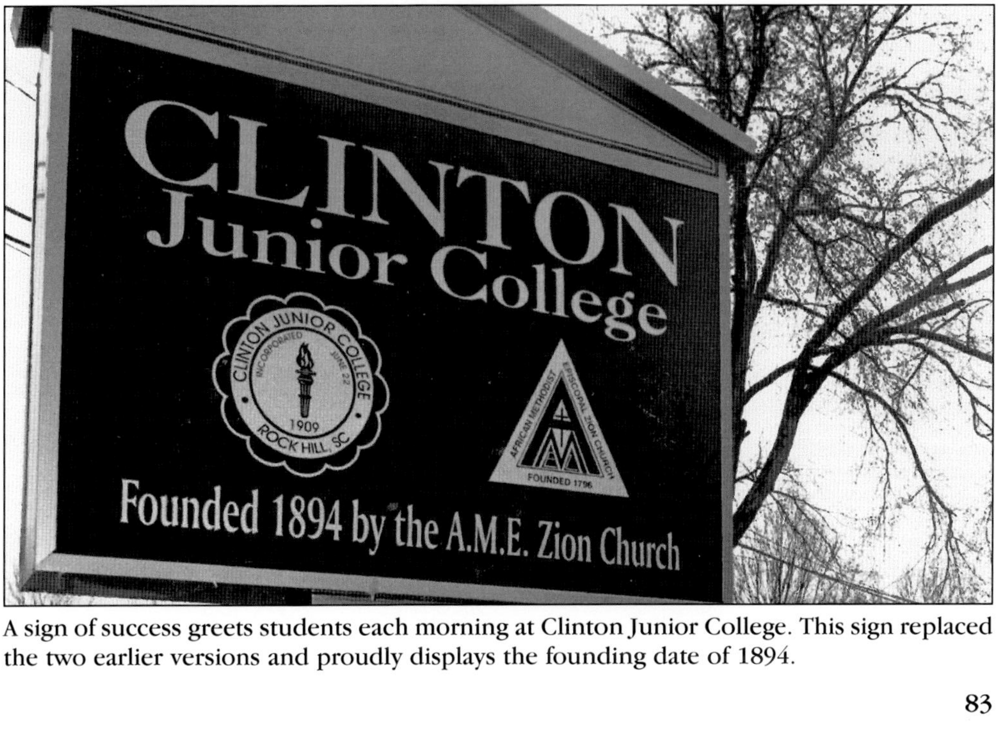

A sign of success greets students each morning at Clinton Junior College. This sign replaced the two earlier versions and proudly displays the founding date of 1894.

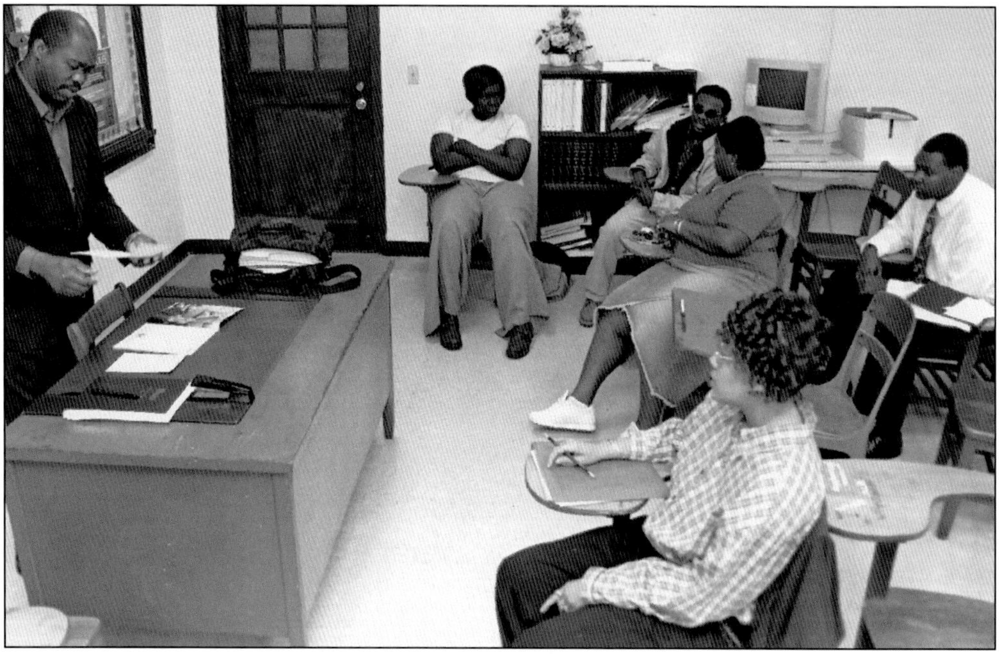

Full-time faculty and student enrollment increased in the early 1990s. Two computer laboratories were established, and the school began to offer computer technology classes. The Russell Honors Leadership Program was established under the leadership of Dr. Bertha Roddey. Pictured is a classroom and students in the Department of Business in 2003. Students successfully interned at the South Carolina legislature during the era that Dr. Russell was president, and the Scholars Programs were established in 2003.

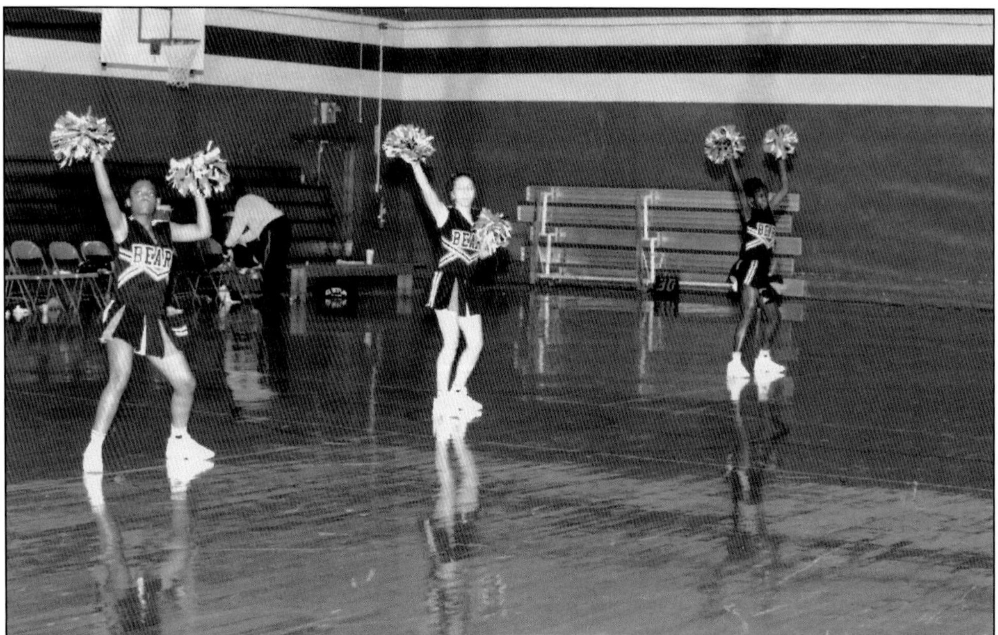

Cheerleaders praise the basketball team that became Division 10 Junior College Champions in 1999.

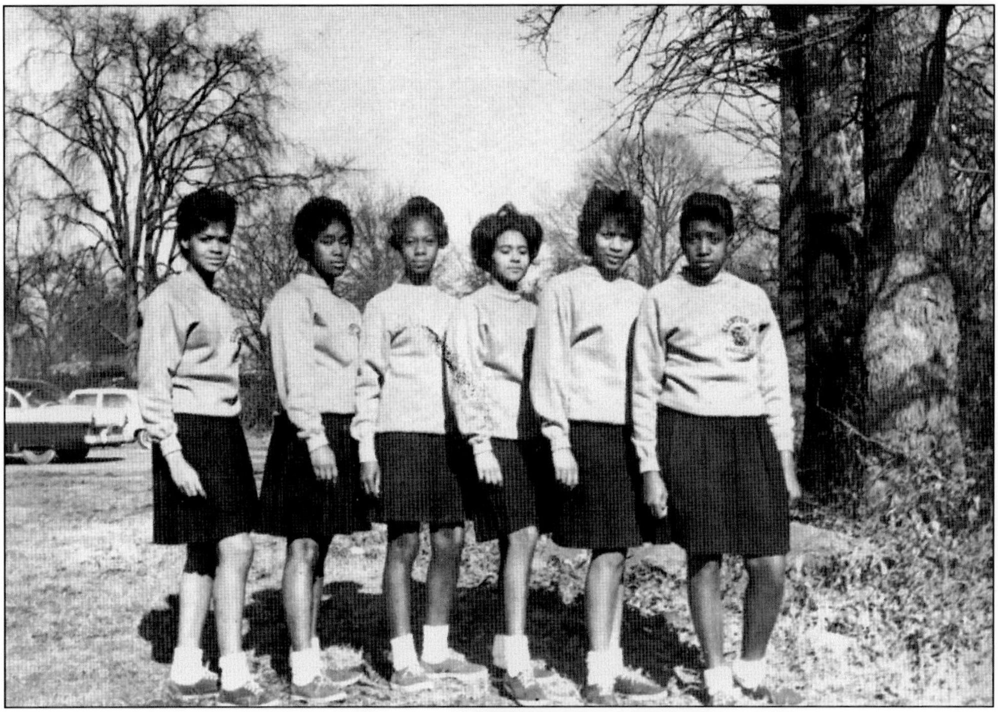

These cheerleaders encouraged the 1964 sports teams to victory.

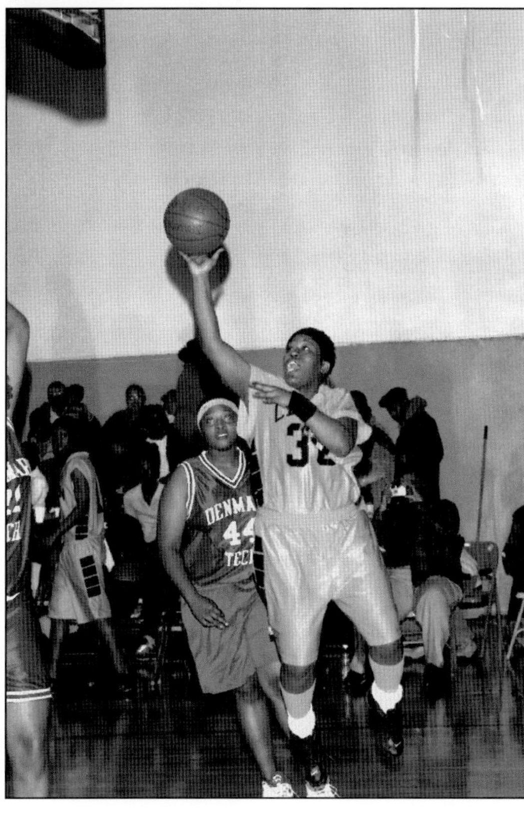

Clinton Junior College Golden Bears play hard, but they always try to exhibit good sportsmanship on the ball court. For more than 60 years, students have been recruited for basketball. A women's team has been fielded for approximately 40 years.

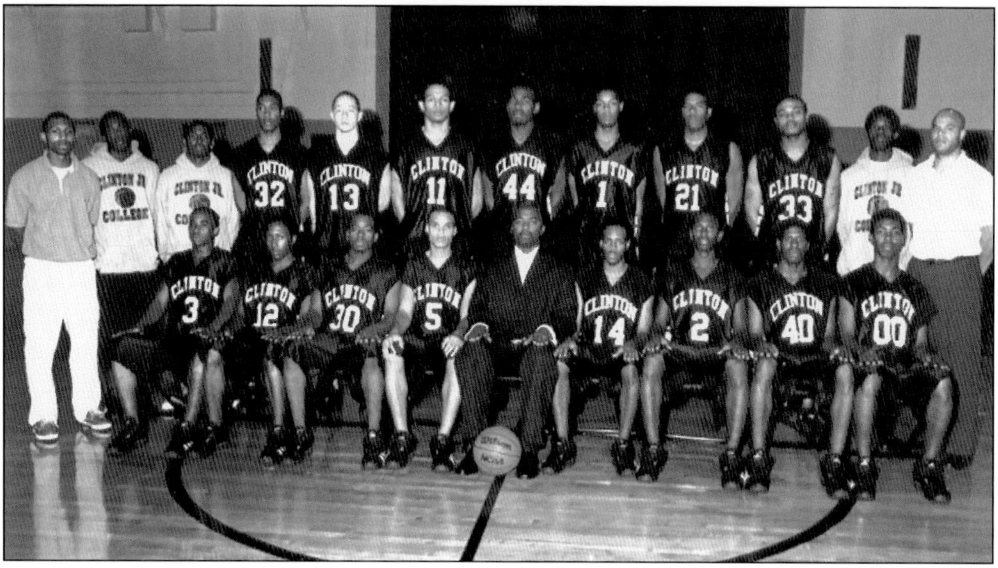

In 1999, the Clinton Junior College men's basketball team won the Region 10 Conference Championship. The team went on to the NJCAA Championship in Illinois, where they finished eighth in the nation. In 2004, the men's team was the Region 10 Champions and traveled to Maryland for post-season play.

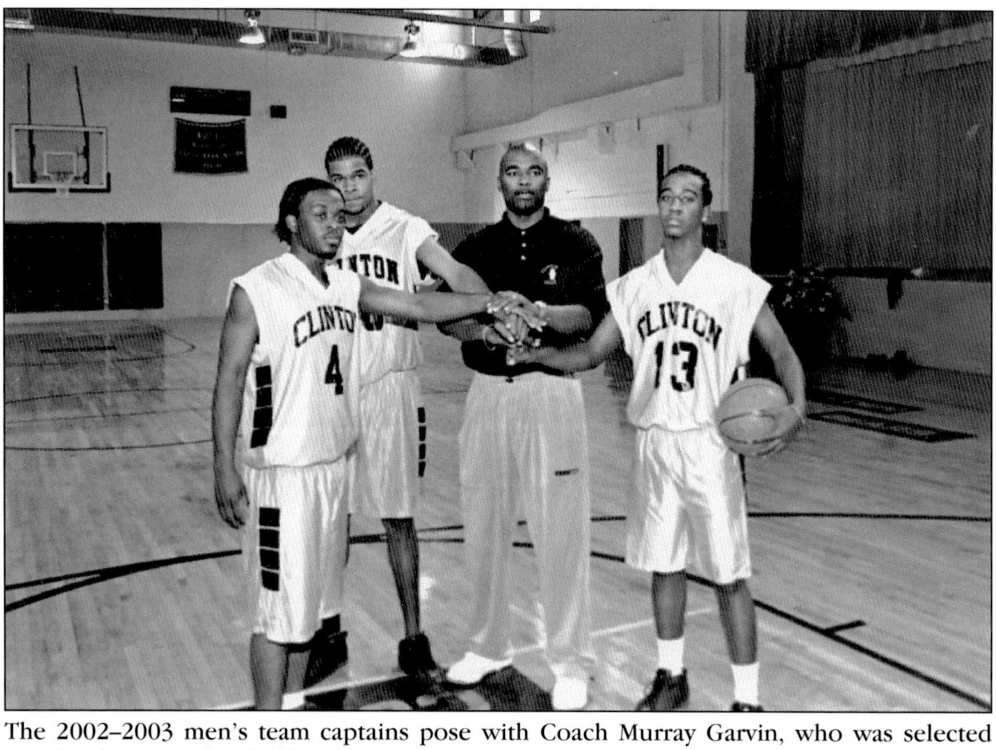

The 2002–2003 men's team captains pose with Coach Murray Garvin, who was selected Coach of the Year in 2004 by the other coaches in Region 10.

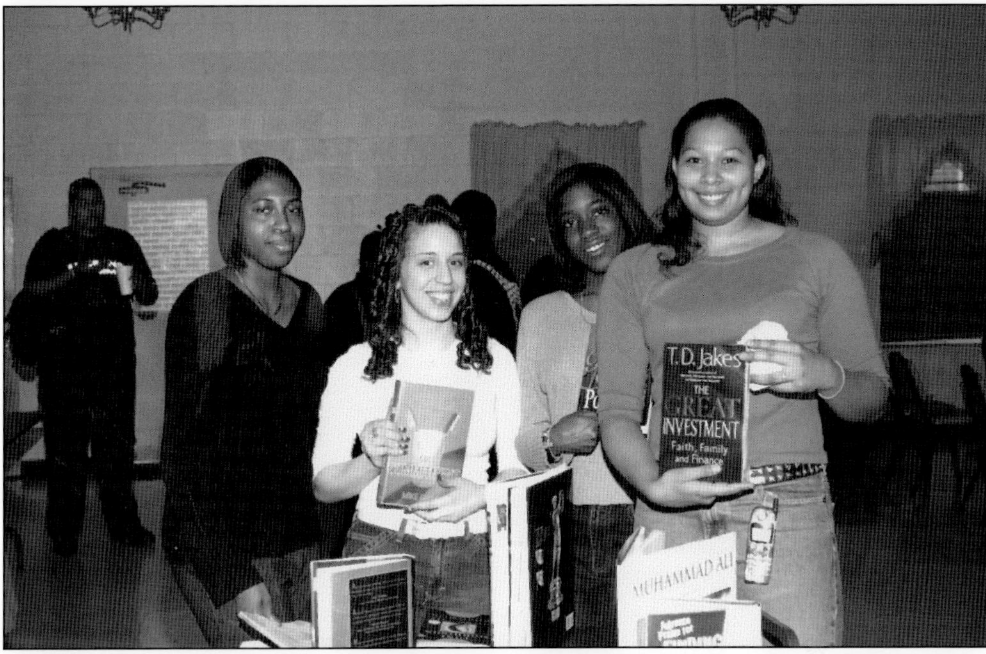

Literacy is essential, and books should be treasured. Clinton Junior College offers courses in reading, creative writing, and composition. Students may also enjoy classes about women in literature, as well as African-American writers. Poetry, drama, and essays are part of the English programs at Clinton and have been since 1894.

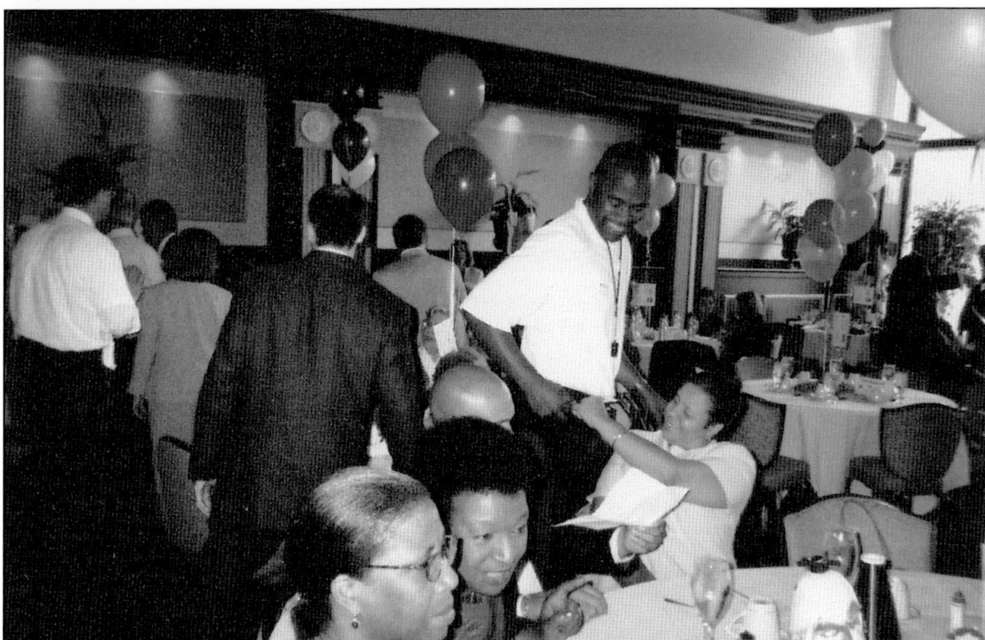

Faculty members of Clinton Junior College and other supporters enjoy fellowship while raising dollars to help in the fight against leukemia. The event was held at the Rock Hill City Club in 2003. Clinton Junior College staff and students strive to help others whenever possible.

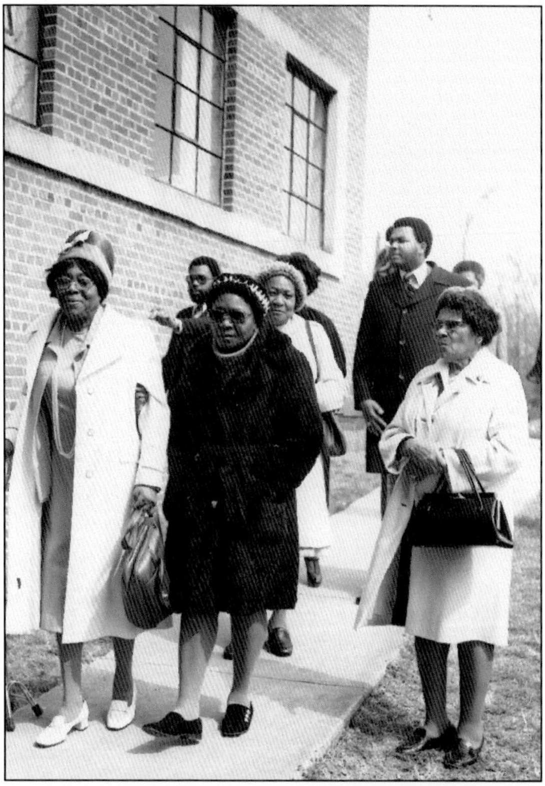

Supporters from the A.M.E. Zion Church attend Founders' Day each year in March, as these people are doing *c.* 1980.

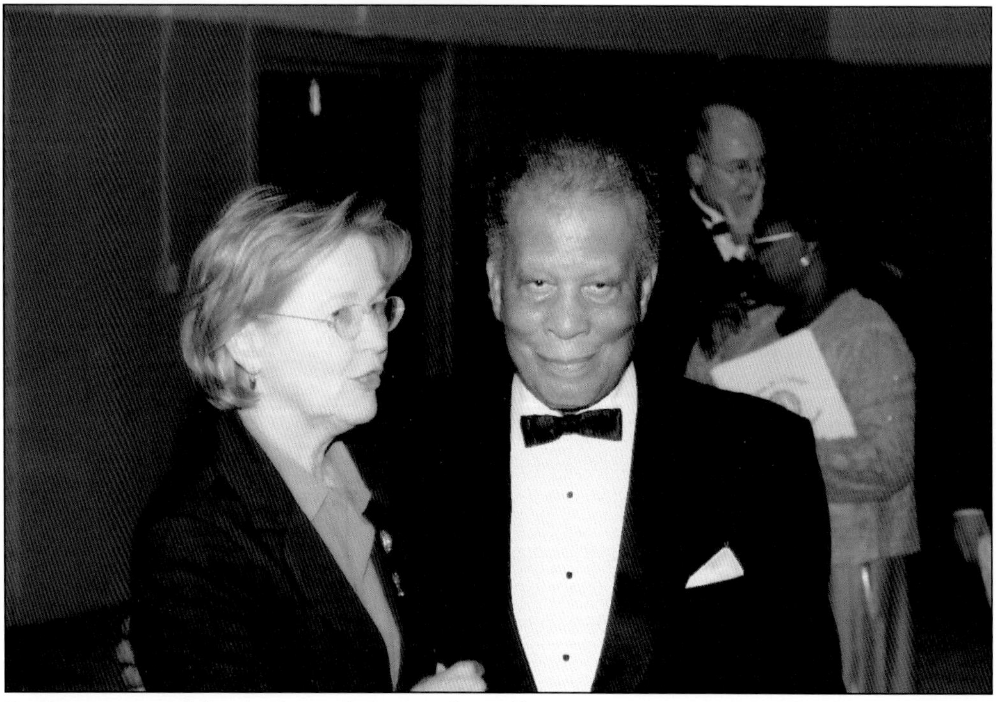

During an annual fund-raising dinner at the college, Mrs. Jane Spratt, wife of Congressman John Spratt, converses with Councilman Winston Searles.

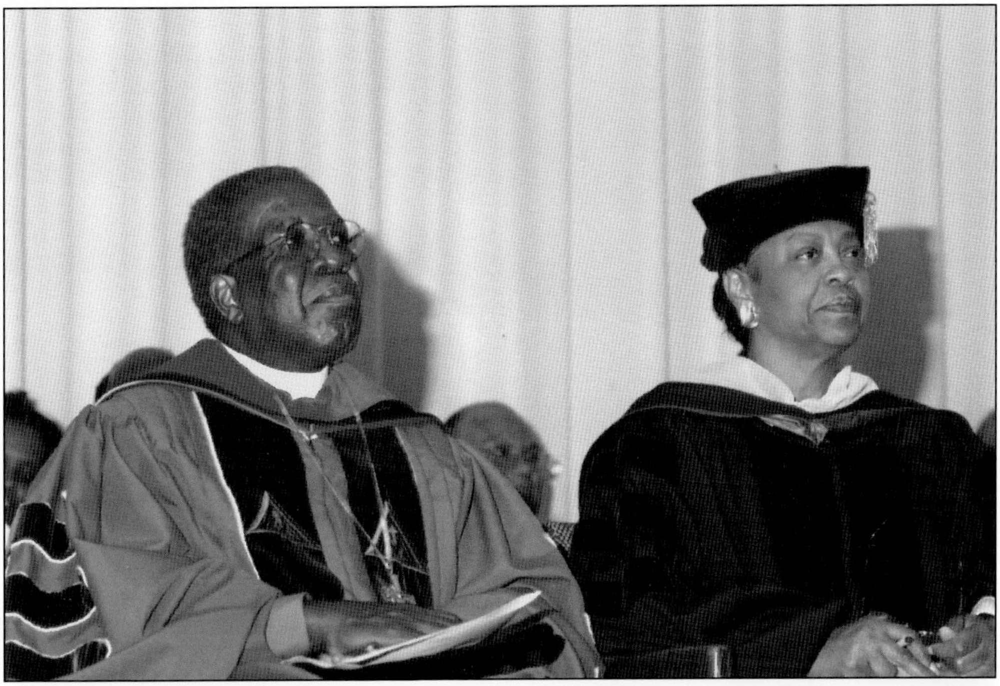

Rep. Bessie Moody-Lawrence was the commencement speaker in 2003. She is pictured here with Bishop Joseph Johnson.

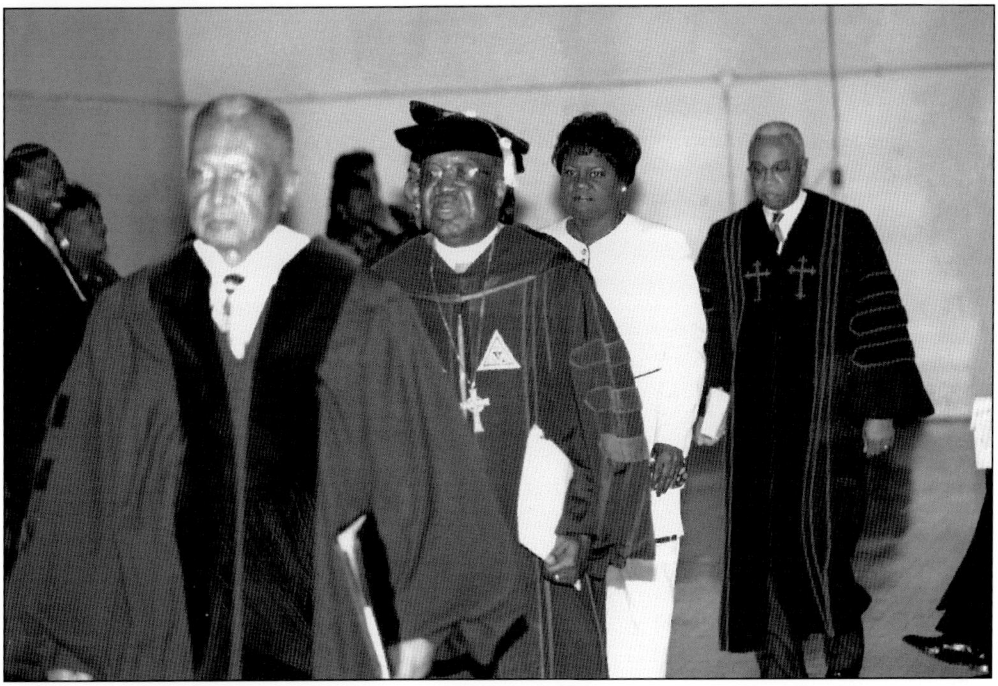

Regional celebrities and nationally prominent ministers frequently visit Clinton Junior College as guest speakers. Pictured from left to right are Rev. Z.B. Wells, Bishop Joseph Johnson, Dr. Cynthia McCullough Russell (partially hidden), Beatrice Thompson, and Rev. Robert Christian. Beatrice Thompson is a Charlotte, North Carolina news radio commentator.

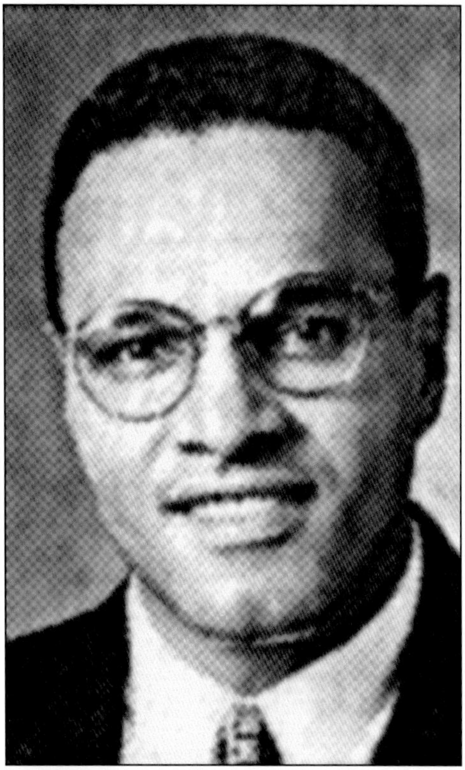

Dr. Freeman Hrabowski, president of the University of Maryland at Baltimore, was the speaker for the 2002 fall convocation.

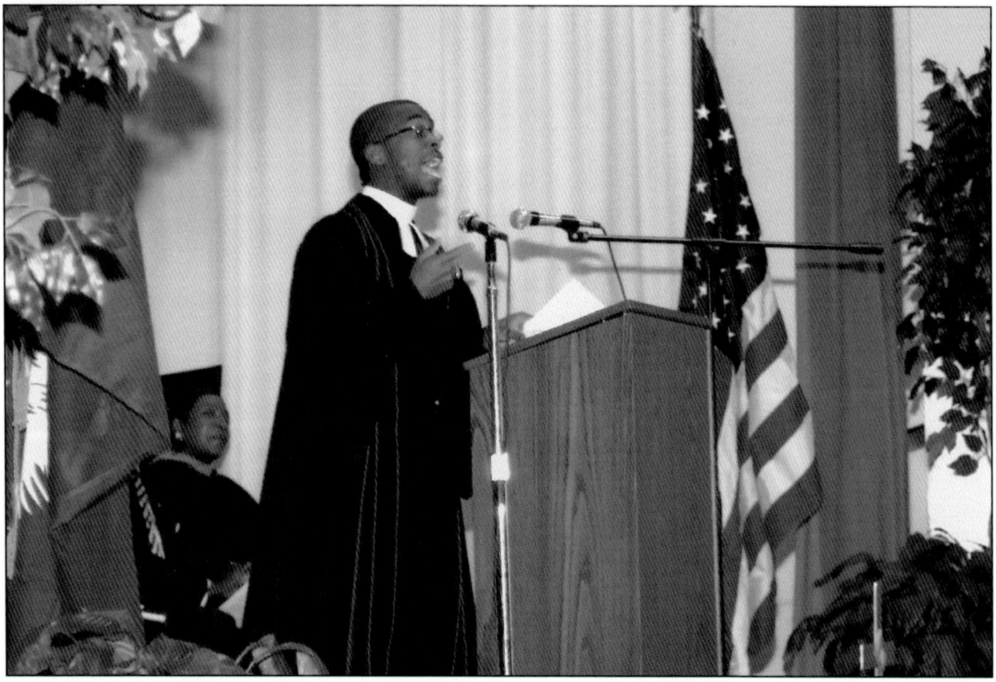

Rev. Eldren Morrison, pastor of Liberty Hill A.M.E. Zion Church in Lake Wylie, South Carolina, and a student at Livingstone College, was the baccalaureate service speaker in 2004.

Rock Hill city councilman Winston Searles (Ward I) is enrolled in computer technology courses at Clinton Junior College. Councilman Searles is a member of the Clinton Junior College Board of Trustees and a strong supporter of the college. His late wife, Willa, was a Clinton College alumnus.

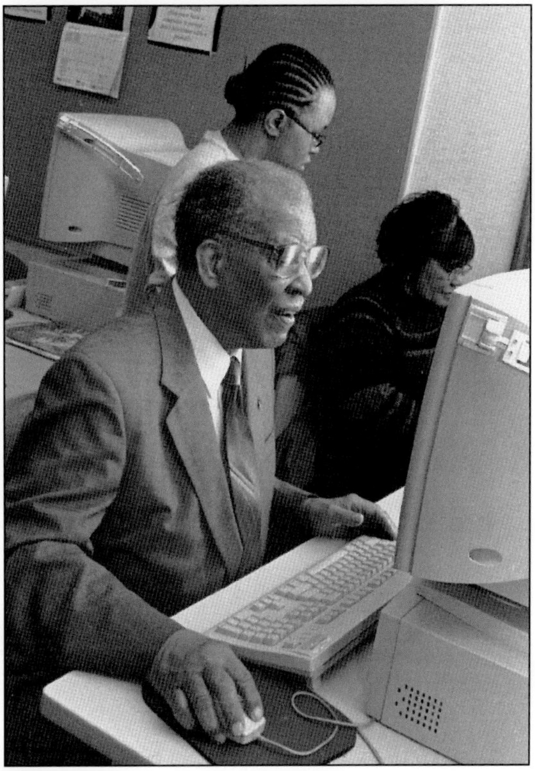

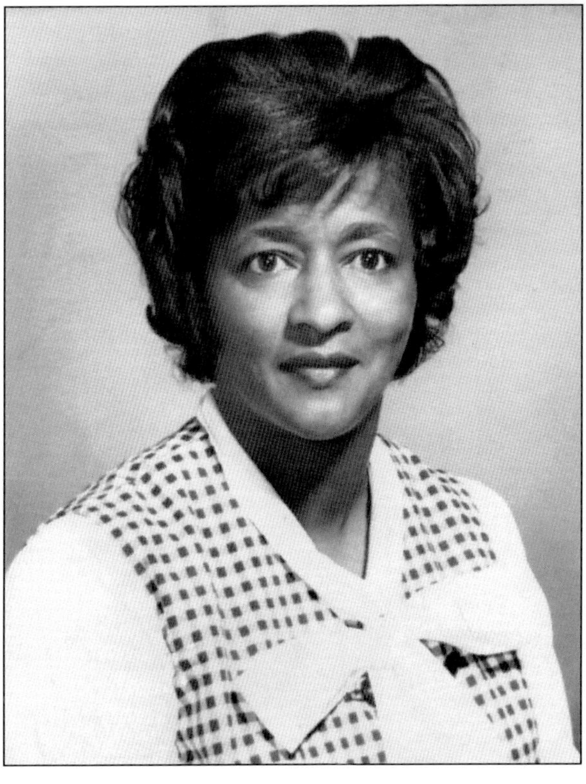

Mrs. Willa Code Searles is a 1941 graduate of Clinton College. She went on to complete a bachelor's degree at Livingstone College and a doctorate at Indiana University.

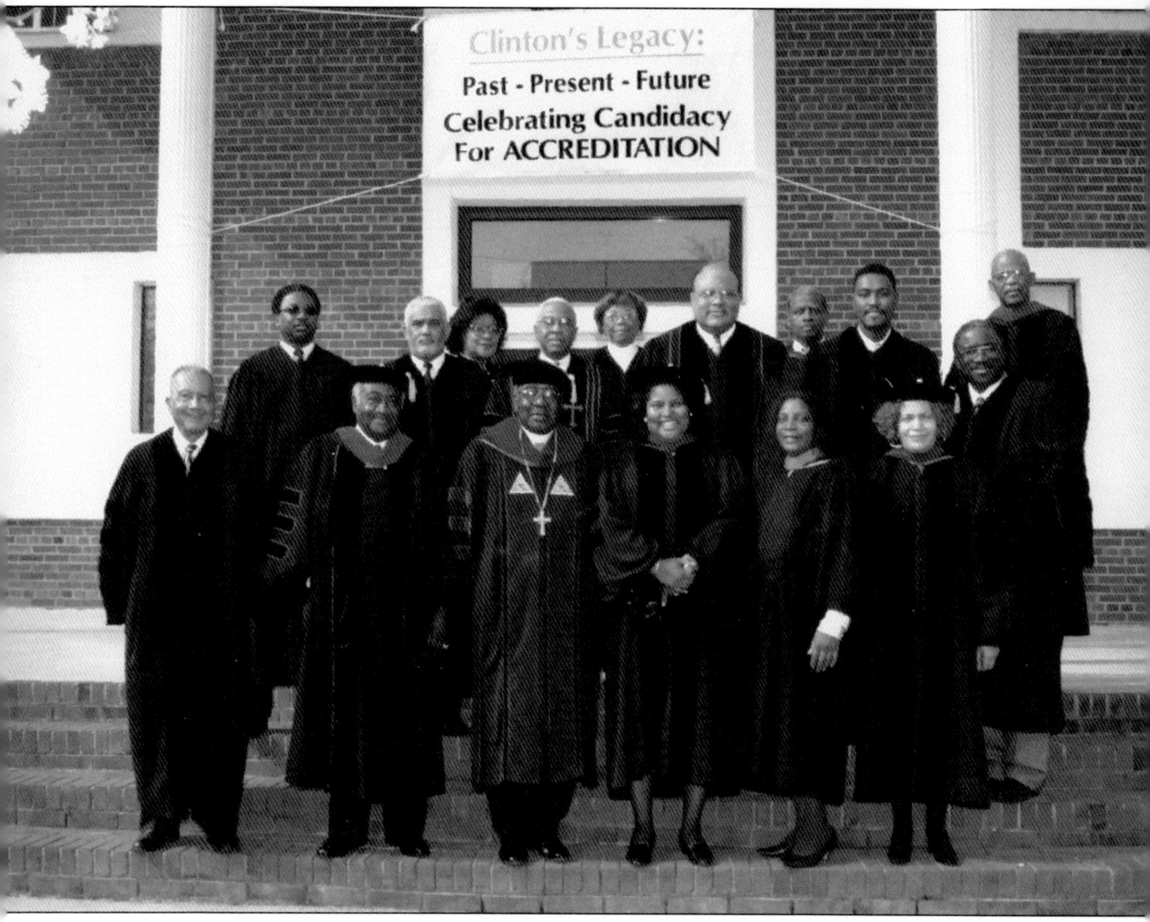

On April 9, 2003, Clinton Junior College received long-awaited good news. The accreditation committee of the Transnational Association of Christian Colleges and Schools (TRACS) approved the school for accreditation. This came after more than three years of hard work and planning that began under the leadership of former college president Dr. Cynthia McCullough Russell and was then championed by the current president, Dr. Elaine Johnson Copeland. Pictured is the board of trustees, then-president Dr. Cynthia McCullough Russell, Dean Janis Pendleton, and self-study chairman Dr. Elaine Johnson Copeland.

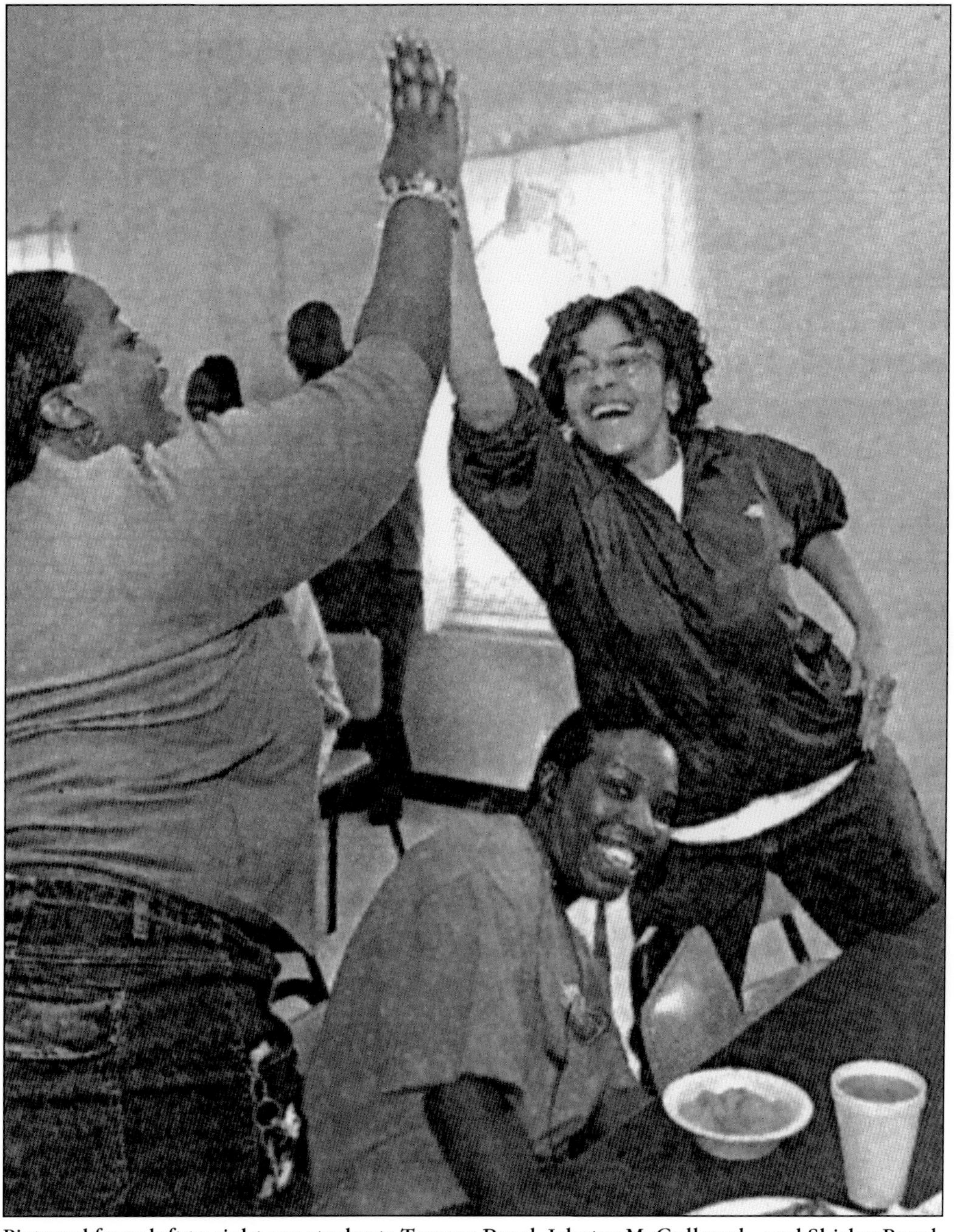

Pictured from left to right are students Tamara Boyd, Ishatay McCullough, and Shirley Royal, celebrating the announcement of accreditation.

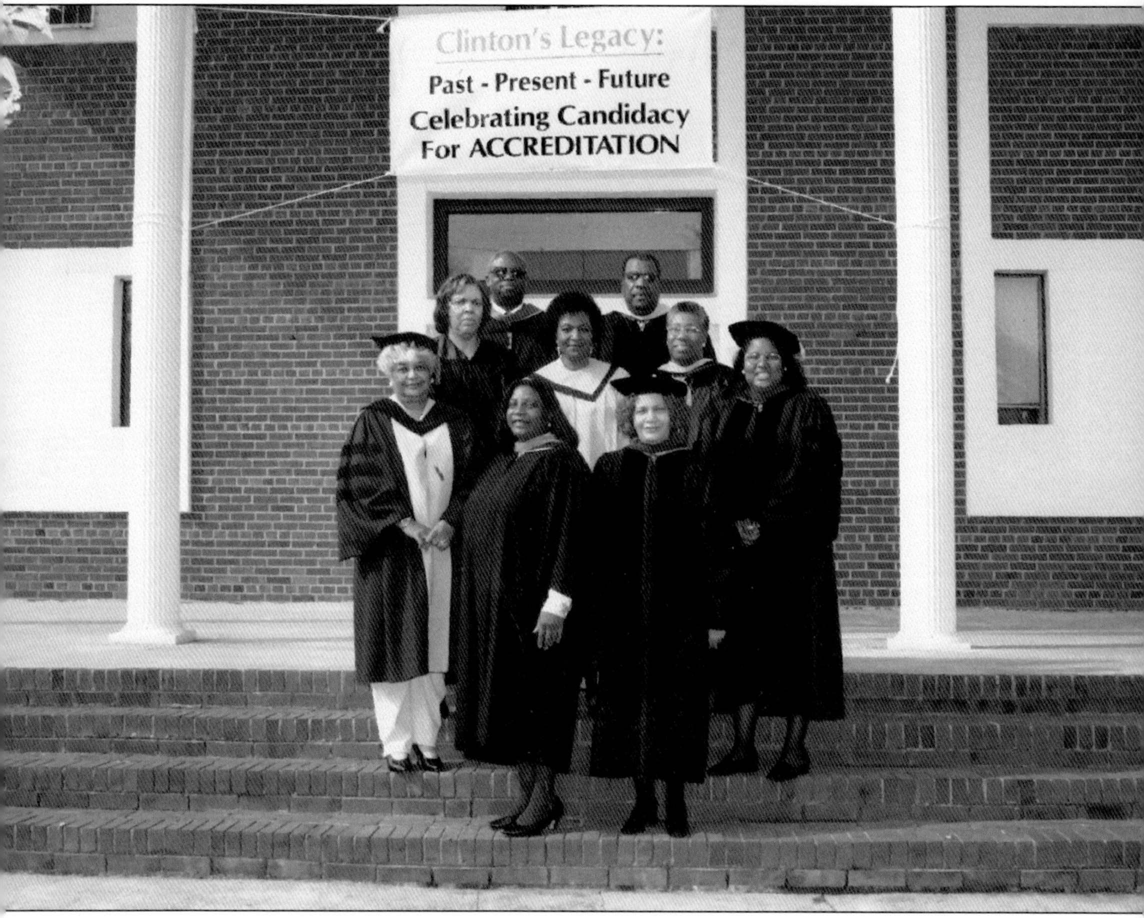

Teamwork means success. Members of the Steering Committee for Accreditation pose for a picture to capture another historical moment. From left to right are (front row) Janis Pendleton and Elaine Johnson Copeland; (middle row) Bertha Roddey, Cynthia Roddey, Sadie Pye-Jumper, Ann Reid, Cynthia McCullough Russell; (back row) David Jenkins and Rev. Richard Graham.

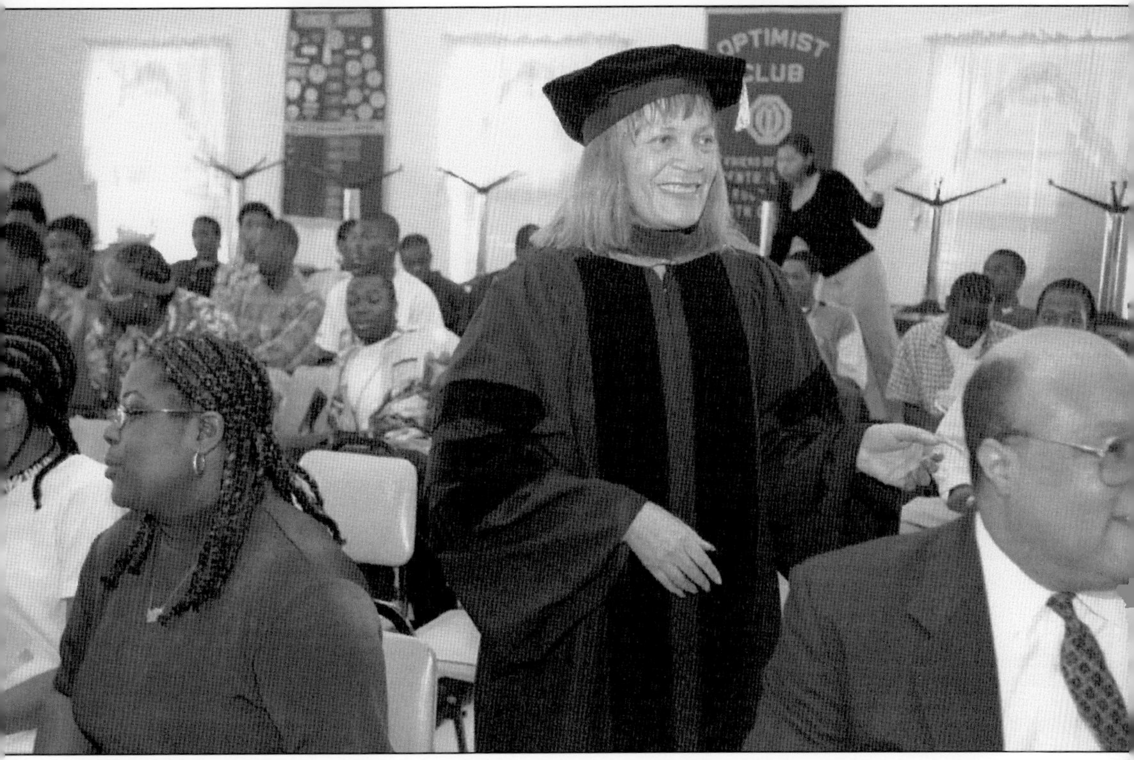

In June 2001, when Dr. Elaine Johnson Copeland was appointed acting president, she immediately and successfully began working toward compliance with TRACS recommendations. She also established a college endowment fund and secured adequate retirement and insurance plans for faculty and staff. A native of South Carolina, Copeland returned to the state after serving as administrator/teacher at Oregon State University for 4 years and the University of Illinois at Urbana-Champaign for 24 years. Having graduated from Emmett Scott High School in 1960, Dr. Copeland has several degrees: a bachelor of science from Livingstone, a master's degree with honors from Winthrop University, a master of business administration from University of Illinois at Urbana-Champaign, and a doctorate with high honors from Oregon State University. She continues to pursue excellence on behalf of the students and administrators at Clinton Junior College.

JOHN M. SPRATT, JR.
5th DISTRICT, SOUTH CAROLINA

1536 LONGWORTH BUILDING
WASHINGTON, D.C. 20515
(202) 225-5501

COMMITTEES:
RANKING MEMBER, BUDGET
ARMED SERVICES

Congress of the United States
House of Representatives
Washington, D.C. 20515

DISTRICT OFFICES:

TOM GETTYS BUILDING
BOX 350
ROCK HILL, SOUTH CAROLINA 29731
(803) 327-1114

39 E. CALHOUN STREET
SUMTER, SOUTH CAROLINA 29150
(803) 773-3362

88 PUBLIC SQUARE
DARLINGTON, SOUTH CAROLINA 29532
(843) 393-3998

September 6, 2002

Dr. Elaine Johnson Copeland
President
Clinton Junior College
1029 Crawford Road
Rock Hill, South Carolina 29730

Dear Dr. Copeland:

I wish that I could be with you to celebrate your inaguration as the President of Clinton College, but Congress is meeting today in special session in New York, to commemorate the tragic events of September 11, 2001. I, nevertheless, join with faculty, students, alumna and friends in wishing you a happy and highly productive tenure at Clinton College.

You have returned to South Carolina, your home, and brought with you extensive experience in higher education. Clinton College is at a critical juncture, and is extremely fortunate to have you to take the helm with your ability, experience, and education.

I not only wish you success, but expect you to achieve it; and to that end, I pledge you and Clinton College my continuing support.

Respectfully,

John Spratt

John M. Spratt Jr.
Members of Congress

JMSj

Congressman John Spratt sent a letter extending his congratulations to Dr. Elaine Copeland on the occasion of her inauguration as the 12th president.

State of South Carolina

Office of the Governor

Jim Hodges
Governor

Post Office Box 11829
COLUMBIA 29211

GREETINGS

On behalf of the State of South Carolina, I am pleased to extend best wishes to you as you celebrate the installation of the twelfth president of Clinton Junior College, Dr. Elaine Copeland.

Clinton Junior College has established itself as a center of learning seeking to equip its students with the knowledge and ability to be successful in a global marketplace. Dr. Copeland has distinguished herself as person of integrity and dedication ready to lead this college to higher levels. She has dedicated her career to higher education and her experience and leadership skills will prove to be great assets as Clinton Junior College carries on its tradition of excellence.

I offer my warmest wishes to you on this memorable occasion, and I hope that you will let me know if I can ever be of help to you in the future.

Jim Hodges

Jim Hodges

Gov. Jim Hodges writes to congratulate Dr. Copeland on her inauguration.

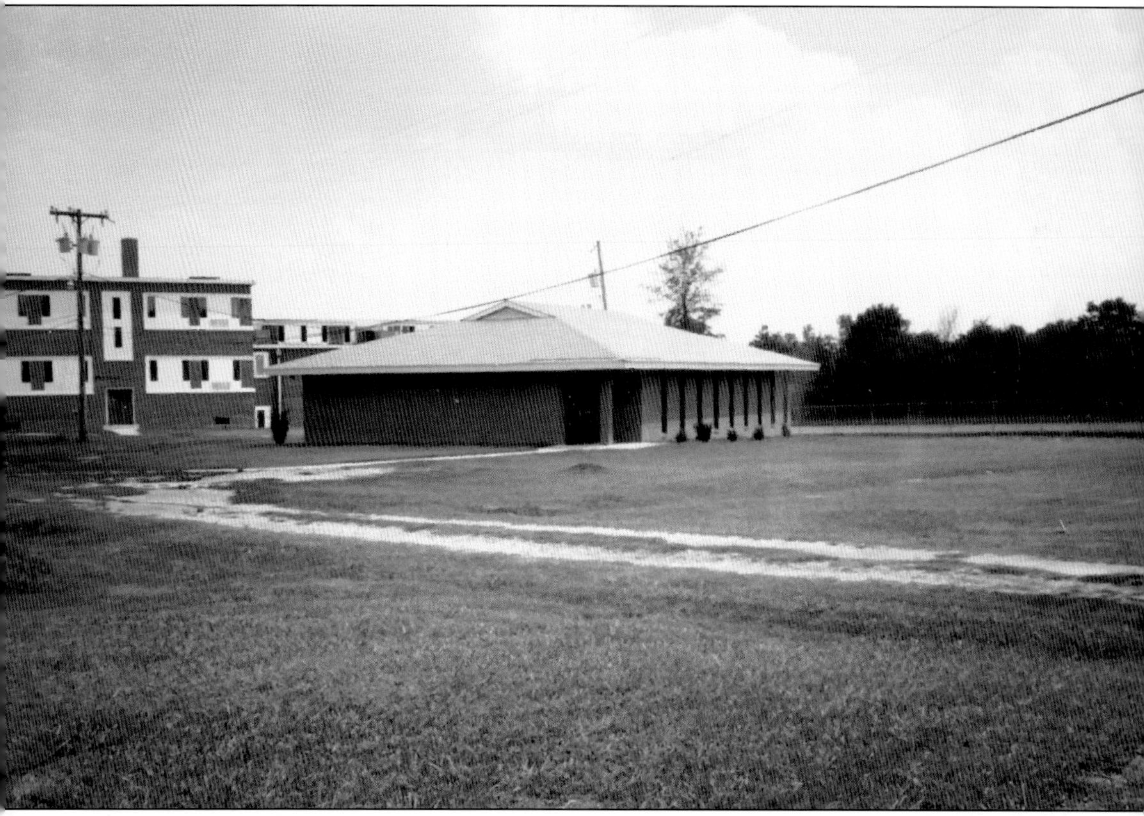

Clinton Junior College has had a library since 1894. The first, housed in Crockett-Robinson Hall, shared the first floor with the dining room, kitchen, and auditorium. The library later moved into the building that is now the Student Center and remained there until the Fisher Memorial Library was completed in the 1980s.

Richard L. Fisher served as bishop of South Carolina and chair of the Clinton Junior College Board of Trustees from 1987 to 1991. He passed away in 1991. The library was named in his memory in 1995.

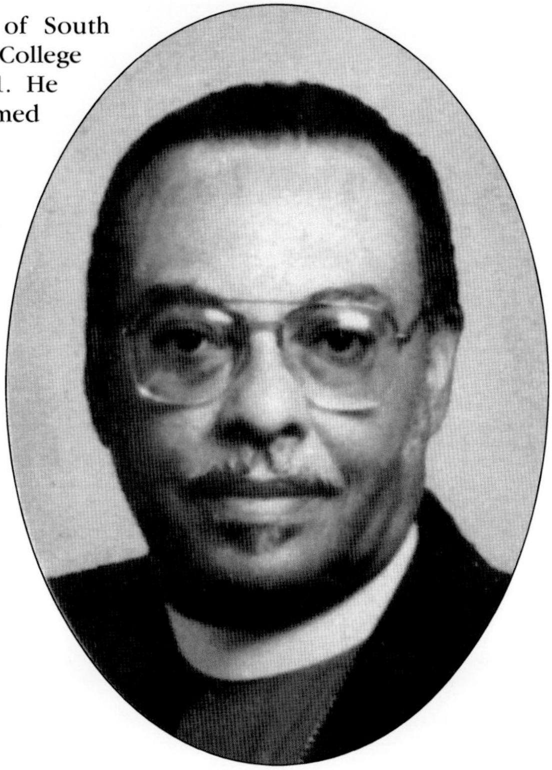

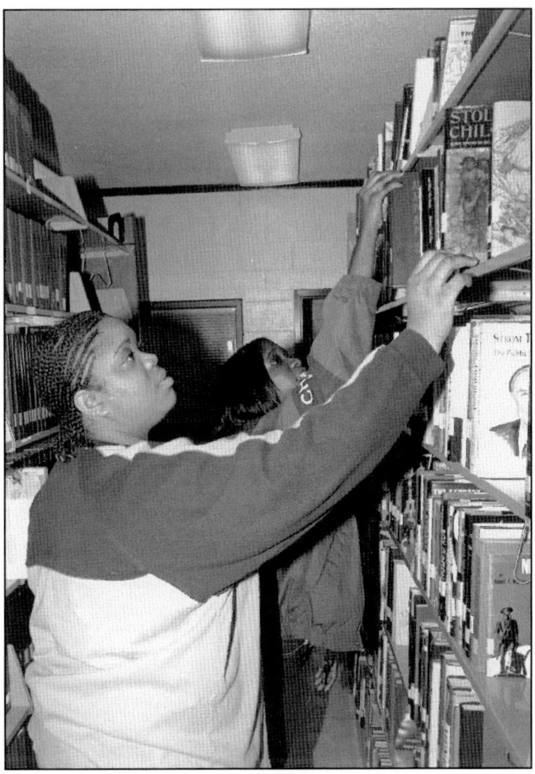

Books are tools for education, and libraries can become obsolete. In 2002, the college launched a $3 million fund-raising campaign in an effort to build a state-of-the-art library and technology center for the college. Shown here are students within the concrete block interior of the Richard L. Fisher Memorial Library. Clinton Junior College's first computer laboratory was also located in the Fisher Memorial Library.

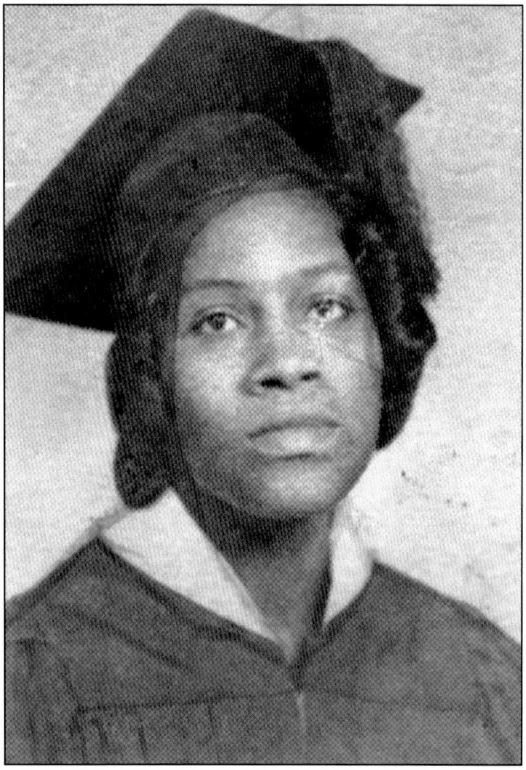

Mrs. Henrietta Barber Wilkes graduated from Clinton in 1942. She transferred to Benedict College.

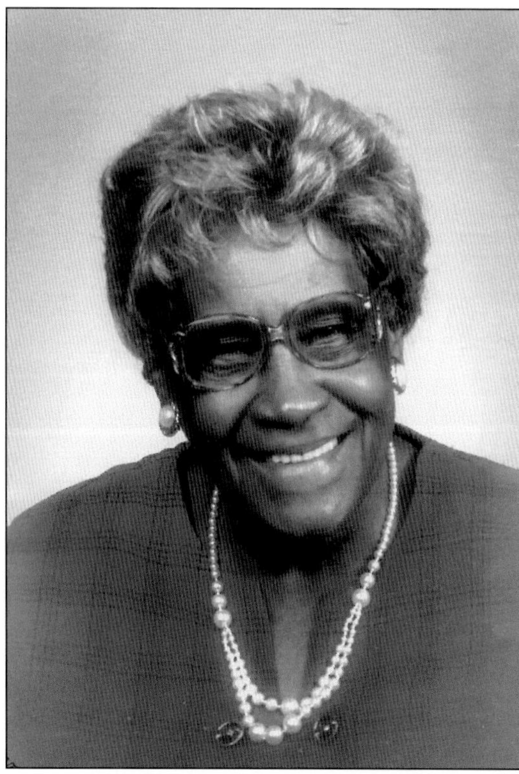

Mrs. Wilkes served as the college librarian for many years and continued to be a great supporter and avid basketball fan after her retirement.

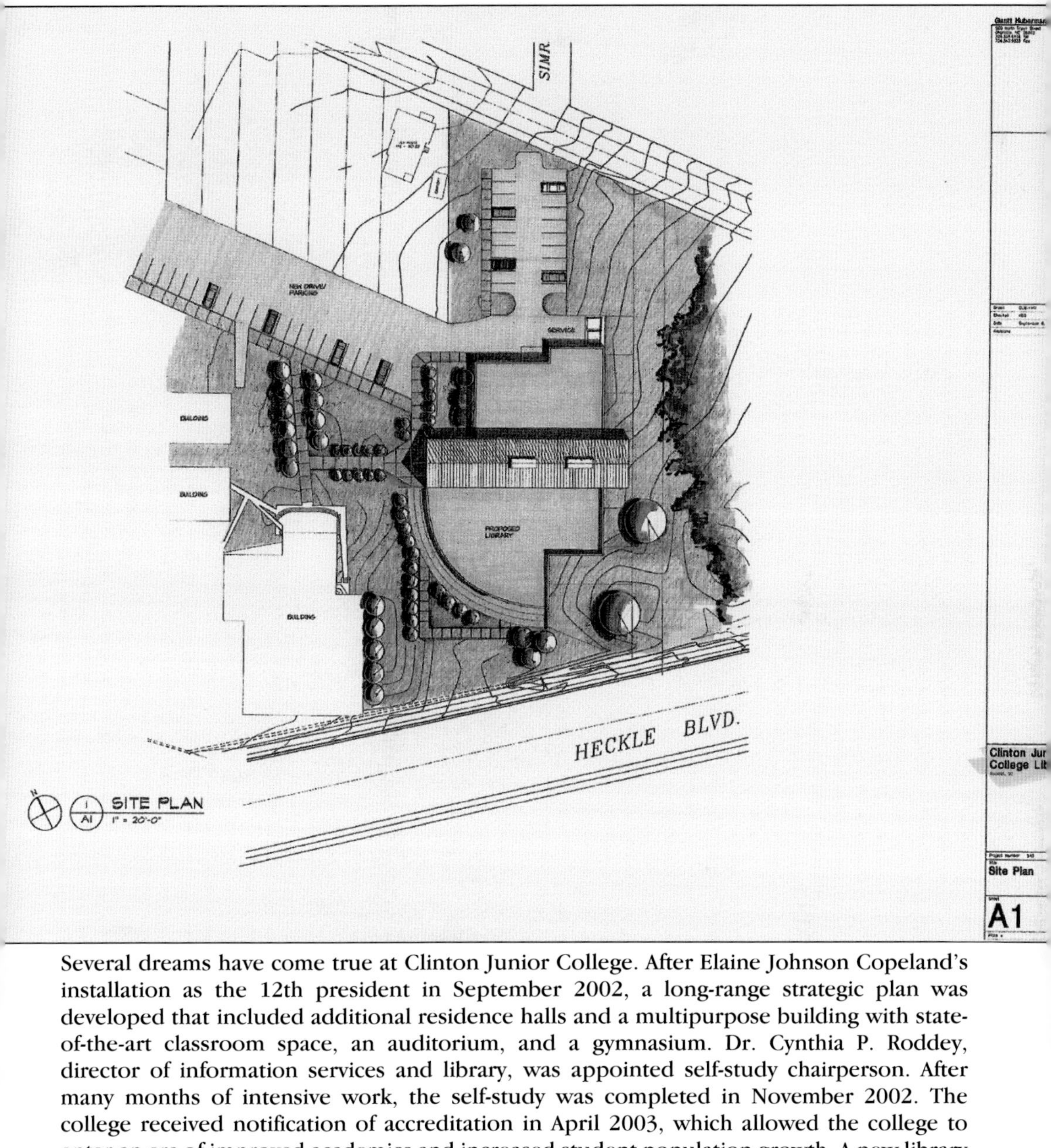

Several dreams have come true at Clinton Junior College. After Elaine Johnson Copeland's installation as the 12th president in September 2002, a long-range strategic plan was developed that included additional residence halls and a multipurpose building with state-of-the-art classroom space, an auditorium, and a gymnasium. Dr. Cynthia P. Roddey, director of information services and library, was appointed self-study chairperson. After many months of intensive work, the self-study was completed in November 2002. The college received notification of accreditation in April 2003, which allowed the college to enter an era of improved academics and increased student population growth. A new library and technology center would meet the challenges of the 21st century according to the feasibility studies. Pictured is the bird's-eye view of the campus envisioned by Gantt-Huberman Architects of Charlotte, North Carolina.

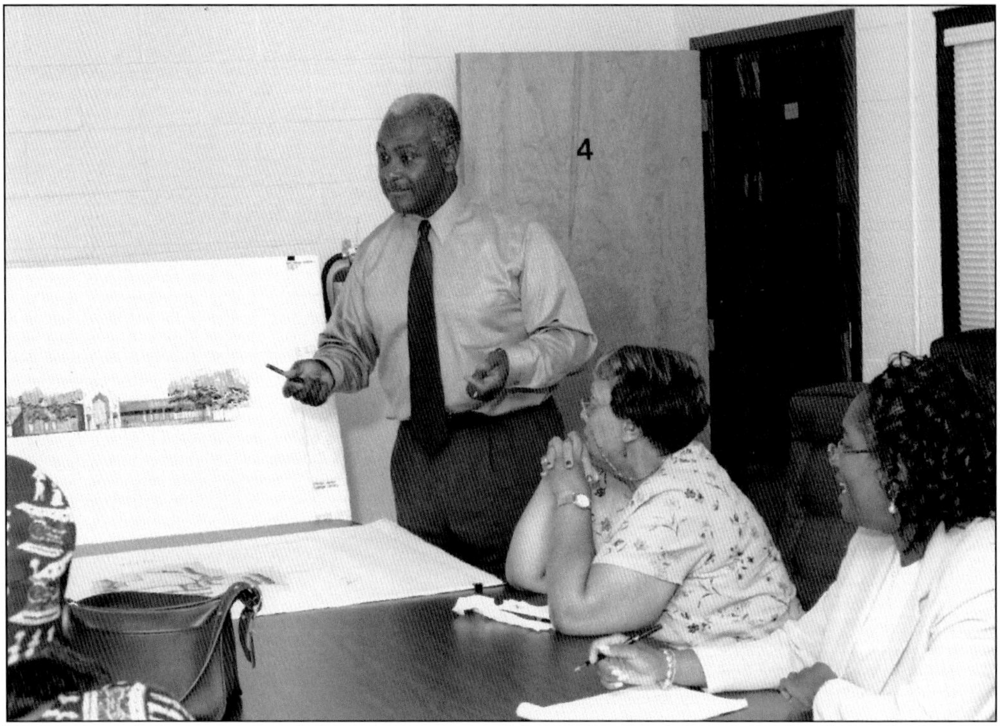

Harvey B. Gantt, chief principal of Gantt-Huberman Architects of Charlotte, North Carolina, unveils the exterior elevation drawings of the new library and technology center that will be constructed at Clinton Junior College to meet the challenges of the 21st century. Harvey Gantt was the first African American to enroll at Clemson University in 1963. He became mayor of Charlotte in 1984 and remains active in the Carolinas, serving as advisor and architect on a multitude of schools and businesses.

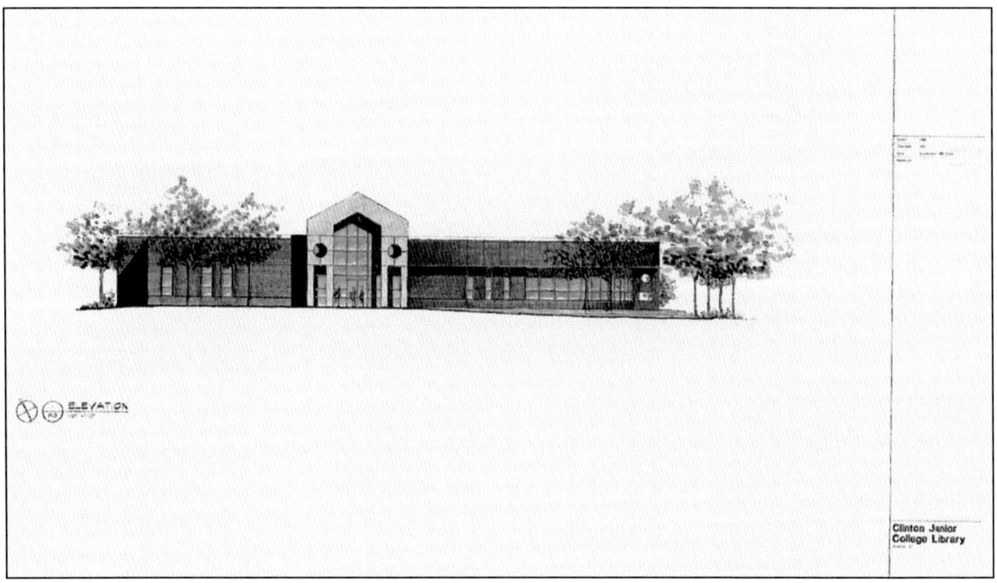

The entrance to the new library is attractive and modern. Enrollment will greatly increase in the 21st century, so the new library will be an asset to the college and to the community.

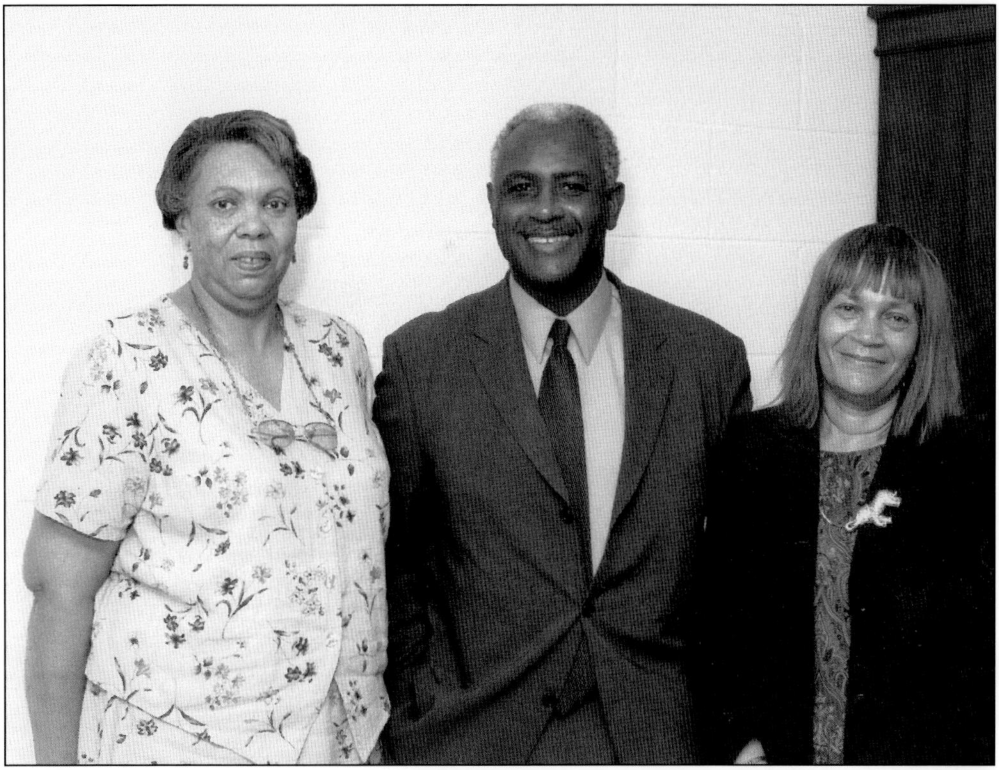

Pictured are two of South Carolina firsts: Cynthia Roddey (left) and Harvey Gantt (center) pose with Elaine Copeland in 2003. Roddey and Gantt integrated Winthrop and Clemson Universities, respectively.

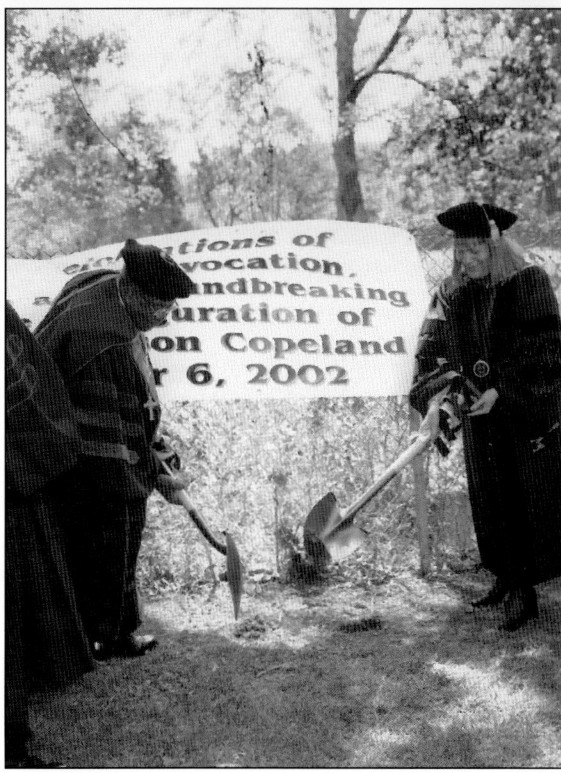

Bishop Johnson and Dr. Copeland break ground for the new library and technology center designed by architect Harvey Gantt. When complete, the library will be valued at approximately $2.5 million. Along with computers and books, it will house vintage photographs and records in the archives area.

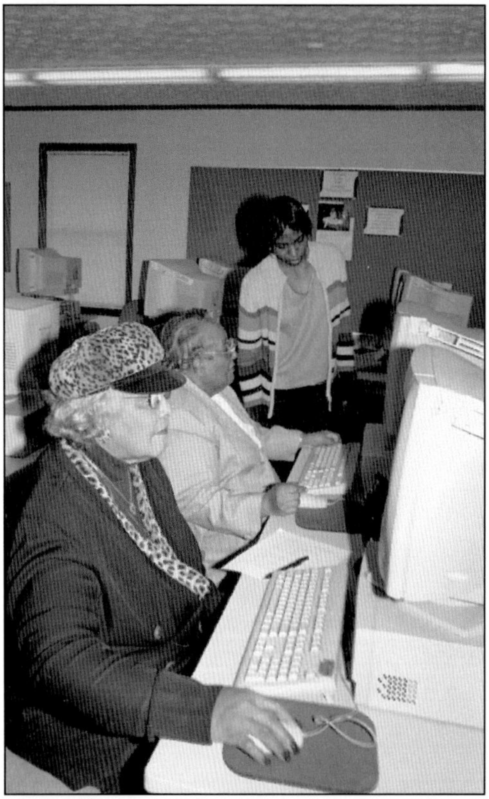

In 1961, IBM introduced the Selectric Typewriter, the standard for all keyboards of future computers. By 1987, Selectrics were obsolete, and personal computers by IBM were the ideal word processor. People had to relearn keyboards' possibilities, as well as hardware and software, hard copy, and the Internet. Clinton Junior College answered the community's need, and now many people enjoy the computer laboratory provided by Clinton Junior College. Pictured is a class for adults who want to update their skills. The college's new library will include a state-of-the-art technology center.

According to a Beloit College survey, people who entered college in 2004 were born in 1982. To this generation, the Kennedy tragedy was a plane crash. To them, African Americans have always been welcomed in retail stores. To them, African Americans have always voted without fear. To the people entering college in the fall of 2004, blacks and whites have always dined in the same places.

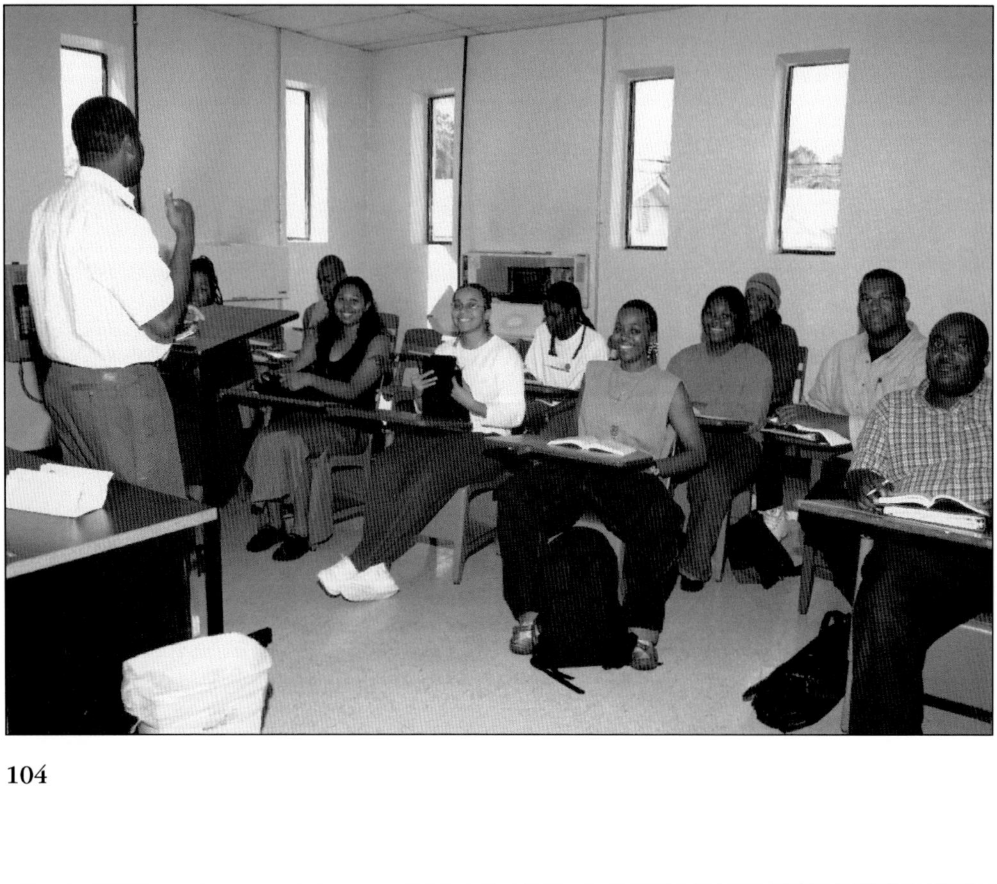

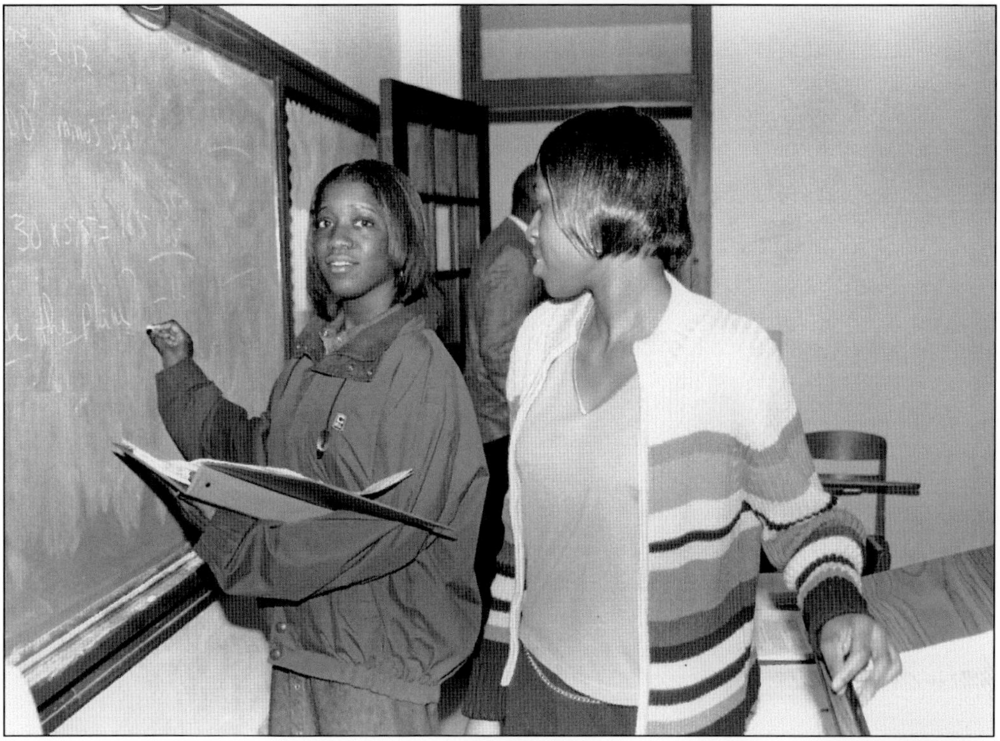

The academic department encourages students to have study partners. Makeba Green and LaTasha Dreher work together on a history project.

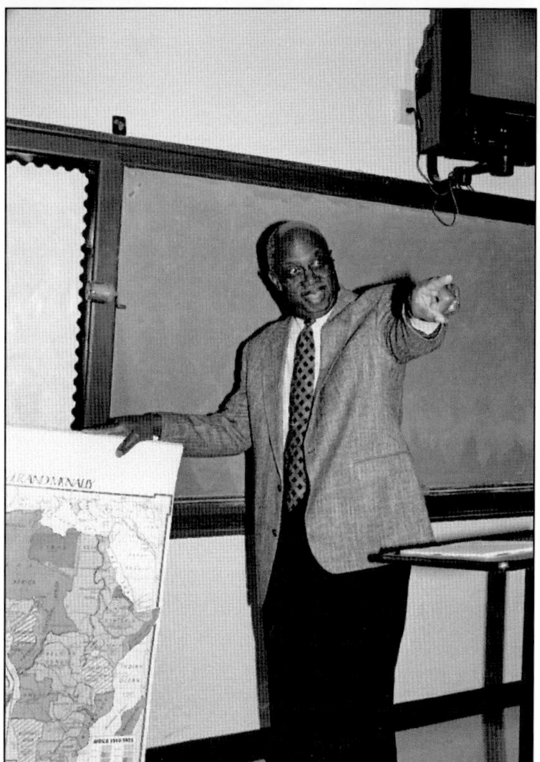

Mr. David L. Jenkins taught U.S. history, world history, and geography for more than 15 years.

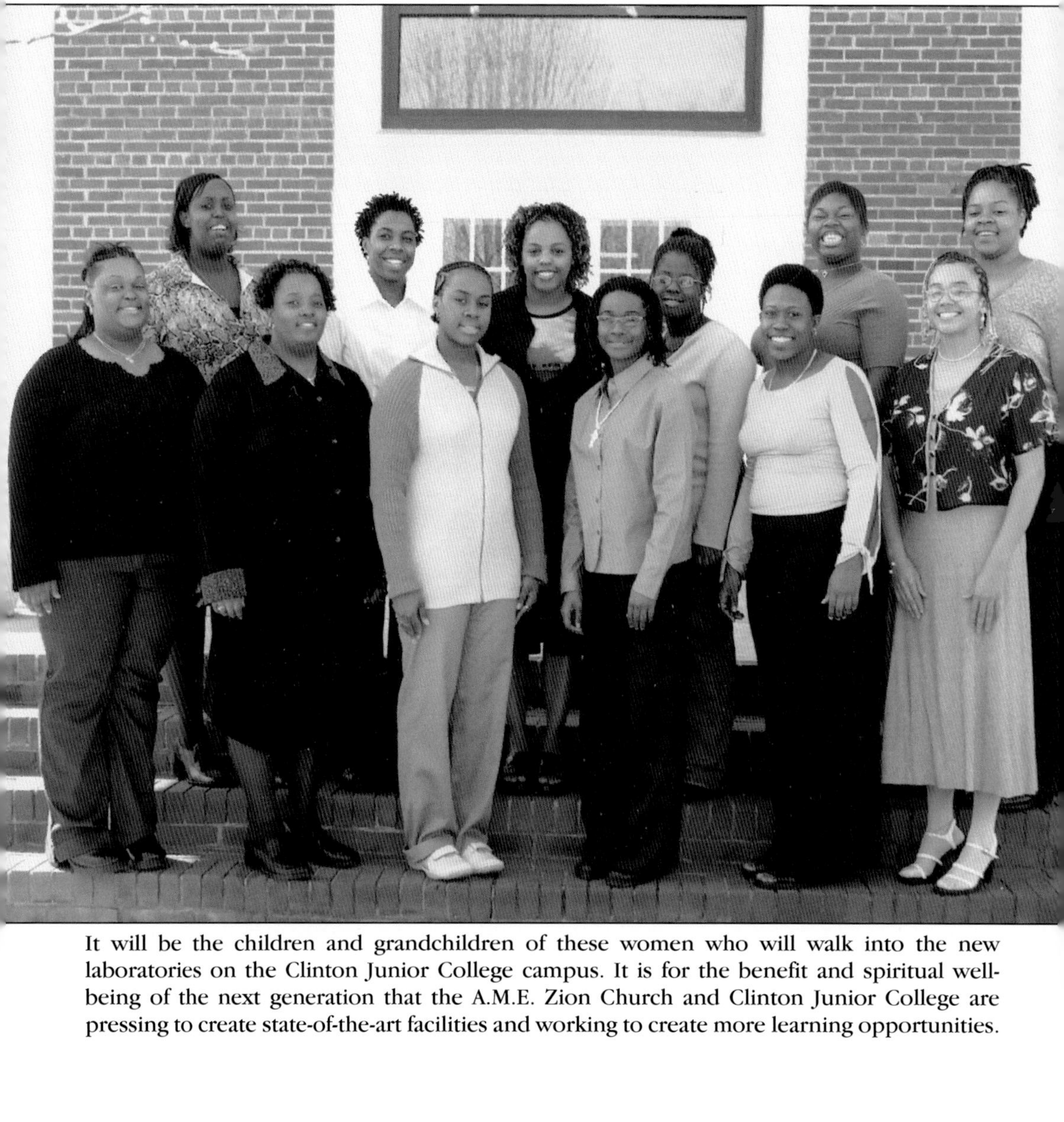

It will be the children and grandchildren of these women who will walk into the new laboratories on the Clinton Junior College campus. It is for the benefit and spiritual well-being of the next generation that the A.M.E. Zion Church and Clinton Junior College are pressing to create state-of-the-art facilities and working to create more learning opportunities.

As technology changes, so does the way students learn. Students Samuel Lightner (left) and LaTasha Dreher (right) watch Rachel Nelson work with new software.

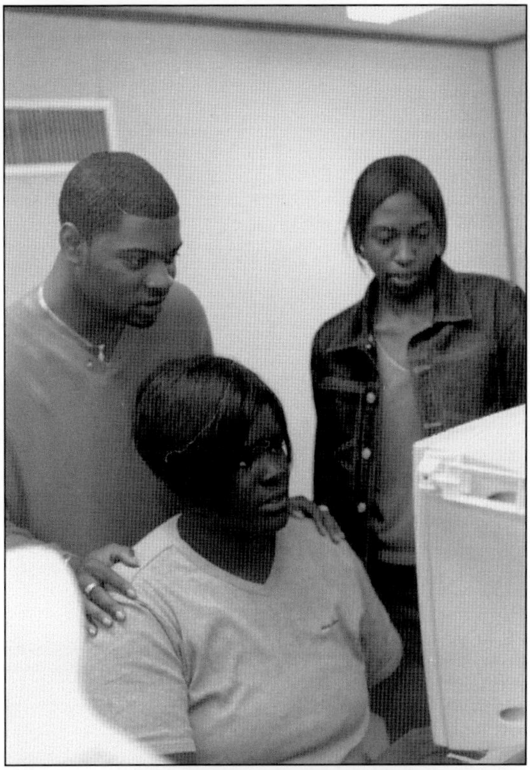

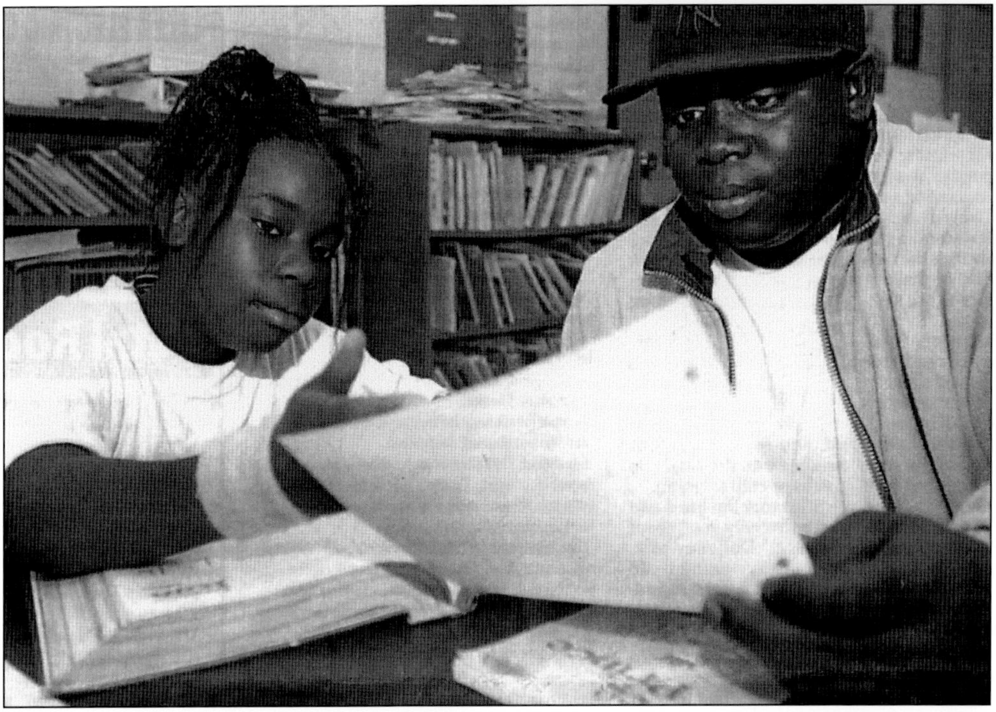

Clinton students are expected to perform community service. Here, Stan Diouf tutors students at the neighborhood Boys and Girls Club.

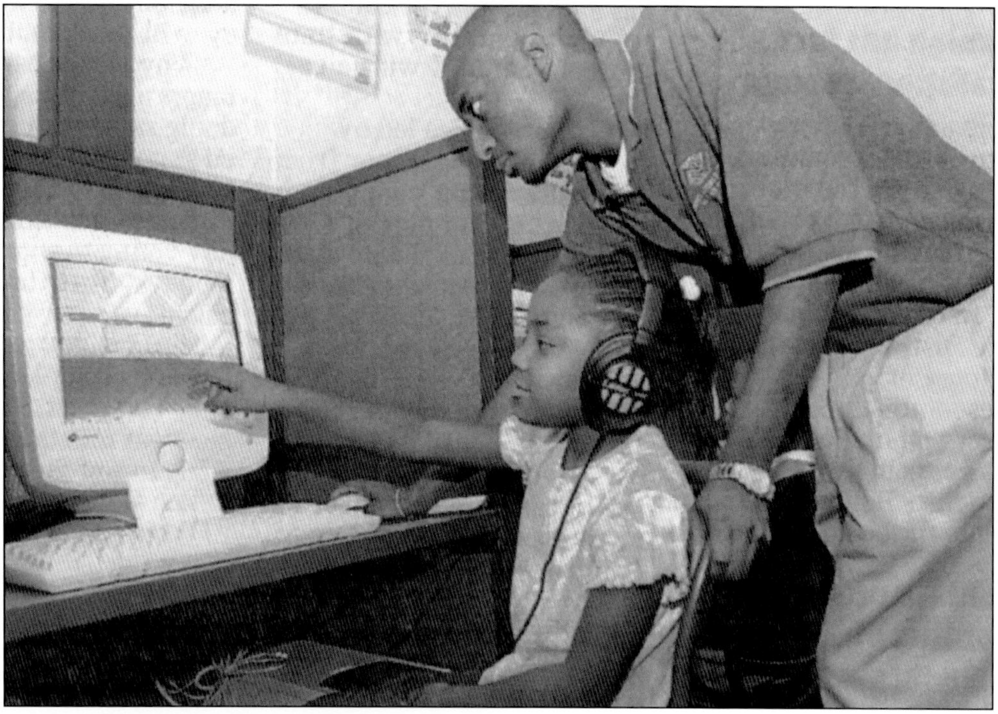

Maurice Herrington also volunteers at the Boys and Girls Club.

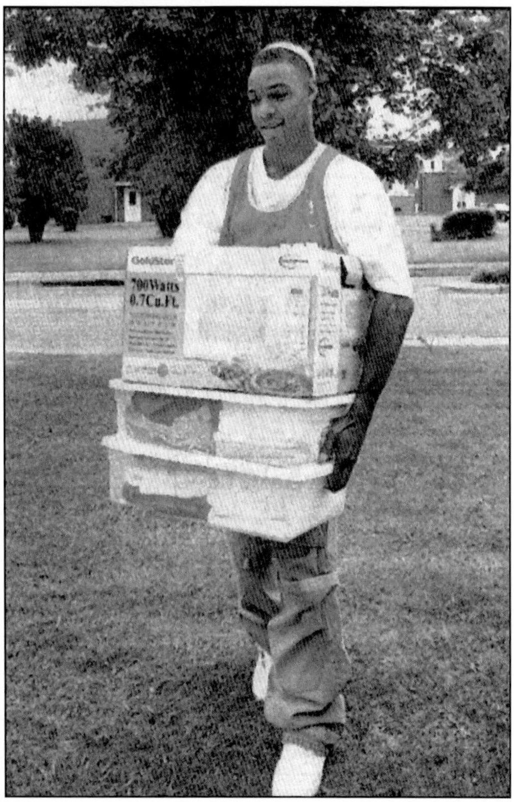

Sammy Monroe moves into his room in the residence hall with some of the comforts of home.

Seven

The Church's Legacy

Clinton Junior College is a part of the legacy of the early organizers of the A.M.E. Zion Church. Many of the buildings on the campus are named in honor of bishops who served South Carolina and were great supporters of the college. These men took seriously the mandate of the founding fathers to make education available in areas where the church is thriving. Other historically black colleges were funded by church denominations. The 135-year-old Claflin University in Orangeburg, South Carolina, was founded in 1869 and supported by Northern whites and Southern black Methodists. In Columbia, South Carolina, two other colleges for the descendants of former slaves were established: Benedict College in 1871 (American Baptist) and Allen University in 1870 (A.M.E. Church). These institutions paved the way for Clinton College.

The bishops who supervise South Carolina also serve as chairmen of the board of trustees at the college.

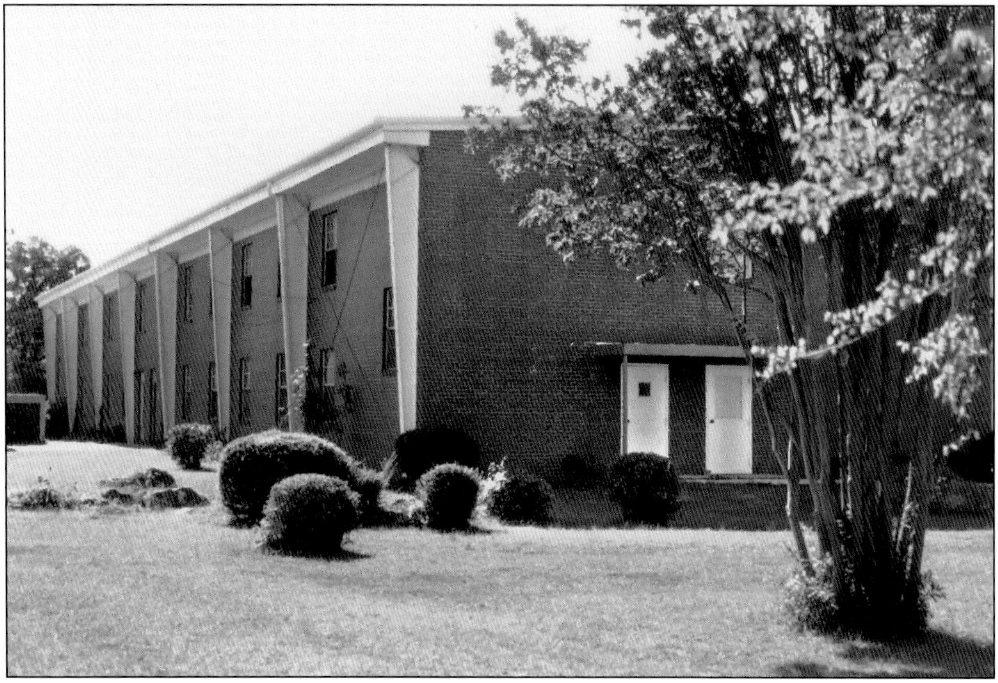

Cauthen Hall is named in honor of Bishop Joseph D. Cauthen. It serves as the ladies' residence hall.

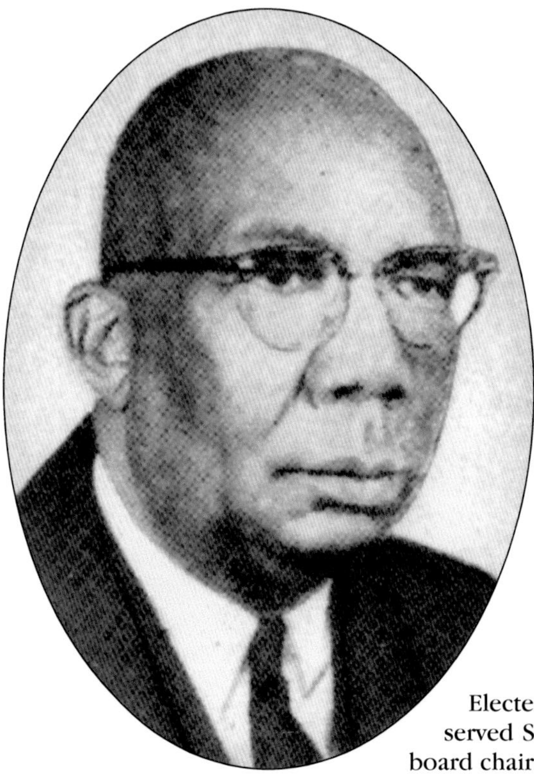

Elected bishop in 1956, Joseph D. Cauthen served South Carolina and as the Clinton College board chairman from 1960 to 1968.

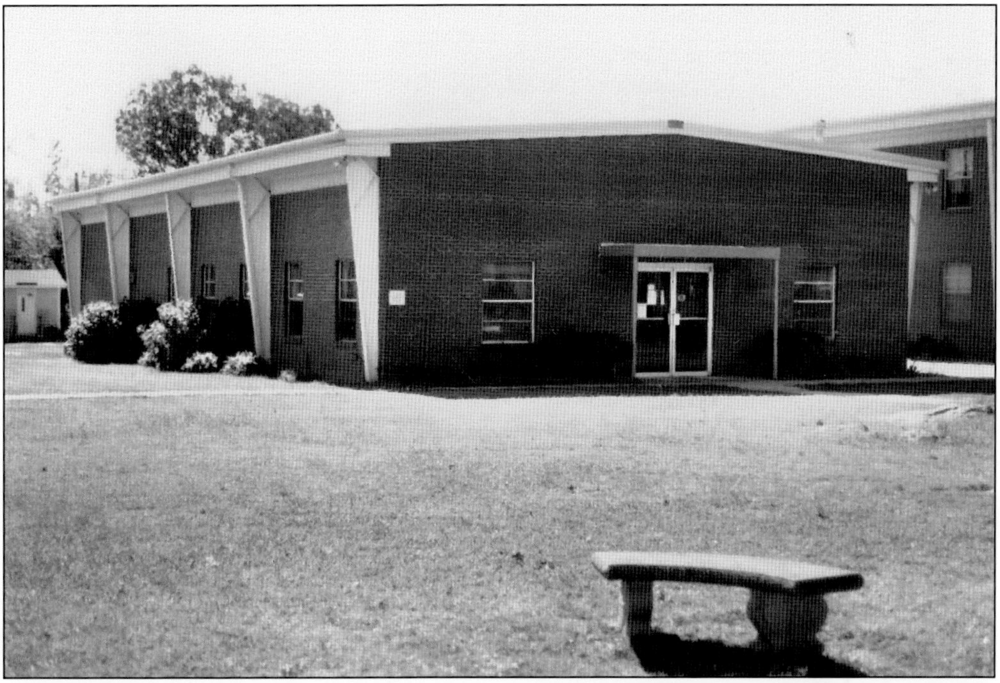

Shaw Dining Hall is named for Bishop Herbert Bell Shaw, who was instrumental in raising the money to build the dining hall and the ladies' residence hall.

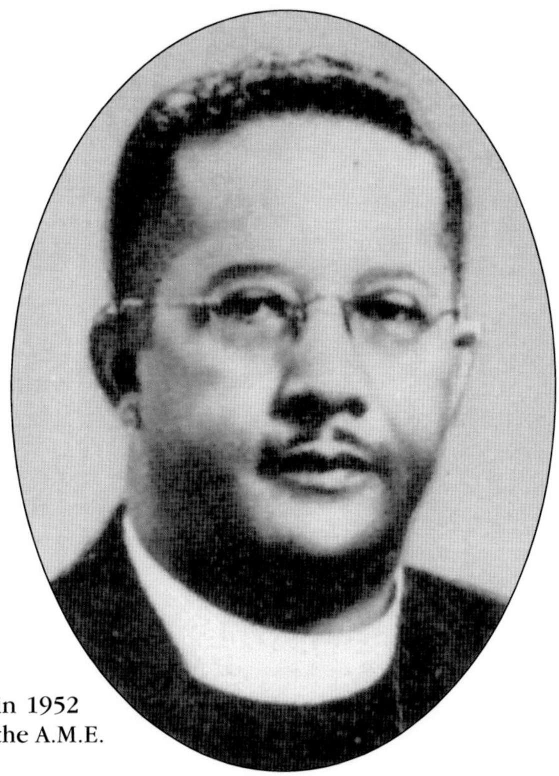

Herbert Bell Shaw was elected bishop in 1952 and served the Palmetto Conference of the A.M.E. Zion Church.

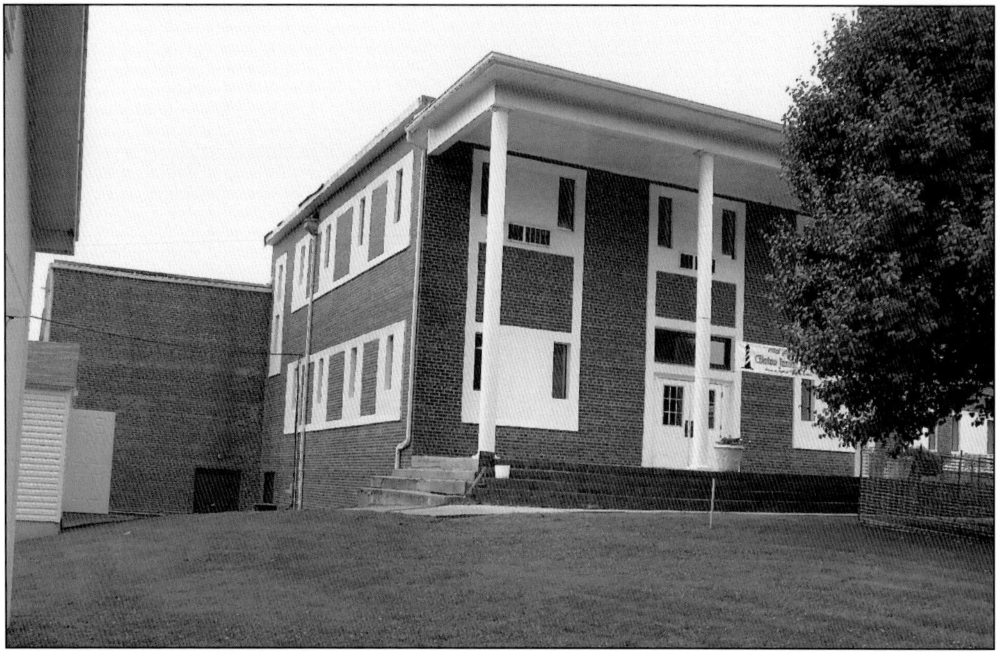

Slade Moreland Administration and Academic Building was named in memory of Bishop W.W. Slade and Dr. Sallie V. Moreland. The gymnasium is named for Bishop J.W. Martin.

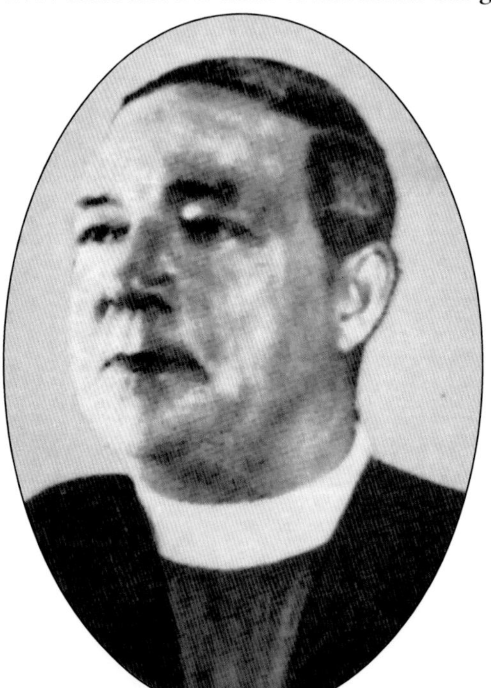

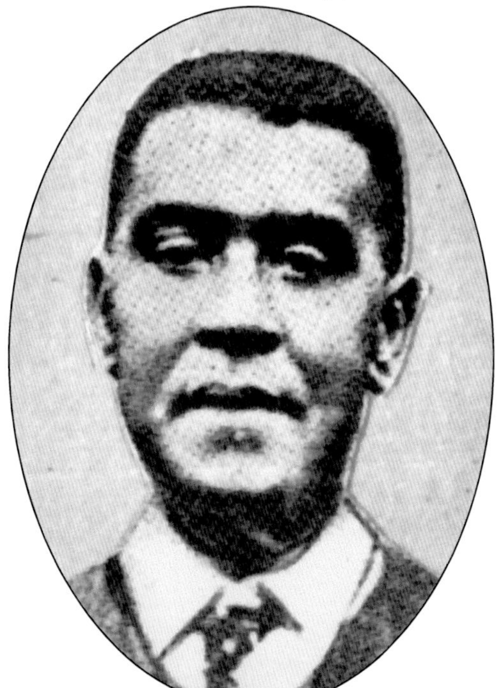

(Left) Bishop John William Martin was elected in 1924. He was known as an outstanding athlete and scholar.
(Right) Bishop W.W. Slade served as chair of the Clinton Junior College Board of Trustees from 1944 to 1960.

Eight
110 Years of Excellence in Education

The 21st century brought Clinton College to its 106th birthday. On September 11, 2001, the United States of America witnessed one of the greatest tragedies in history. Two airplanes deliberately crashed into the towers of the World Trade Center in New York City. Another plan crashed into the Pentagon in Washington, D.C., and another crashed into a wooded area in Pennsylvania. Terrorists had attacked the United States. Life as we knew it had changed.

In the days and years that followed, the Clinton College family adjusted to a new way of life and fought to move forward. In 2004, the college celebrated its 110th birthday.

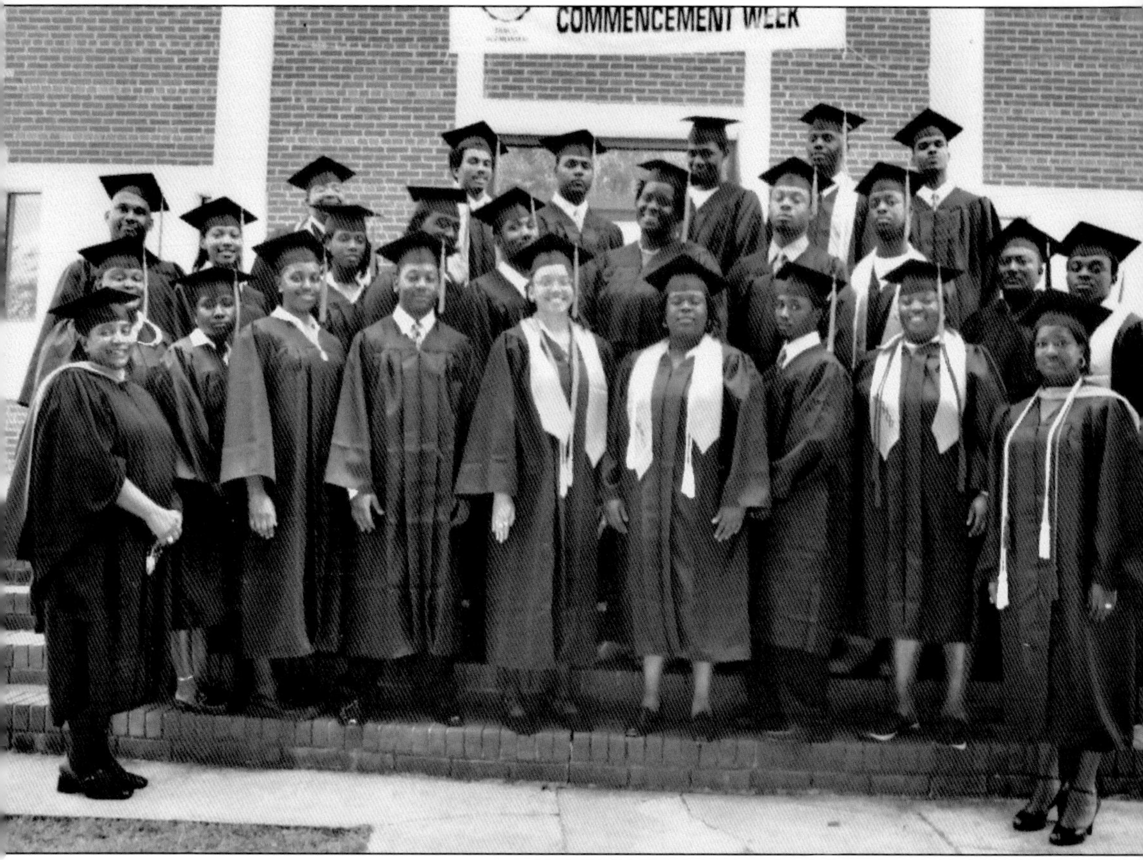

Pictured here are the 23 students who graduated as the Class of 2003.

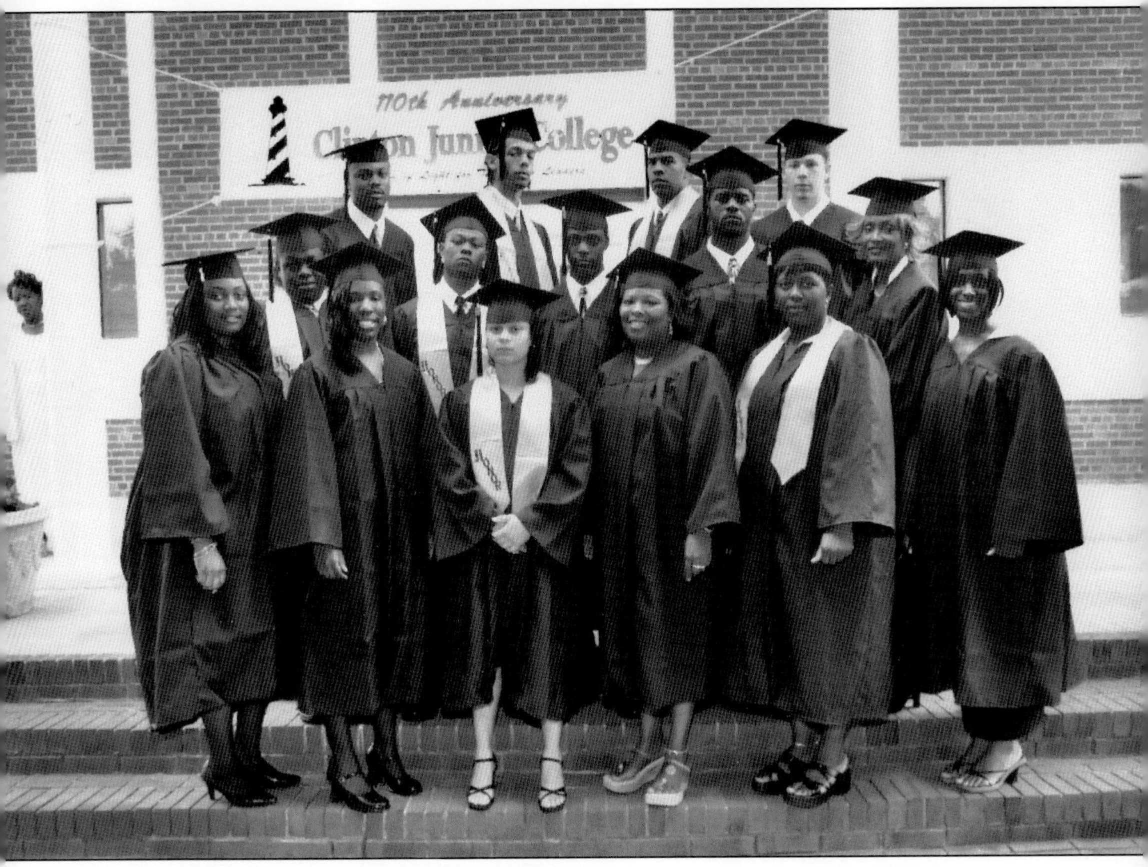

Fifteen graduates comprised the Class of 2004.

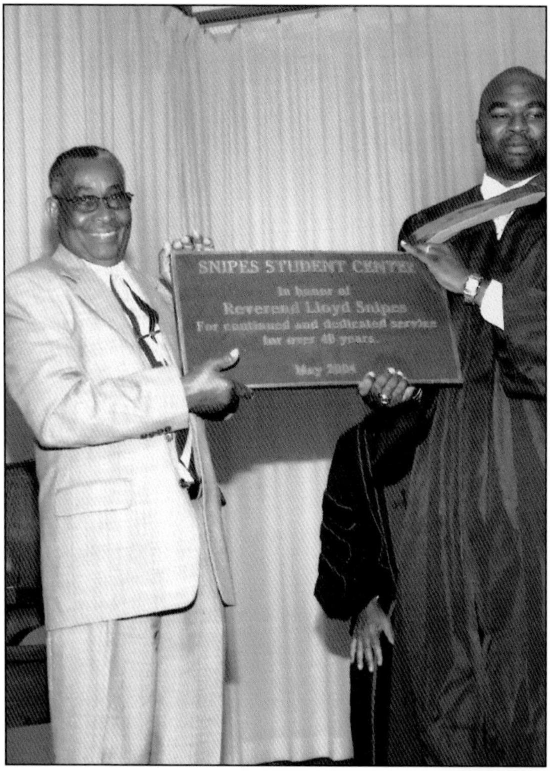

At the 2004 Commencement, the student center was named in honor of Rev. Lloyd Snipes for more than 40 years of service to the college. Reverend Snipes (left) holds the wall plaque with Coach Murray Garvin.

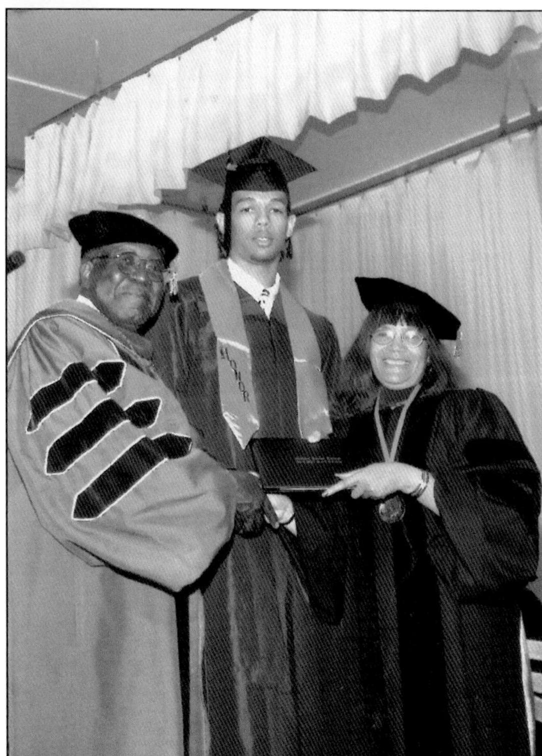

All Clinton College athletes know they are students first. Pictured in the center is Pierre Steins, who graduated with honors and is also an outstanding basketball player. He is flanked by Bishop Joseph Johnson on the left and President Copeland on the right.

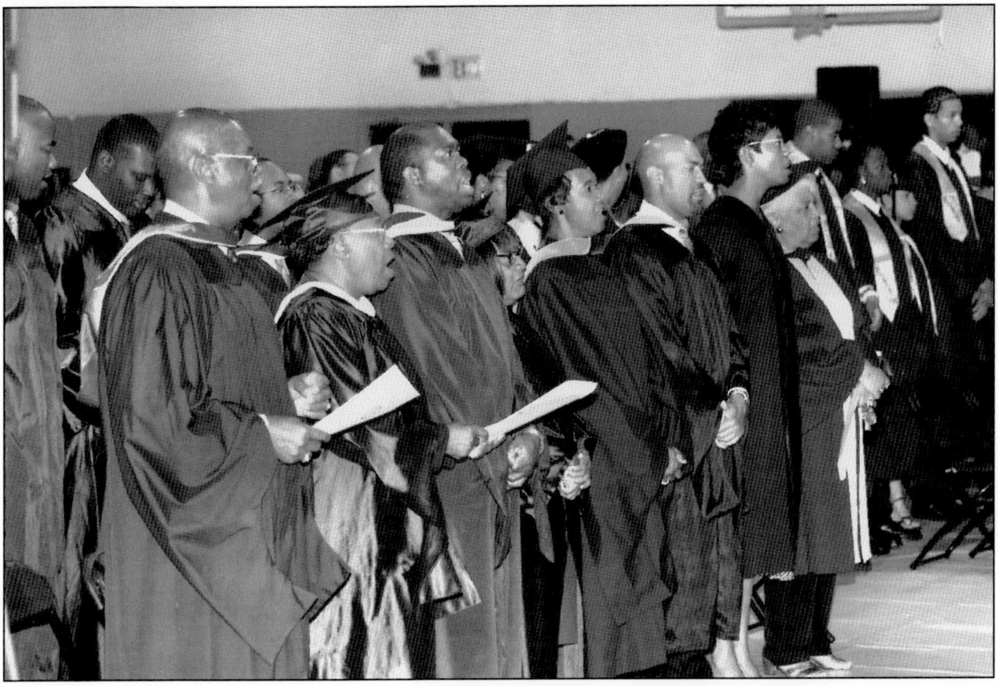

Pictured here are members of the faculty and staff participating in the 2004 commencement exercises.

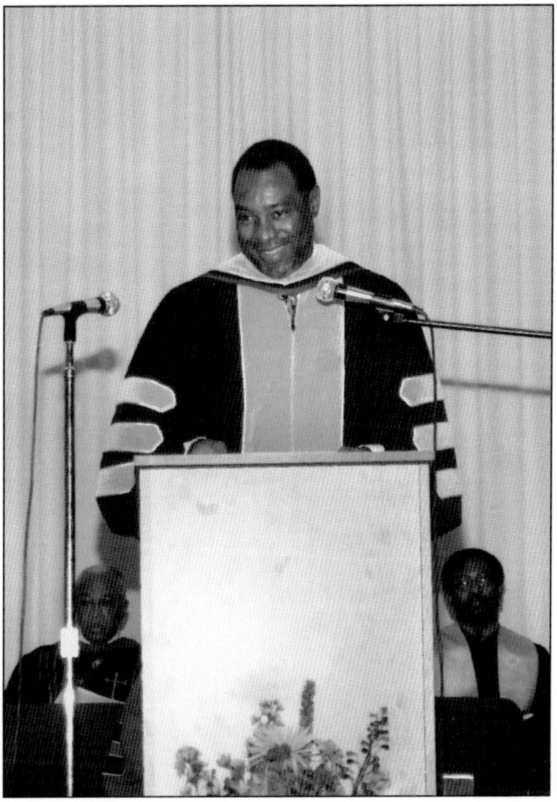

The speaker for the 2004 commencement exercises, which celebrated the 110th year of the college, was Dr. Randy Bridges, superintendent of Rock Hill Public Schools.

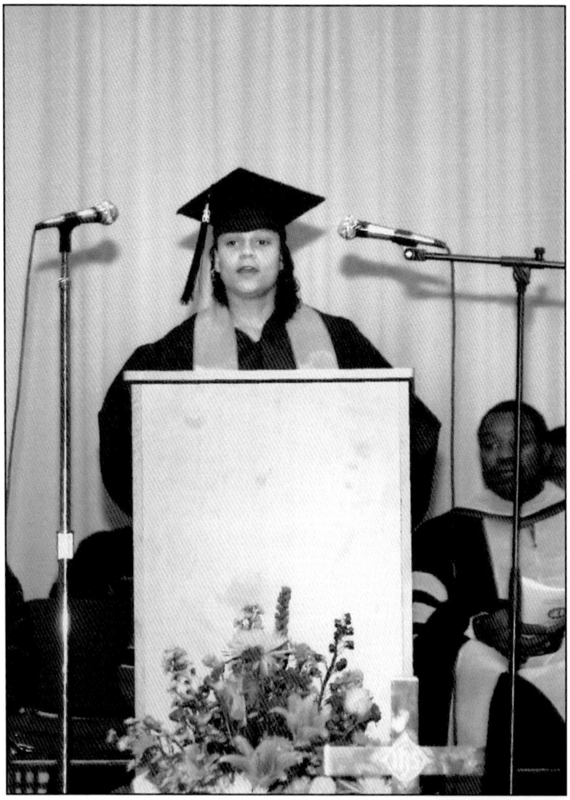

Esperanza Visbal greets the 2004 Commencement crowd. "Essie" was the Class of 2004 valedictorian.

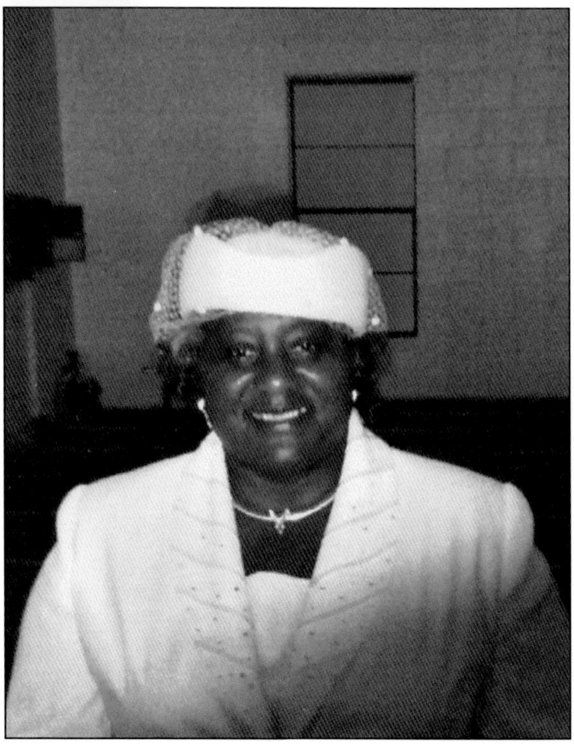

Mrs. Daisy Carter Wylie, Class of 1967, was the alumni representative on the 110th anniversary committee.

Nine

The Mission of the College

The stated mission of Clinton Junior College is to "design and implement an educational program that will help all students lead moral, spiritual and productive lives." The college believes that education is a continuing process and encourages the students to pursue bachelor's degrees and beyond.

Students from all over the United States, the Bahamas, the Virgin Islands, and Africa have matriculated at Clinton. In 2003, after Clinton received accreditation, the U.S. Immigration Department approved Clinton to admit international students. With the use of the Internet, recruiting these students will be easier, making the Clinton student population more diverse.

The leadership of the church supports the leadership of the college to make the mission a reality.

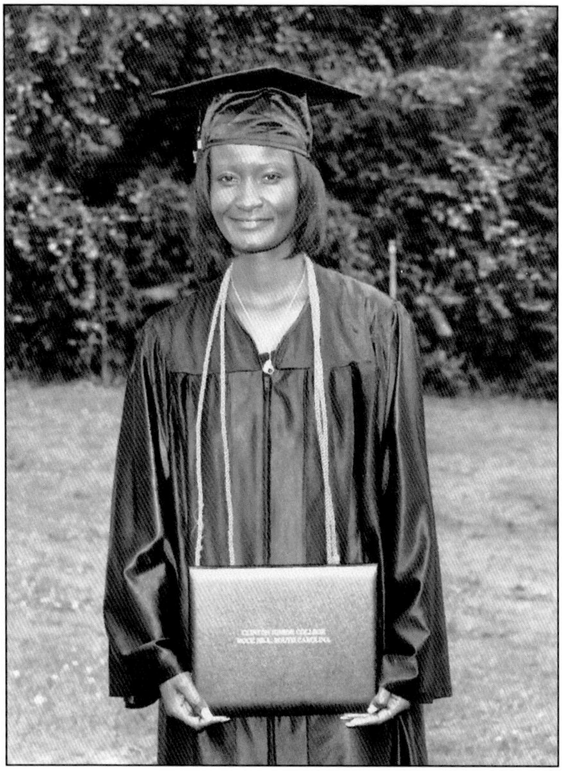

Kenya Kamara was part of the Class of 2000, the last class of the 20th century. Here, she shows off her degree. Kenya is from Nigeria, and her degree from Clinton carried her to Howard University in Washington, D.C.

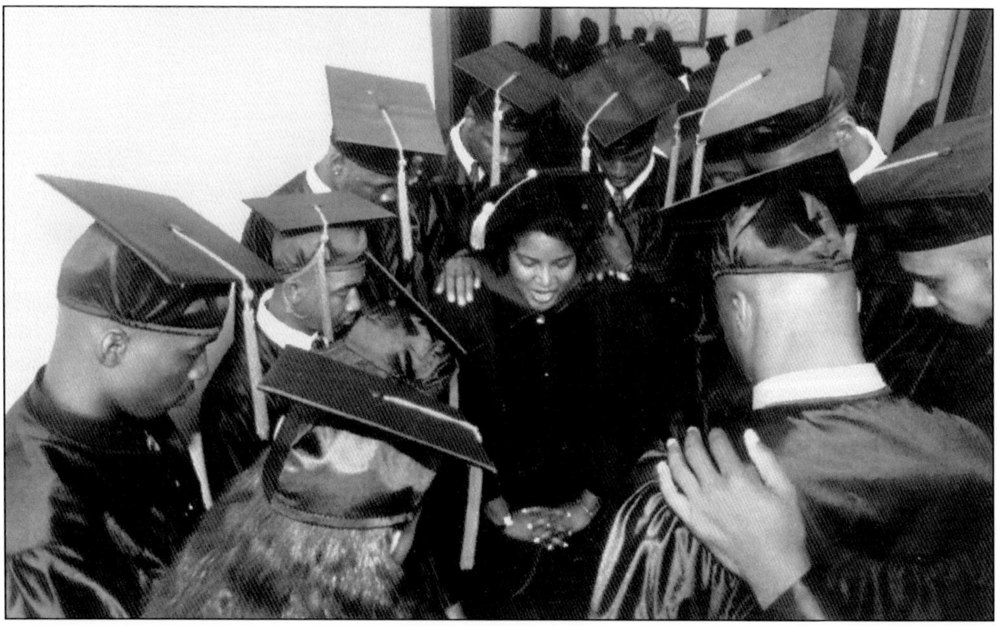

Clinton Junior College's mission is exemplified as Dr. Cynthia McCullough Russell prays with and for the Class of 1998. For more than 110 years, Clinton Junior College's mission has been to develop students academically, physically, socially, emotionally, and spiritually. This mission begins with enrollment and is realized with Commencement. It is finalized throughout one's life because education is a never-ending process.

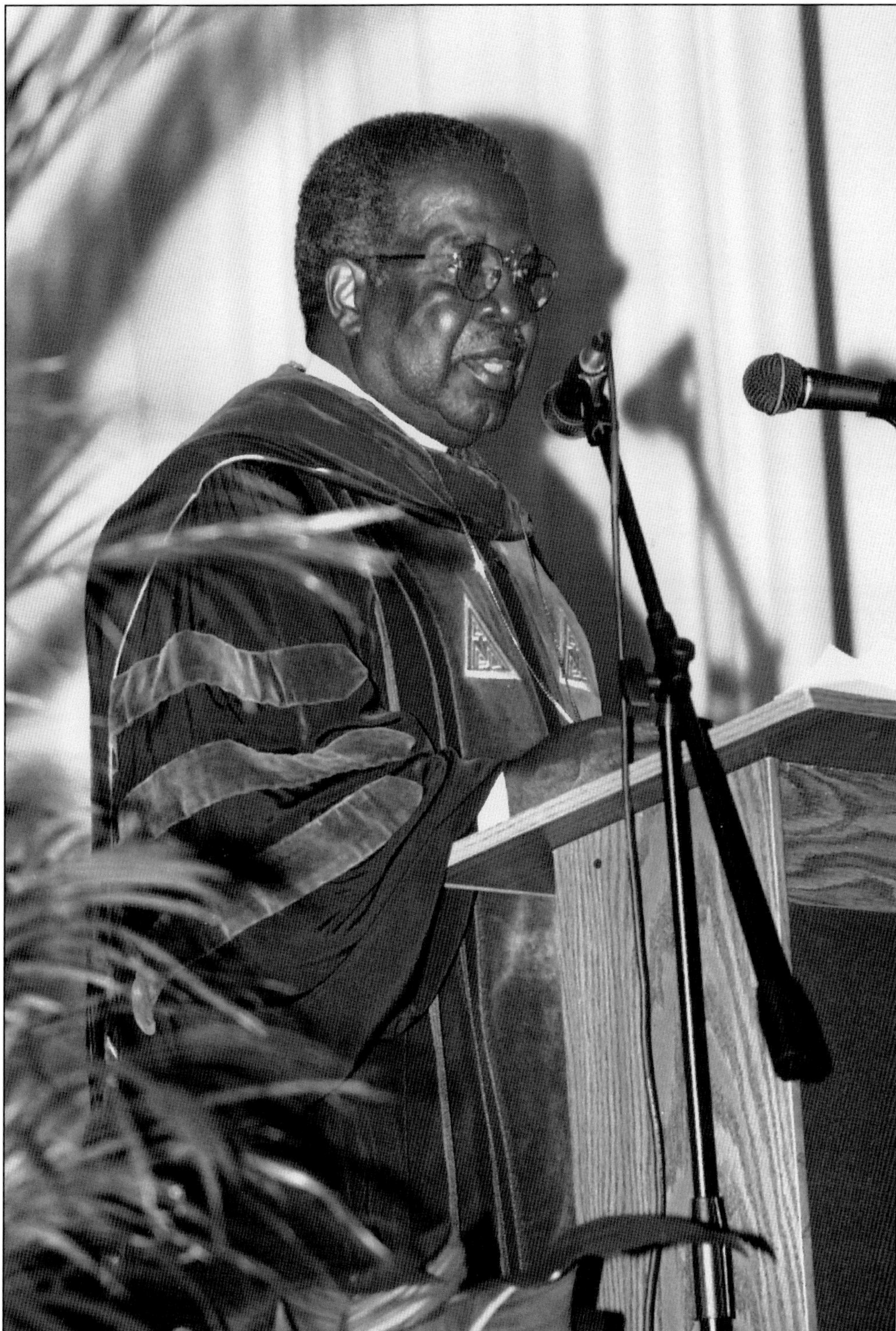

Bishop Joseph Johnson chaired the board of trustees from 1996 to 2004 and served as presiding bishop of the South Atlantic Episcopal District of the A.M.E. Zion Church.

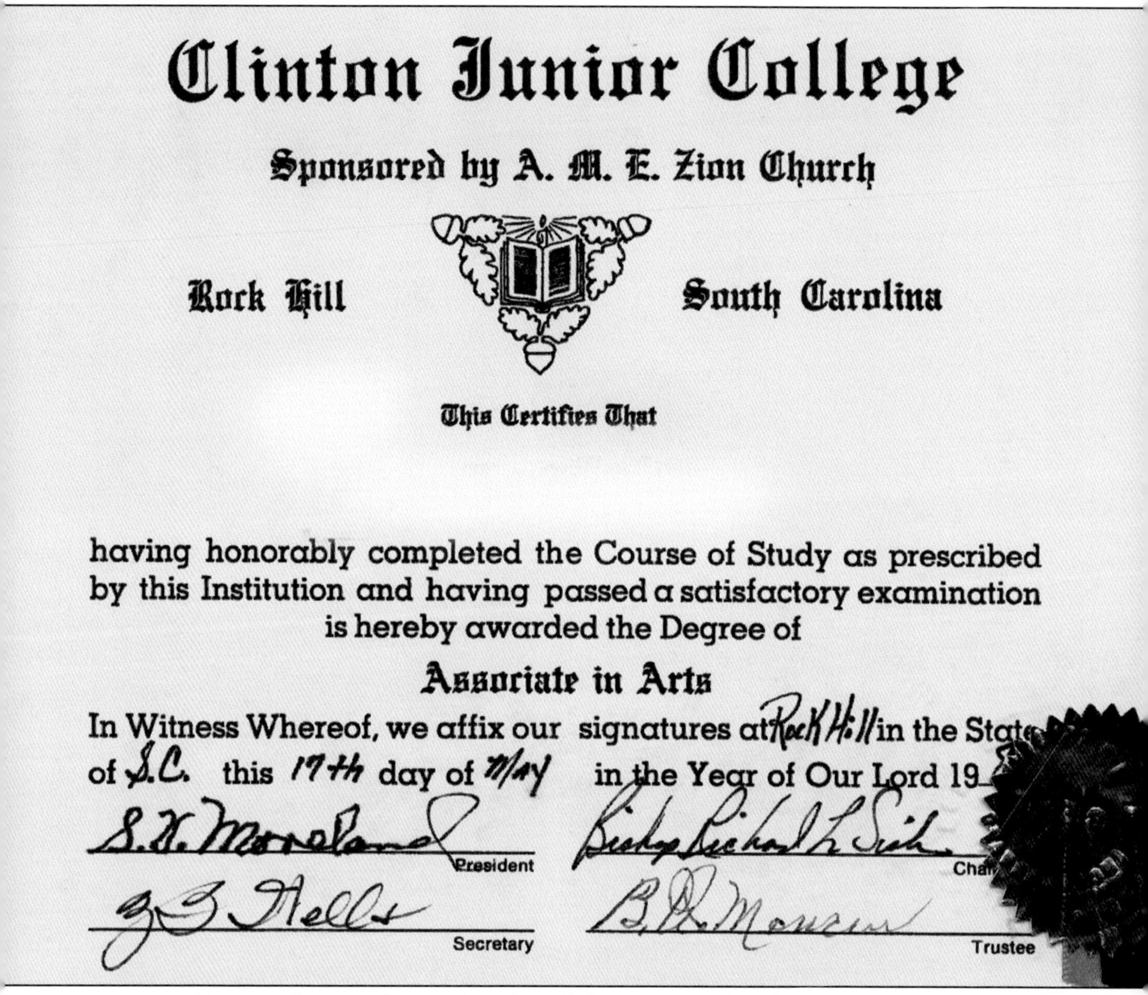

Clinton Junior College

Sponsored by A. M. E. Zion Church

Rock Hill South Carolina

This Certifies That

having honorably completed the Course of Study as prescribed by this Institution and having passed a satisfactory examination is hereby awarded the Degree of

Associate in Arts

In Witness Whereof, we affix our signatures at Rock Hill in the State of S.C. this 17th day of May in the Year of Our Lord 19

President

Secretary

Cha

Trustee

It's a small piece of paper that packs a lot of clout. Pictured is the type of diploma issued in the latter of half of the 20th century. This diploma, from 1987, has Dr. Sallie Moreland's signature. She was one of the most active and dedicated presidents at Clinton Junior College.

Ten

THE PRESIDENTS

Clinton Junior College has had 12 distinguished presidents in its 110 years of service. Three presidents served as acting presidents for short periods. They were Mr. E.P. Gist in 1942 and Reverends W.J. Campbell and Booker Medford in 1946. According to Bishop Walls, Mr. Gist was an "alumnus and trustee of the institution" and served for "several months." He says of the Reverends Campbell and Medford that they were "assiduous in their brief tenure." Mr. C.T. Hinton was also recorded to be an acting president, but his term lasted three years, 1937–1940. Dr. Sallie Moreland served an unprecedented 48 years. Traditionally, the presidents of Clinton College have served not only at the helm, but also as professors before and during their tenure as president.

The information on the first 10 presidents of the college is chronicled by Bishop W.J. Walls in his book The African Methodist Episcopal Zion Church: Reality of the Black Church *(1974).*

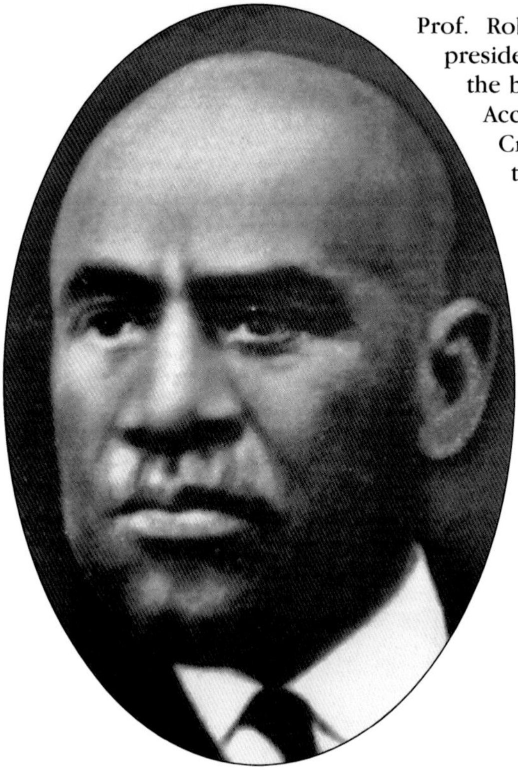

Prof. Robert J. Crockett was the college's first president. His term was 1894–1908. He was also the brother of the founder, Rev. Nero Crockett. According to Bishop W.J. Walls, Professor Crockett was an "energetic and enthusiastic tutor" and, under his administration, did "praiseworthy work." His tenure ended in 1908 when he became principal of Lancaster Normal and Industrial School.

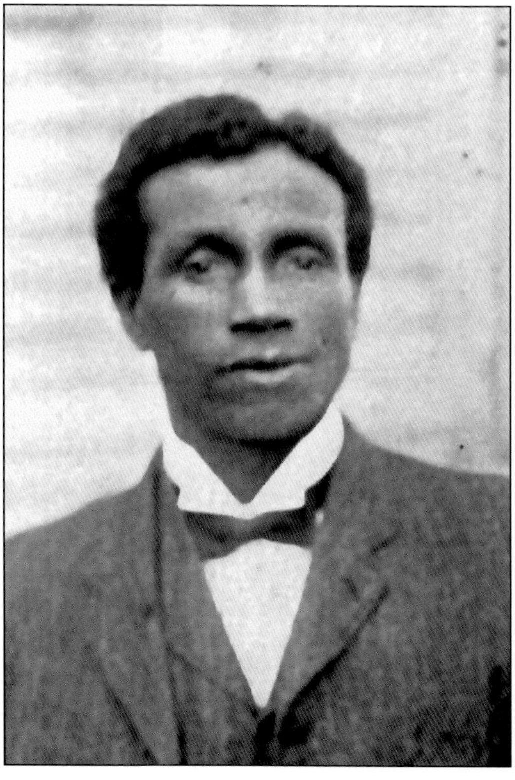

Prof. Robert James Boulware served as the college's second president from 1908 to 1931. Bishop Walls calls him a "good man and laudable educator." He served until he passed on in 1931. The school lapsed for a brief period after his death.

The third president was Prof. James Stephen Stanback from 1931 to *c.* 1937. He was "drafted as president" by the Board of Christian Education of the church. He was an "ardent reader" and conducted the institution with "anxious solicitude without a fixed salary." He served until his health failed. Stanback died shortly after his resignation in 1937.

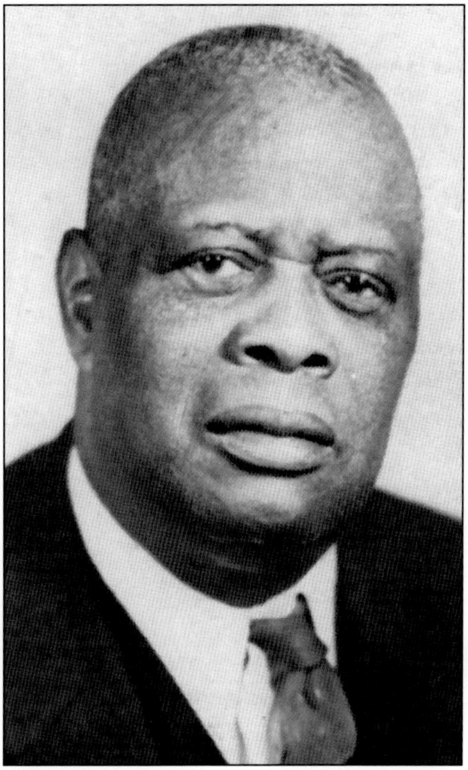

The Rev. C. T. Hinton Dies

The death in Rock Hill last Friday of the Rev. Dr. C. T. Hinton removes from Zion Methodism one of the most colorful figures of this generation. Dr. Hinton, graduate of Livingstone College, was for many years president of Clinton College, and brought to that institution many improvements in its curricula and physical equipment.

Prior to his election as president he had been head of the music department, and brought that department to an extraordinary high state of excellence.

He was held in high esteem by educators throughout his own denomination and by educational authorities in the area where he labored so long and effectively.

Despite the fact that Dr. Hinton had suffered the loss of his legs, he was possessed with a wealth of hopefulness and determination, which not only brought great buoyancy to his own great spirit, but was the constant and never-failing inspiration to thousands who came in touch with him. He was a living example of the courageous soul, who not only overcame a tremendous handicap, but in spite of it, made an outstanding contribution to society.

The world is poorer by the passing of

Rev. C.T. Hinton served as acting president from 1937 to 1940. Said Bishop Walls, "He brought to the work understanding and enthusiasm." According to a newspaper article about his death, he had been head of the music department and brought excellence to the department prior to becoming president. He died around 1940.

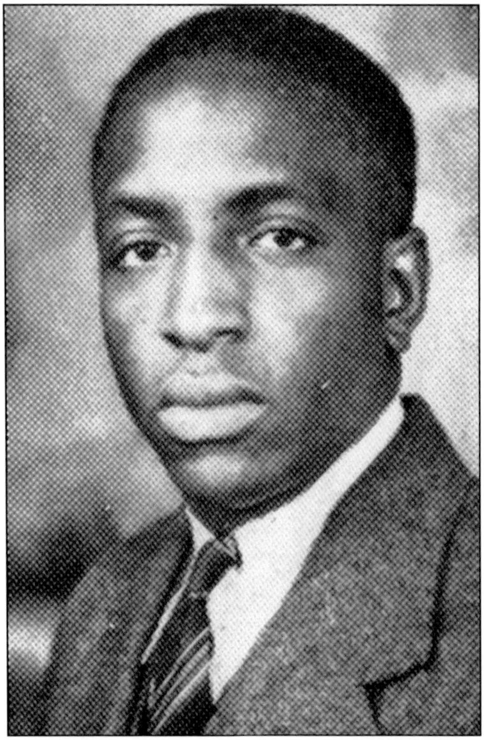

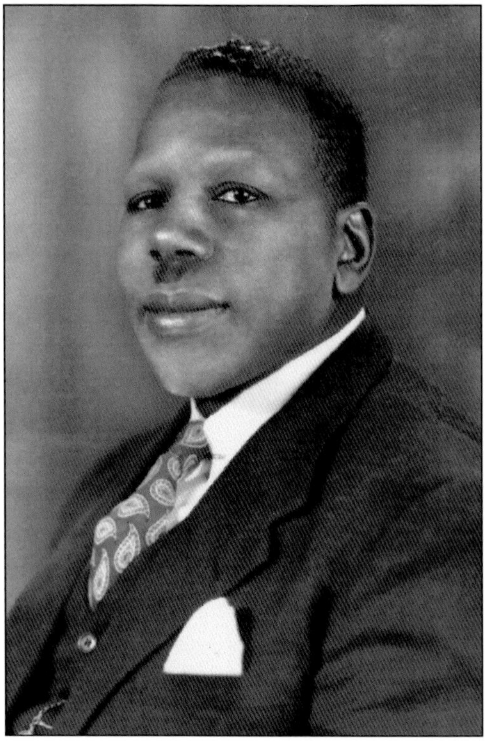

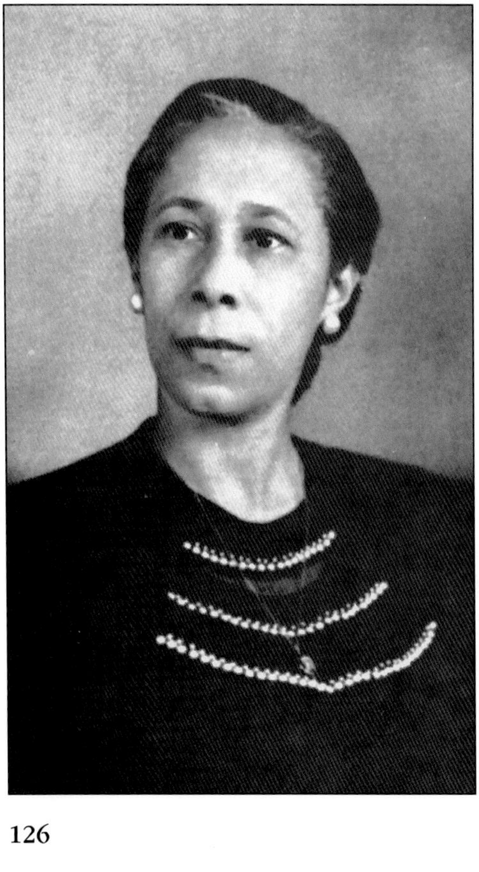

(Above left) Rev. James W. Shaw was elected president of the college in 1942. He was a churchman and educator and served successfully for two years until 1946. *(Above right)* The college had a resurgence under the leadership of the fifth president, Edward Warner Brice Jr. He served from 1940 to 1942. He "intensified the scholastic standards, and Clinton Junior College received accreditation from the South Carolina State Department of Education and the American Association of Junior Colleges; it also granted State Teachers' Certificates." Professor Brice served with "effulgence" for two years until he was drafted into the army.

In 1946, Dr. Sallie V. Moreland was requested to serve as acting president. She was a teacher in the Clinton College high school department. Later that year, she was elected by the joint Board of Education–Schools and Colleges of the church and the college's board of trustees, and she became the 10th president, serving from 1946 to 1994. Bishop Walls says of her administration, she "imbued many scholars with accurate and well-disciplined learning."

In July 1994, the board of trustees, under the leadership of Bishop George Battle, asked Dr. Cynthia McCullough Russell to serve as interim president of the college. She became president in 1995. During her six-year tenure until 2001, the college moved forward at a rapid pace.

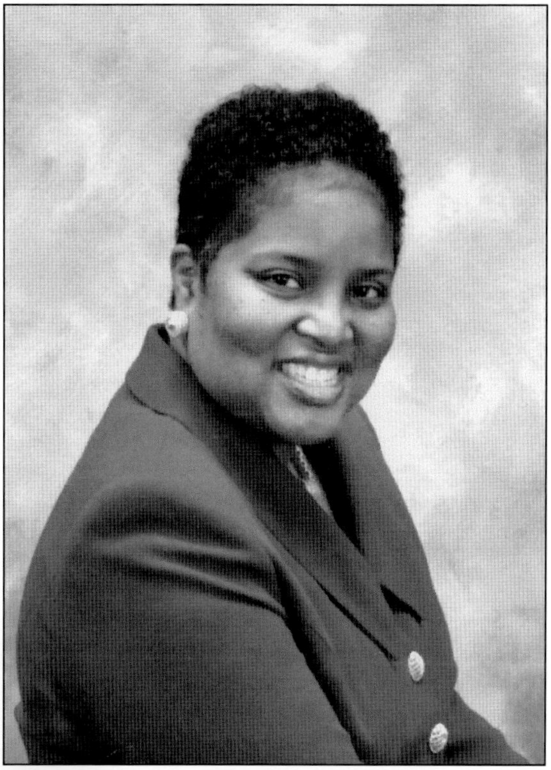

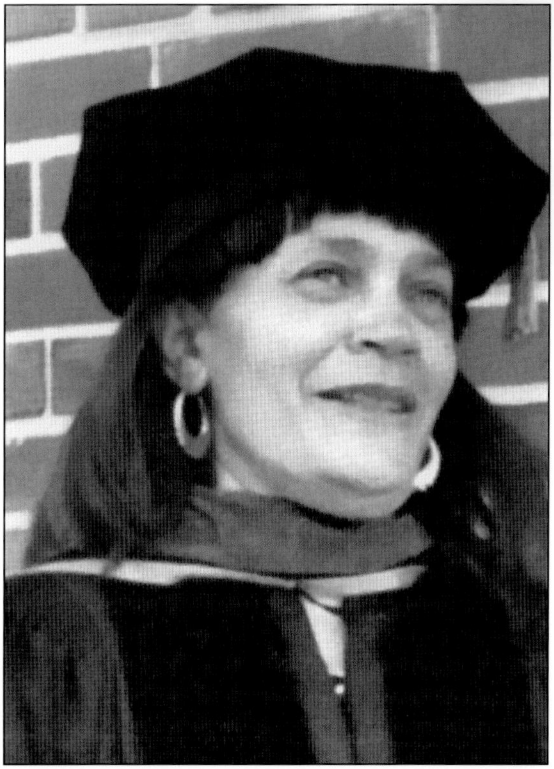

In June 2001, Dr. Elaine Johnson Copeland became the 12th president of the college. She serves in that role currently. Under her leadership, accreditation was realized, a new library was built, and the college is moving forward.

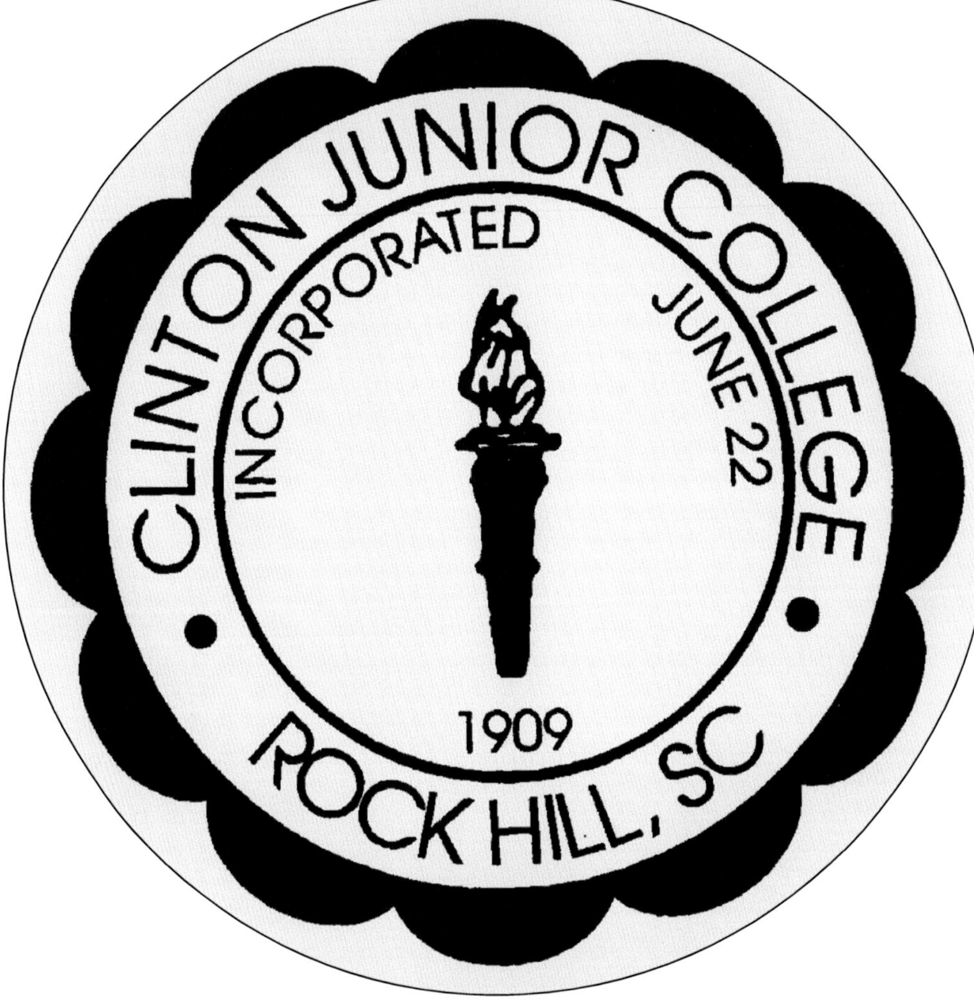

The official seal of the college was redesigned in 1995 by Dr. Cynthia McCullough Russell. It shows the date of incorporation and a flaming torch to signify the light of education never going out.